Goethe's Elective Affinities *and the Critics*

From the time of its publication to the present, Goethe's famous novel *The Elective Affinities* (*Die Wahlverwandtschaften,* 1809), has aroused a storm of critical confusion. Critics in every age have vehemently disagreed about its content (whether it defends the institution of marriage, radically supports its dissolution, or even whether it is about marriage at all), its style (whether it is romantic, realistic, modern, or post-modern) and its tone (whether it is tragic, anti-romantic, or ironic). The present study begins by focusing upon the reaction of Goethe's contemporaries, and then discusses Goethe's own efforts — in light of the initial negative critical reaction — to shape the novel's reception. It continues by viewing the novel through the lens of nineteenth-century Hegelianism, positivism, and biographical studies, and by exploring the relationship between the novel's nineteenth-century reception and the growth of psychoanalytic theory and German nationalism. Moving on to the twentieth century, the book considers the re-evaluation of Goethe's scientific works, the impact of the Second World War on the novel's interpreters, and the growing influence of literary theory. Here particular emphasis is placed upon Walter Benjamin's seminal essay on the novel and upon the criticism that the essay has inspired.

Astrida Orle Tantillo is associate professor of Germanic Studies at the University of Illinois at Chicago.

Studies in German Literature, Linguistics, and Culture
Literary Criticism in Perspective

Literary Criticism in Perspective

James Hardin (*South Carolina*), General Editor

About *Literary Criticism in Perspective*

Books in the series *Literary Criticism in Perspective* trace literary scholarship and criticism on major and neglected writers alike, or on a single major work, a group of writers, a literary school or movement. In so doing the authors — authorities on the topic in question who are also well-versed in the principles and history of literary criticism — address a readership consisting of scholars, students of literature at the graduate and undergraduate level, and the general reader. One of the primary purposes of the series is to illuminate the nature of literary criticism itself, to gauge the influence of social and historic currents on aesthetic judgments once thought objective and normative.

Goethe's *Elective Affinities* and the Critics

Astrida Orle Tantillo

CAMDEN HOUSE

First published 2001
by Camden House

Camden House is an imprint of Boydell & Brewer Inc.
PO Box 41026, Rochester, NY 14604–4126 USA
and of Boydell & Brewer Limited
PO Box 9, Woodbridge, Suffolk IP12 3DF, UK

ISBN: 1–57113–212–0

Library of Congress Cataloging-in-Publication Data

Tantillo, Astrida Orle.
    Goethe's Elective affinities and the critics / Astrida Orle Tantillo
    p. cm. — (Studies in German literature, linguistics, and culture. Lit-
erary criticism in perspective)
Includes bibliographical references and index.
ISBN 1–57113–212–0 (alk. paper)
    1. Goethe, Johann Wolfgang von, 1749–1832. Wahlverwandtschaften.
2. Goethe, Johann Wolfgang von, 1749–1832—Criticism and interpre-
tation—History. 3. Benjamin, Walter, 1892–1940. I. Title.
II. Studies in German literature, linguistics, and culture (Unnumbered).
Literary criticism in perspective.

PT1971.W4 T36 2001
833'.6—dc21

                                                        2001037378

A catalogue record for this title is available from the British Library.

This publication is printed on acid-free paper.
Printed in the United States of America

For my parents

Contents

Preface

THIS BOOK FOLLOWS THE GUIDELINES of the Literary Criticism in Perspective Series in listing the entries of the final bibliography in chronological order. In order to assist the reader in locating individual works, each chapter also contains a list of works cited in alphabetical order. In addition, the index also lists the names of authors discussed. Because this series attempts to reach a broad audience, I have provided English translations of all German quotations. Whenever possible, I quote from published English translations as these translations are themselves part of the historical reception.

Acknowledgments

THIS BOOK WOULD NOT HAVE BEEN POSSIBLE without the help of several individuals. I would especially like to thank Jim Hardin for his support of the project and his generous assistance with secondary materials. My friends John F. Cornell, Daryl Koehn, Imke Meyer, and Susanne Rott provided much needed advice and help throughout the project. Lilian Friedberg, my research assistant, did an excellent job in assisting me during the book's final stage. And finally, I would like to thank my husband, Steve Tantillo, for his invaluable comments and assistance in writing and editing the manuscript.

A. O. T.
February 2001

Abbreviations of Goethe editions

FA   *Sämtliche Werke.* Ed. Hendrik Birus et al. 40 vols. Frank-
        furt: Deutscher Klassiker Verlag, 1985–.

GG   *Goethes Gespräche.* 5 vols. Ed. Wolfgang Herwig. Zurich:
        Artemis, 1965–87.

HA   *Goethes Werke.* Ed. Erich Trunz. 14 vols. Hamburg: Chris-
        tian Wenger Verlag, 1949–71. Cited here from the reissued
        thirteenth edition, Munich: Verlag C. H. Beck.

Unless otherwise noted, all translations from Goethe's works are
taken from *Goethe's Collected Works.* 12 vols. New York: Suhrkamp,
1983–89. Citations are listed according to volume number and
page of this edition.

Introduction

FROM THE TIME OF ITS PUBLICATION to today, Goethe's novel, *Die Wahlverwandtschaften* (Elective Affinities, 1809), has aroused a storm of interpretive confusion. Its readers have disagreed about its main message, themes, and even its style. Many critics have argued that the novel contains an endorsement of the loose sexual practices of the nearby Jena Romantics, while many others have maintained that the tragic end of the novel offers a conservative defense of traditional marriage. Beginning with Walter Benjamin, several critics have even disputed that the novel is about marriage at all. Readers have also fiercely debated the role of the chemical theory of elective affinities presented in the novel. Some argue that it suggests a philosophy of nature that is rooted in fate. Others maintain it is about free choice. Others still believe that the chemical theory is merely a structural device that allows the author to foreshadow events in the novel and bears no relevance to the greater issues of the novel. And while several generations of scholars have searched for the elusive single, all-pervasive idea that Goethe maintained ran through his entire novel, more recent scholars have argued that the novel is a prototypical postmodern text, whose numerous strands and very structure preclude a single interpretation.

One would naturally expect that the interpretation of any novel would undergo substantial revisions over the course of nearly two hundred years as each new generation of readers sees it from within a different cultural and historical perspective. What is particularly striking about *Die Wahlverwandtschaften*, however, is the lack of agreement *within* almost every age about even the novel's most basic elements. Goethe's contemporaries argued over whether it was a moral or immoral book and whether the style was romantic or classical. Such major interpretive disagreements were not only characteristic of Goethe's time, but have marked nearly every generation of scholarship. Because the novel has never experienced a consistent interpretive reading on even its main points, the study of its reception illustrates perhaps better than any other work by Goethe the shifts in the cultural and intellectual atmosphere over the past two hundred years. Each age has presented a conflicting story about the novel, and these conflicts, in turn, tell us as much about the society and culture that produced them as about the novel. Thus, moral issues were prominent during the novel's debut (as much of the material was considered shocking and inappropriate for young women) as well as during the period following the Second World War (as many were trying to analyze, if not reconcile, the role of German culture within German politics). So too, did biographical details become important for the novel's interpretation during the reign of positivism and psychoanalytic theory. The development of literary theory, beginning with Benjamin, marked a definite break with past traditions and heralded a new approach to interpretation. The author was no longer placed in the center, but the text itself became the focus. Biography became less important as the philosophical and theoretical issues within the text gained prominence. Scholars in the second half of the twentieth century concentrated on the text, whether addressing formal issues of genre, character analysis, or close textual reading, much more than upon the author or his life. By the end of the twentieth century, the move away from the author that Benjamin had advocated had become more absolute. Authorial intentions were placed aside, and the novel was hailed not as a classical or romantic text, but as a postmodern one that highlighted the futility of closure and the search for meaning.

The general reception of Goethe, of course, has also undergone marked changes throughout the past two hundred years. The connection between his changing status and the interpretation of the novel is a complicated one. His critical popularity reached its zenith during his lifetime after his success with *Die Leiden des jungen Werthers* (The Sorrows of Young Werther, 1774) and again at the end of the nineteenth century during the rise of German nationalism, and fell to its nadir in the time directly following his death and again today, when he has come under attack for his conservative ideas and canonical status. Today, he is most criticized for his hierarchical and patriarchal views — views that contemporary scholars have linked to the political conservatism during his day, the rise of National Socialism one hundred years later, and finally the perpetuation of traditional, Western values. During his own day, however, his harshest critics were conservative and religious leaders who viewed him as a danger to traditional values. And rather than viewing him as politically influential, the Young Germans found him to be irrelevant precisely because he did not take a political stand. What makes the study of the *Die Wahlverwandt-schaften*'s critical reception especially interesting against this backdrop, however, is that it is often directly at odds with the prevailing attitude toward Goethe in general. The two ends of the spectrum are illustrated by the book's initial reception and its reception today. When *Die Wahlverwandtschaften* was published, Goethe was popular with the general reading public, but critical opinion was largely against it. Many critics thought the book was not written for a high audience, but that Goethe had pandered to the public and compromised his aesthetic standards in order to appeal to a larger and more popular audience. Today, Goethe is largely unpopular within the academic community, but his novel is one of his few works that still enjoys a great deal of theoretical attention. And while many of his major works are criticized for their representative conservative views, *Die Wahlverwandtschaften* is more often viewed as progressive.

This study examines the interpretive issues that surround the novel's reception. A brief overview of the novel's main characteristics points to some of the reasons inherent within the text that have lead to its controversial reception. First, the novel is complex. Although not long, it is tightly written. Interpreters, therefore, have a wealth of material to mine. Numerous events recur several times, whether musical duets or drownings. The use of mirroring pervades the whole, whether Ottilie's features on the ceiling of the chapel, the characters' propensity to see nature as a reflection of themselves, Ottilie's handwriting and piano playing, or the two symmetrical halves of the novel itself. Not only do symbols appear throughout the novel for the reader to interpret, but the characters themselves often offer several interpretations of them. For example, every main character gives a different interpretation of the meaning of the baby's strange appearance, two characters analyze the meaning of the unbroken chalice, and three provide views on the significance of grafting shoots. There is further a strange paucity of proper names: the four main characters and the child that is born share the same root name, Otto. Many of the other characters are known simply by their status or occupation, such as the Count, the Gardener, the Schoolmaster, etc. If commentators have agreed on any aspect of the novel, it is perhaps the fact that Goethe provides an unusual amount of detail. One learns quite specifically about the characters' likes and dislikes: Eduard is fond of plane trees, likes sugar in his tea, and hates draughts; Ottilie is partial to asters; Charlotte cannot stand it when people rock in their chairs; the Captain is bothered to the core if anyone marks on a map that he has drawn. Similarly, many of the most prevalent artistic trends of the time are catalogued within the novel, from sentimental garden designs that are taken directly from Hirschfeld's book to the descriptions of evening entertainments. During the course of the novel, the reader is provided with the theories behind the laying of pathways, the use of moss huts, and the ultimate goal of planned "naturalness" within garden designs. One also learns about *tableaux vivants* (complete with discussions of particular paintings and etchings), musical evenings, and the social interest in magnetic experiments of the day.

Second, numerous conflicting interpretations arise from the fact that the characters of *Die Wahlverwandtschaften* present opposing views on such central topics as marriage, nature, and aesthetics. The institution of marriage is both ridiculed and defended, and despite the fact that several characters strongly desire to marry, the novel itself does not provide an example of a single happy marriage. Those who wish to argue for a conservative defense of marriage may turn to Mittler's words on it, while those who wish to argue that Goethe intended to undermine the institution may turn to the Count's proposal of five-year marriage contracts. In discussing the chemical theory of elective affinities, the characters generally agree that human beings mirror nature's activities. They disagree, however, on how exactly nature acts. The Captain sees nature as primarily free. He views the chemical theory as one that promises freedom of choice to even the most minute of nature's particles. Charlotte, in contrast, sees nothing but predetermined actions. In her mind, chemicals, like people, are largely determined by necessity. And while many of Goethe's contemporaries commented on the accurate picture of country life presented within the novel, the novel itself presents myriad opinions on the activities of the characters. The educated Schoolmaster is critical of both the chapel design and the *tableaux vivants*, while the practical-minded Captain must redo many of the landscape projects that Charlotte has implemented. His changes, in turn, appear to be ominous as they lead to two drowning accidents.

A third interpretive complication within *Die Wahlverwandt-schaften* is that it contains satire, irony, and black humor. The one true defender of traditional marriage is an eccentric bachelor, Mittler. Goethe further satirizes this character by providing his history: he was once a clergyman, but left his religious calling — because he won the lottery. A close look at Mittler's defense of marriage even reflects Mittler's monetary interests. He discusses marriage in terms of debts and receipts. The harshest critic of marriage, the Count, cannot wait to be married again, and his adulterous lover, the Baroness, who wishes that the Count's wife would give him a divorce, does everything within her power to salvage Charlotte's marriage. Ottilie is at times characterized as an ideal mother, is symbolically linked to the Virgin Mary, and at one point believes that her true calling in life is to care for children. Yet, her careless-ness ultimately kills the child, and even before the accident, she is not an ideal nanny. She simultaneously reads, carries the baby, and walks along the uneven paths of the manor.

Even the title of the novel has been a source of critical confu-sion: it points to both a scientific theory and to a meaning of mar-riage. While modern readers are more likely to see the compound words within it, "Wahl" meaning "choice" and "Verwandtschaft" meaning "relatives," Goethe's readers also associated the word with a scientific theory. The term "Wahlverwandtschaften" origi-nates from a 1782 translation of a chemical treatise by Torbern Bergman, *De attractionibus electivas*. One anonymous reviewer even questioned Goethe's taste in choosing such a bizarre and practically incomprehensible title (148). Similarly, another thought that Goethe had chosen such a title in order to generate conversa-tion about the novel (Böttiger 189). The confusion over the term is even reflected within the novel. Charlotte hears the word "Wahl-verwandtschaften" and mentally breaks the word into its parts. The conversation about the theory begins because she has confused the chemical term with its more humanistic meaning. She hears the term and thinks about some near relations experiencing marital difficulties. The men attempt to enlighten her about the scientific meaning of the term, but the ensuing discussion further obfuscates the borders between human and chemical behavior. The characters set up analogies between themselves and the chemicals addressed in the theory. Commentators, moreover, have never been in agreement as to the ultimate function of this analogy. Some argue that it is of central importance to the novel and its structure (Adler 274; Steer 39; Nemec 53–54, 61; Milfull 83), while others have argued that it plays but a minor role in the novel (Gray 217; Clark 244).

Another contributing factor to the interpretive confusion is the advertisement that Goethe wrote for *Die Wahlverwandtschaften*. In order to help promote his novel and undoubtedly to help shape its reception, he published the following, anonymous advertisement in the *Morgenblatt für gebildete Stände:*

> Es scheint, daß den Verfasser seine fortgesetzten physikalischen Arbeiten zu diesem seltsamen Titel veranlaßten. Er mochte bemerkt haben, daß man in der Naturlehre sich sehr oft ethischer Gleichnisse bedient, um etwas von dem Kreise menschlichen Wissens weit Entferntes näher heranzubringen, und so hat er auch wohl in einem sittlichen Falle, eine chemische Gleichnisrede zu ihrem geistigen Ursprunge zurückführen mögen, um so mehr, als doch überall nur *eine* Natur ist und auch durch das Reich der heitern Vernunftfreiheit die Spuren trüber, leidenschaftlicher Notwendigkeit sich unaufhaltsam hindurchziehen, die nur durch eine höhere Hand und vielleicht auch nicht in diesem Leben völlig auszulöschen sind. (quoted from *HA*, 6:639, emphasis in original)

> [It seems as if the author's continued natural studies have caused him to use this unusual title. He may have noticed that in the natural sciences one often uses ethical parables in order to bring closer what is quite distant from the circle of human knowledge; and so he also probably wanted, in a moral case, to bring a chemical figure of speech back to its spiritual origins, especially since there is only *one* nature overall, and also since throughout the realm of cheerful freedom of reason the traces of sad, passionate necessity irresistibly pull themselves and may only be erased by a higher hand, and perhaps even then not in this life.]

Goethe's "explanation" of the role of nature within the novel has only spurred scholarly debates. I have given the quote in full, be-

cause in many ways it foreshadows several of the main critical approaches that have been taken to the novel.[1] First, Goethe's advertisement gives credence to one of the oldest and most traditional
ways of reading the work: as a portrayal of the ethical battleground
between duty and passion, reason and necessity, and culture and
nature. Goethe's reference to a higher power may even seem to
endorse a victory of reason, although we may have to wait for the
afterlife for its ultimate triumph. His statement also implies a
straight reading of the end of the novel: Ottilie could not triumph
over her love in this life, but a promise is held out for her happiness
(as well as Eduard's) in the next one.

Conversely, a closer look at the quotation allows a certain dose
of irony to creep in and leads to a more modern and ironic interpretation of the novel. That the author of *Werther* and *Faust* and
the creator of such characters as Albert and Wagner could characterize the realm of reason as "cheerful" should surely give one
some pause. In addition, once one recalls Goethe's own views on
immortality, views that did not include a Christian notion of
heaven, but a more classical notion of ceaseless activity, then one
has further grounds to mistrust Goethe's advertisement as speaking
to his aims within the novel. Ottilie's portrayal as a Christian saint
and the narrator's optimism about her condition in the afterlife
could therefore be seen as irony or even black humor. After all, as
several scholars, including Benjamin, have noted, Ottilie and Eduard bear similarities to the lovers, Francesca and Paolo, who in
Dante's *Inferno* wind up not in heaven, but in hell.

Third, Goethe's propensity to mix such oppositional terms as
reason and passion and freedom and necessity have given deconstructionists (Miller) the springboard from which to argue that
Goethe's language, whether consciously or unconsciously, col-
lapses upon itself and leaves us with no particular meaning or
teaching and therefore questions the very viability of closure within
the novel. What does freedom mean, in the end, if in Goethe's
view it is never separable from necessity?

Finally, the advertisement strongly suggests that Goethe's scientific studies and natural philosophy play an important role within
the novel. This reading of the advertisement encourages a comparison of Goethe's scientific texts and natural philosophy with the
novel. If he indeed links human morality with an understanding of

nature, then his understanding of nature, as evidenced in his scientific texts, may provide information on interpreting the novel.

Goethe further contributed to the interpretive disagreements with his numerous and often cryptic comments on the novel, from his claim that he wrote it for young girls (reported by Varnhagen von Ense 321) to his repeated assertions that there was not a line within the novel that he had not personally experienced (*FA 2*, 12:303, 385). The hunt for a definitive interpretation was therefore fueled by Goethe's own, at times contradictory, comments on the novel. On the one hand, he speaks of his deep love for Ottilie (*FA 2*, 7:528), on the other hand, he rather flippantly talks about letting her starve to death (Varnhagen von Ense 321). Similarly, at times he speaks of not being able to abide Eduard (*FA 2*, 12:215–16), while at others he admires his capacity to love (*FA 2*, 6:535–36). A unifying theme in many of Goethe's statements, however, is his emphasis upon the novel's complexity. From his earliest remarks to friends to his later conversations with Johann Peter Eckermann (1792–1854), Goethe stressed over and again the novel's intricate structure and veiled meaning. Even before the novel was published, he began to shape its reception. On 1 June 1809, he wrote to his friend, the composer Karl Friedrich Zelter (1758–1832), that he not only placed numerous different elements within the text, but that many of these were hidden within it (*FA 2*, 6:459). A few months later (*FA 2*, 6:485; 26 August 1809), he followed up on his comments, and again wrote to Zelter of the veiled quality of the work. He expressed the hope, moreover, that Zelter would not be hindered by either the transparent or the non-transparent veils within the novel from seeing "the truly intended *Gestalt.*" To Christoph Martin Wieland (1733–1813), his fellow author and neighbor, he indicated that the novel had to be read at least three times before it could be understood (Wieland 239). Similarly, to his publisher, Johann Friedrich Cotta (1764–1832), Goethe wrote that much is hidden within the novel and hoped that this aspect would spur readers to read and reread it (*FA 2*, 6:496; 1 October 1809). In his letter to the French diplomat, Karl Friedrich von Reinhard (1761–1837), Goethe even predicted that the novel's meaning might remain incomprehensible for a time, only to be rediscovered through multiple rereadings at a later date (*FA 2*, 6:522–23; 31 December 1809). Nearly twenty years after the novel's publication, Goethe still stressed to Eckermann that he had placed more within his novel than could ever be comprehended in a single reading of it. In addition, scholars have been particularly intrigued by the structure of the novel given the fact that Goethe, contrary to his general practice, destroyed the drafts of it.

The present study examines the major critical approaches to the novel across the changing cultural and intellectual landscapes of the past two hundred years. The book begins with the earliest unpublished comments on the novel, proceeds to the earliest reviews of it, and concludes with the most recent studies that emphasize theory and interdisciplinary approaches. Chapter 1 begins with the novel's early reception, a reception that was marked by moral issues and focused upon the dichotomy between duty and passion. It begins by examining the first critical works of the novel and discusses some of the reasons behind the predominance of this critical approach. This chapter also investigates Goethe's own attempts to promote the novel and fashion the direction of its interpretation.

Chapter 2 begins by analyzing the critical reception following Goethe's death. It takes up the historical and biographical approaches that characterized the nineteenth and early twentieth centuries. Although the period directly after Goethe's death marked a low point in his popularity, two main theoretical schools of nineteenth-century Germany, the Hegelians and the positivists, wrote several influential pieces on *Die Wahlverwandtschaften*. By the end of the nineteenth century, the positivist school as well as the burgeoning interest in psychoanalysis led to a veritable industry of Goethe biographies where his works became intertwined with his life. In many ways, the biographical approach may be seen as a natural outgrowth from the duty-versus-passion debate that marked the novel's early reception. It is an easy step to take to go from arguing about the morality or immorality of the work to the morality or the immorality of the author. Goethe's life story began to be analyzed as a means of unraveling the "meaning" of the work. Conversely, with the rise in the interest in psychoanalytic theory, Goethe's works began to be analyzed as a means of understanding his life.

Chapter 3 focuses exclusively upon Walter Benjamin's seminal essay on *Die Wahlverwandtschaften*. I have devoted an entire chapter to this work not only because of its immense influence on the novel's reception in the twentieth century, but also because of its overall theoretical importance. Benjamin's essay is both a critique and a philosophical treatise and is without question the most important piece ever written on *Die Wahlverwandtschaften*. The essay is also perhaps one of Benjamin's most esoteric works; it is therefore impossible, I believe, to appreciate its significance without closely analyzing its details. In particular, this chapter seeks to explain the connection between Benjamin's literary theory and his interpretation of the novel. In the essay, Benjamin openly breaks with the mainstream theoretical approaches that characterized the late nineteenth and the early twentieth centuries. His essay could be considered the first truly modern approach to the novel in that it seeks to sever the author's life and intentions from the work. For Benjamin the work is not about the moral issues of marriage, nor is it — nor should any work of art be — inextricably linked to its author's life, nor is it even character-driven. Instead Benjamin looks to the mythical and the dark elements of Goethe's novel. This essay was particularly influential in the reception of *Die Wahlverwandtschaften* because a renewed interest in Benjamin in the latter part of the twentieth century helped fuel a revival of interest in the novel. In the 1980s many of the most prominent German and American literary theorists took their direction in interpreting the novel from Benjamin.

Chapter 4 explores the reception of the novel from 1925 until the end of the twentieth century. The Second World War exercised a clear influence on the novel's interpretation. In particular, critics began to raise the issue of the novel's morality as they were grappling with the effects of the war. These postwar critics, however, did not see the novel in terms of the black and white moral issues of Goethe's contemporaries, nor did they strive to elevate Goethe, as their nineteenth-century predecessors had done, as a German ethical demigod. Instead many of these critics tried to paint a more complicated moral picture of the novel in light of their experiences during the war. These critics began to emphasize the concerns of the individual over those of society. The generations that followed the war continued to distance themselves from Goethe as well as from the traditional German canon in general. The chapter examines this trend during the 1970s and 1980s before turning to the clashes in the 1980s and 1990s between the deconstructionists and those who opposed them. It concludes by analyzing the most recent interpretive trends, from reading the novel in light of literary theory to viewing it within the context of the history and philosophy of science.

During the course of the book, I attempt to give a critical overview of different interpretive approaches. The purpose of this book, however, is not to argue for a particular theory or approach, but to show that the novel's staying power stems, at least in part, from its ability to maintain numerous interpretations.

Notes

[1] This advertisement itself has also become an important influence in the shaping of the novel's criticism. It is often reprinted in collections of Goethe's works and is often cited in critical discussions. Julius W. Braun also includes it in his edited work that quotes the reactions of Goethe's contemporaries on his works (211).

Works Cited

Adler, Jeremy. "Goethe's Use of Chemical Theory in His *Elective Affinities*." *Romanticism and the Sciences*. Ed. Andrew Cunningham and Nicholas Jardine. Cambridge: Cambridge UP, 1990.

Anonymous. "Französisches Urtheil über Goethes *Wahlverwandtschaften*." *Morgenblatt für gebildete Stände*. No. 71. Tübingen. 23 March 1810. Quoted here from Härtl 1983, 146–50.

Benjamin, Walter. "Goethes *Wahlverwandtschaften*." *Neue deutsche Beiträge* (1924/25). Quoted here from *Walter Benjamin: Gesammelte Schriften* I, i. Ed. Rolf Tiedemann and Hermann Schweppenhäuser. Frankfurt: Suhrkamp, 1974. English from *Walter Benjamin: Selected Writings (1913–1926)*. Vol. 1. Ed. Marcus Bullock and Michael W. Jennings. Essay trans. Stanley Corngold. Cambridge: Belknap Press, 1996.

Bergman, Torbern. *Disquisitio de attractionibus electivis.* Vol. 2. Nova acta Regiæ societatis scientiarium upsaliensis, 1775.

[Böttiger, Karl August]. "*Die Wahlverwandtschaften;* ein Roman von Göthe." *Bibliothek der redenden und bildenden Künste*. Leipzig, 1810. Quoted here from Härtl 1983, 176–98. Also reprinted in Braun 1885, 265–69.

Braun, Julius W. *Goethe im Urtheile seiner Zeitgenossen: Zeitungskritiken, Berichte, Notizen, Goethe und seine Werke betreffend, aus den Jahren 1772–1812.* 3 vols. Berlin: Friedrich Luckhardt, 1885.

Clark, Robert T., Jr. "The Metamorphosis of Character in *Die Wahlverwandtschaften.*" *Germanic Review* 29 (1954): 243–53.

[Goethe]. Advertisement for *Die Wahlverwandtschaften. Morgenblatt für gebildete Stände.* 4 September 1809. Cited here from *HA*, 6:639. Also reprinted in Härtl 1983, 50–51 and Braun 1885, 211.

Gray, Ronald D. *Goethe: A Critical Introduction.* Cambridge: Cambridge UP, 1967.

Härtl, Heinz. *Die Wahlverwandtschaften: Eine Dokumentation der Wirkung von Goethes Roman 1808–1832.* Weinheim: Acta humaniora, 1983.

Hirschfeld, Christian Cay Laurenz. *Theorie der Gartenkunst.* 5 vols. Leipzig: Weidmann, 1779–1785.

Milfull, John. "The 'Idea' of Goethe's *Wahlverwandtschaften.*" *Germanic Review* 47 (1972): 83–94.

Miller, J. Hillis. "A 'Buchstäbliches' Reading of *The Elective Affinities.*" *Glyph* 6 (1979): 1–23.

———. *Ariadne's Thread: Story Lines.* New Haven: Yale UP, 1992.

———. "Interlude as Anastomosis in *Die Wahlverwandtschaften.*" *Goethe Yearbook* 6 (1992): 115–22.

Nemec, Friedrich. *Die Ökonomie der Wahlverwandtschaften.* Münchner Germanistische Beiträge. Vol. 10. Munich: Fink Verlag, 1973.

Steer, A. G., Jr. *Goethe's Elective Affinities: The Robe of Nessus.* Heidelberg: Carl Winter Universitätsverlag, 1990.

Varnhagen von Ense, Karl August. Diary Entry. 28 June 1843. Quoted here from *Karl August Varnhagen von Ense Werke.* 5 vols. Frankfurt: Deutscher Klassiker Verlag, 1994. 5:320–21. Also reprinted in *HA*, 6:641.

Wieland, Christoph Martin. Letter to Charlotte Geßner. 10 February 1810. Weimar. Quoted here from *Goethe in vertraulichen Briefen seiner Zeitgenossen: Die Zeit Napoleons 1803–1816.* Ed. Wilhelm Bode. Berlin: Mittler & Sohn, 1921. 238–39. Also reprinted in Härtl 1983, 137 and *HA*, 6:663.

1: 1809–1832:
The Morality of Art

GOETHE'S *DIE WAHLVERWANDTSCHAFTEN* WAS begun in the spring of 1808, finished in the fall of 1809, and published in October of the same year. Goethe was sixty years old, and this period was one of the most fruitful of his life. *Faust I* (1808) had finally been published. Around this time, he was also working on *Zur Farbenlehre* (The Theory of Colors, 1810), *Pandora* (1807/ 1808), his autobiography, *Dichtung und Wahrheit* (Poetry and Truth — the first part of which was published in 1811), and *Wilhelm Meisters Wanderjahre* (Wilhelm Meister's Journeyman Years, 1821). Many of his readers expected that *Die Wahlverwandtschaften* was to be the long-awaited sequel to *Wilhelm Meisters Lehrjahre* (Wilhelm Meister's Apprenticeship, 1795), and indeed, Goethe had initially conceived of *Die Wahlverwandtschaften* as one of the stories within the *Wanderjahre*. The poems of this period include "Metamorphose der Tiere" (Metamorphosis of Animals, 1806), "Natur und Kunst" (Nature and Art, 1807), "Mächtiges Überraschen" (Immense Astonishment, 1807–8), "Abschied" (The Farewell, 1807–8), and "Das Tagebuch" (The Diary, 1810).

Goethe's life had been somewhat unsettled during the years directly preceding those of the novel's composition. In particular, his marital status changed due to the unrest of the times. In 1806, Weimar and nearby Jena had come under attack by French forces. Five days after the Battle of Jena, Goethe finally married his lover of nearly twenty years, Christiane Vulpius. Their sixteen-year-old son, August, attended the wedding. There are several different versions about why Goethe finally married Vulpius. According to one version, he married her out of gratitude for saving his life from drunken French soldiers who were occupying the town. According to another version, he married her because he wanted to ensure her legal rights should anything have happened to him. At the time before the novel's composition, Goethe was also said to have fallen in love, like his character Eduard, with a much younger woman —

although there is some disagreement as to who that woman might have been. Many have speculated that Ottilie was based on Bettina von Arnim, Wilhelmine (Minna) Herzlieb, and/or Silvie von Ziegesar.

Prior to their marriage, Christiane was not an accepted part of Weimar society. Nor was it a given that marriage would open societal doors for her. One of Goethe's earliest biographers, George Henry Lewes (who himself was involved in a rather unconventional relationship with George Eliot), reports that Goethe's attempt to legitimize his relationship to Vulpius was a greater scandal than the original liaison (490). The first time the couple appeared publicly together as husband and wife was at a tea at the house of Johanna Schopenhauer (1766–1838). (Johanna, the mother of Arthur, would shortly become a famous author in her own right.) She had only recently moved to Weimar and believed that Goethe had chosen her house for the occasion because of her urbanity and outsider status. Needless to say, she was quite gracious to Christiane, and Goethe seemed grateful to Schopenhauer. As Schopenhauer later quipped, if Goethe could give that woman his name, she certainly could give her a cup of tea (Köhler 27).

Goethe's own way of life and his relationship to the state of matrimony were much discussed. He was criticized both for living together with a woman without marrying her and for then finally marrying her. What is striking about the early reception of the novel, however, was that scarcely anyone referred to Goethe's personal life in their discussion of it, even in private letters. This is especially noteworthy since one of the main criticisms of *Die Wahlverwandtschaften* during Goethe's lifetime was that it was an immoral work. The early critics, however, did not read Goethe's life into the novel, but kept the author's life and work in separate categories. This treatment is in sharp contrast to the novel's later reception, especially in the last twenty years of the nineteenth century. Then, it would be treated almost exclusively in respect to Goethe's own life.

Die Wahlverwandtschaften initially caused a sensation. Several of Goethe's contemporaries compared the public's reaction to that of *Die Leiden des jungen Werthers* (Böttiger, *"Die Wahlverwandtschaften,"* 189) and many noted the controversy that surrounded its interpretation (Böttiger, "Ueber Göthe's," 108; F. Schlegel,

"Über Liebe," 252; Abeken, *Goethe*, 109). A fierce debate emerged almost immediately between those readers who loved and admired the book and those who hated it. Several reviewers thought that the novel signaled Goethe's decline as an author (Rehberg 101–7; Wieland, Letter to Böttiger, 165). For example, the literary historian Franz Christoph Horn (1781–1837) argues that although the book was much read, it was so bad that it could not be liked even by those who normally admired Goethe (225). The Bishop of Konstanz declared that *Die Wahlverwandtschaften* could do more moral damage than Laclos's *Liaisons dangereuses* (Dangerous Liaisons, 1782) (Wessenberg 108). Others, in contrast, compared *Die Wahlverwandtschaften* to the *Odyssey* and Goethe to Homer (Anonymous, Advertisement 84; Meißner, *Allgemeine*, 383; Ancillon 376). Many critics argued that the novel contained a vigorous defense of marriage and was therefore an extremely moral text (Conz, "Noch einige," 256; Eckermann 153, 155–56). The controversy surrounding the novel's interpretations was so intense that not only was the novel itself critiqued, but several of the reviews were hotly debated both privately and in the press. Over twenty reviews were published solely on *Die Wahlverwandtschaften* in Goethe's time. Numerous other published accounts further addressed the novel in the context of Goethe's other works or of German literature generally.[1] Eckermann's extremely positive interpretation of the novel, one that stressed its moral strains, led in part to his future role as the official recorder of Goethe's thoughts.

Die Wahlverwandtschaften was also actively canvassed in the letters of the time. Perhaps one of the strangest, and certainly one of the most anecdotal, reactions to the novel was that of Zacharias Werner (1768–1823), the Romantic author. He wrote to Goethe that reading the novel lead to his conversion to Catholicism. In particular, he cites these lines from the novel as having been inspired by God and as the cause of his religious awakening: "Nur unter der Bedingung einer völligen Entsagung hatte Ottilie sich verziehen, und diese Bedingung war für ihre ganze Lebenszeit unerläßlich"[2] [Only under the condition of complete renunciation had Ottilie forgiven herself; and this condition was binding for the rest of her life]. The list of the famous contemporaries who gave their opinions on the novel include Friedrich Heinrich Jacobi (1743–1819), Wieland, August Wilhelm (1767–1845) and Friedrich Schlegel (1772–1829), Alexander (1769–1859) and Wilhelm von Humboldt (1767–1835), Friedrich Heinrich Karl Baron de la Motte Fouqué (1777–1843), Rahel Varnhagen (1771–1833), Bettina von Arnim (1785–1859), Theresa Huber (1764–1829), Achim von Arnim (1781–1831), and Clemens Brentano (1778–1842).

Several critics even tried to analyze the virulence of the critical response to the novel. Already in 1814, one anonymous critic — possibly Adolph Wagner (1774–1835), the uncle of Richard Wagner — saw two reigning propensities in the reception of the work, both of which he characterized as prejudices of the time: the first is the notion that all artwork should have a moral tendency; the second regards the romantic expectations of the contents and style of the work. Readers of the time who expected to find a more fantastic style or impassioned, idealistic expressions of yearnings were disappointed in a novel that seemed middle-class and prosaic (A. Wagner? 230–31).

This anonymous critic was right in his characterization of the two main branches of the early criticism. The most important aspect of criticism of this time was the debate over the novel's morality. Those who defended and those who criticized Goethe's work placed central importance on the moral function of the novel. For critics on both sides of the fence, art did not exist for art's sake (and indeed, one of Goethe's fiercest critics, de Valenti, condemned this view of art as extremely dangerous to public mores). Instead, they tended to emphasize the didactic function of art and apply a moral litmus test to the novel. Thus, it became of utmost importance to "decide" upon the morality of the whole work. Goethe's critics declared that he had failed the test in that his novel attacked the very foundation of society, while his proponents hailed Ottilie's death as the triumph of reason over passion. The debates over the central issues of the novel, as whether the novel was meant as a defense or an attack of marriage, or even whether it ultimately is about the triumph of human free will or of natural passion and necessity, therefore were not simply about interpretive disagreements but about the moral and hence "aesthetic" worth of the novel.

A second critical divide of the early reception was the assessment of the overall quality of the novel. Critics could not even agree on whether it was a popular, crowd-pleaser or an esoteric novel written for the elite. They further either hailed it as Goethe's best or worst. The harshest published criticism thought the writing so bad that it was intended to be an insult to the German people (Rehberg; cf. Wieland, Letter to Böttiger, 164). Many found the characters to be unrealistic, flat, and cold. The fiercest proponents of the novel, and often those closely personally associated with Goethe himself, proclaimed the novel riveting and highly moving. They would repeatedly attest to the lifelike qualities of the characters that Goethe had created. Several early readers found Goethe's latest work boring and too laden with details (Rehberg; Wieland; Anonymous, "Französisches"). Other critics praised the details, especially in Goethe's ability to use them to paint an accurate portrait of contemporary life (Solger 180). Notably, several critics (even at least one who was negatively disposed toward the novel) believed that the novel was too much a mirror of its time to be judged by its current generation (Savigny, Letter to Creuzer; Solger; A. Wagner).

What is perhaps most surprising about the early reception of the novel was the degree to which Goethe attempted to fashion public opinion about it. Not only did he write his own advertisement for the novel, but he attempted to solicit reviews for publication from those who would be favorably disposed towards it. He also tried to receive permission from his personal correspondents to publish their positive words on the novel.[3] Then, when he came across a review that he particularly liked, that of Bernhard Rudolf Abeken (1780–1866), he had it reprinted at his own cost and handed it en masse to friends and acquaintances for further dispersal. Goethe also kept copies of it on hand and would send it to anyone who would inquire about the novel or to anyone who had said something disagreeable about it.

Although many of the more negative reactions to the novel were not printed, but bandied about in private correspondence, Goethe quickly became aware that the book aroused a great deal of antipathy and criticism. Some of his acquaintances told him face to face of their displeasure. For example, when Goethe asked Karl Ludwig von Knebel (1744–1834, the former tutor of Karl August who had brought Goethe to Weimar), what he thought of the book, Knebel bluntly answered that he could not stomach [verdauen] it (Härtl 56, 171, 394; and *HA*, 6:641). To which Goethe ironically and perhaps somewhat sardonically replied that Knebel was not his intended audience: he had written the novel for young girls. As Wilhelm von Humboldt noted on another occasion, one could never voice a criticism or even make jokes to Goethe about his works (Letter to Caroline von Humboldt).

It did not take long for critiques of the novel to appear. Already in December of 1809, just two months after the novel's publication date, Riemer complains to Goethe of the "Philister-Kritiker" [philistine critics] who have reviewed the book. He is particularly upset that many do not see the battle between morality and passion contained within the book (*FA 2*, 6:516–17). A few weeks later, on 31 December 1809, Goethe complains rather bitterly of his reading public to Karl Friedrich Graf von Reinhard (1761–1837), Napoleon's ambassador to Cassel. Goethe writes:

> Das Publicum, besonders das deutsche, ist eine närrische Karikatur des demos; es bildet sich wirklich ein, eine Art von Instanz, von Senat auszumachen, und im Leben und Lesen dieses oder jenes wegvotieren zu können was ihm nicht gefällt. Dagegen ist kein Mittel als ein stilles Ausharren. Wie ich mich denn auf die Wirkung freue, welche dieser Roman [*Die Wahlverwandtschaften*] in ein paar Jahren auf manchen beim Wiederlesen machen wird. (*FA 2*, 6:523)

> [The public, especially the German one, is a foolish caricature of the demos. It really imagines that it forms a kind of court or senate and can vote down in life or in reading this or that which it does not like. The only remedy against this is quietly to hold out. How I look forward to the effect that this novel [*Elective Affinities*] will have in a few years on many people upon rereading it.]

The novel indeed received harsh criticism. It was poorly received by several different sectors of the German population. Members of the clergy condemned it, and anonymous reviews savagely attacked it. But what perhaps hurt the most, many of the other German literary figures had negative or lukewarm reactions to it. Before I turn to the published reviews, it is interesting to note the early reactions within the letters of Goethe's contemporaries. While it is difficult to measure the influence that such comments may have had, they nevertheless indicate certain tendencies within the age and reflect many of the same issues present within published criticism. Thus, while one might expect Goethe's fellow writers and acquaintances to treat the style of the novel with a critical eye, one may be surprised at the type of moralism present within their letters. Some of the harshest words spoken about the morality of *Die Wahlverwandtschaften* came from this group of Goethe's peers.

Unpublished Comments

The reactions to Goethe's novel by Germany's elite were mixed. Although Wilhelm Grimm (1786–1859) tells his brother Jacob (1785–1863) that he found much to praise within the novel, he also explains that he found the first half of it boring (28 October 1809; 22 November 1809). His brother Ludwig Emil Grimm (1790–1863) similarly found the book so boring that he nearly fell asleep while it was being read aloud (42). Friedrich Schlegel writes his brother that the novel is ingenious and therefore appealing, but he also complains that it is cold, that the ending seems forced, and that the effect of the whole is "seltsam" [strange] and "gemein" [common/mean]. In addition, he finds that it gives little consolation or joy (Letter to A. W. Schlegel, 102). Although Wilhelm von Humboldt praises aspects of the work and notes that he will enjoy rereading it, he finds fault with the excessive details about the landscaping and everyday lives of the characters. He also writes to Welcker that Goethe has not properly prepared his readers for some of the main events in the novel and further predicts that many will find it immoral (88). The novelist Johann Ernst Wagner (1769–1812) writes that although he would like to be pleased with the work by the master, he is dissatisfied with it. He admires several of the details, but complains that the novel handles sin as something holy. He also likes none of the female characters and believes that he could have created better ones (339–40). Friederike Helene Unger (1741–1813) writes August Wilhelm Schlegel that the morality of the book is "abscheulich" [atrocious] and that even aesthetically it is below the standard of Goethe's other works. Tieck, according to Leopold von Gerlach, called it "Qualverwandtschaften" [Torture Affinities] — a fact that Bettina Brentano let Goethe know (Riemer 166). And when Jean Paul was asked whether he would have liked to have written the novel, he replied that he would have — except for the immoral parts (W. von Gerlach 462).

Although Rahel Levin (later Varnhagen) had initially given a positive endorsement of the novel, she is highly critical of it four-

teen years later. In May of 1823, she records in her diary that although she admires much of the details within the novel, she finds
the topic distasteful. She is particularly critical of Ottilie because of
her headache, dark connection with nature, and lack of talent
(259). She finds it revolting that Ottilie holds a child in her arms
while reading and walking around: "Gerechter Gott, wie kann
einem das einfallen, wenn man ein holdes Kind zu besorgen hat
und im Freien ist!" (259) [Good God, how can that occur to
someone, when one is outdoors and has a sweet child to take care
of!]. Almost twenty years after *Die Wahlverwandtschaften* was published, the novel was still condemned in private letters on moral
grounds. Heine is said to have claimed that Goethe was a corrupter
of religion. Specifically, he believed that the novel overturned "alles
Heilige" [everything holy] and was an attack against religion, morality, and the social forms (Diepenbrock-Grüter 146).

Two of the harshest criticisms of the novel on moral grounds
came from men quite close to Goethe: Jacobi and Wieland. Both
condemned the book because of its possible immoral influence and
both questioned its aesthetic merits. Jacobi reports to his corre-
spondent, the translator and poet, Johann Heinrich Voß (1751–
1826), that Schelling is quite enchanted with the novel (43; cf.
Schelling). Jacobi personally, however, finds the book an "Är-
gernis" [scandal]. Theresa Huber further relates (Letter to Böttiger) that Jacobi's sisters told her that their brother would have
been ashamed to have written such "ein unanständiges unsittliches
Buch" [an improper, immoral book]. In a letter a few weeks later
to Friedrich Köppen (1775–1858), professor of philosophy at
Landshut, Jacobi gives a more detailed account of his dissatisfaction (44–45). The double resemblance of the child to Ottilie and
the Captain, which he holds to be the soul of the book, shocks
him. He finds nothing at all godlike or heavenly in Ottilie's character and in general claims that one can find none of the characters
appealing. The ending of the novel, however, most offends him,
and his statements about it became quite famous and influential in
later criticism. He is disturbed at the seeming metamorphosis of
"Fleischlichkeit in Geistlichkeit" [carnality into spirituality] and
"die Himmelfahrt der bösen Lust" [the ascension of evil desire].
He concludes his comments on the novel by alluding to Bettina
von Arnim's connection to it. He dismisses the discussion of

whether Bettina is an inspiration for Ottilie's or Luciane's character as not worthy of notice.

Wieland's exposition on the novel was much lengthier, and although some of his dissatisfaction is expressed ironically, he nevertheless fiercely objects to the book's immoral tone. To Goethe himself, however, he spoke in a friendly manner about the novel (*FA* 2, 6:511). Wieland wrote two letters in which he discussed the novel at length. To a countess, who has expressed a desire to know his opinion on the novel, he both praises and criticizes it (158–59). He begins first by characterizing Goethe as the most beloved and the most feared of German authors. After giving a word of caution on prospective readers (no woman younger than fifty ought to be allowed to read it), he praises several of the characters, including the Captain, the English Lord, and Mittler. He then quickly begins a lively criticism of the novel. He believes Goethe's desire to write an instructive novel misled him into including too many details from the arts and sciences. He even suggests that Goethe used these details as padding to produce a longer work so that he would receive more money from the publisher! As irritated as he seems to be with the details, however, he also humorously claims that they are the best part of the book. For respectable female readers, these details are the only things that can compensate "für den Verdruß und Eckel an einer so bisarren . . . unsittlichen und scandalosen Geschichte" [for the annoyance and the disgust of such a bizarre, immoral, and scandalous story].

Wieland's harshest words about the novel were expressed to his close friend Karl August Böttiger (1760–1835), a philologist, archeologist, and headmaster of the Weimar Gymnasium from 1791–1804. He writes even more openly to his friend than to the countess, especially since he believed that the letter would be destroyed after it had been read. In this letter, he writes that thanks to Goethe's fame and the public's subsequent sheep-like and "asininische Zufriedenheit mit jedem Futter" [asinine satisfaction with every fodder] that he gives them, he has no incentive to produce great works any more. As far as Wieland is concerned, the only reason that Goethe has written *Die Wahlverwandtschaften* is to make some extra money. He refers to the novel as a "Machwerk" [bad job or concoction] and argues that Goethe's scorn for his readers is evident from the very title of the novel to the development of the story. To all rational readers, the use of the chemical theory is nonsense and childish fooling around. He further asks how Goethe could call this "concoction" a novel and expect that we would take it to be a real work of art. He continues:

> Wissen wir denn etwa nicht was ein Roman ist? Sein Buch ist ein farrago, ein Mischmasch von Dialogen und Vorlesungen über Gartenkunst, Baukunst, Decorationskunst, Mahlerei, Bildnerei, Musik, Mimische Kunst, u. Gott weiß über wie vielerlei Künste, und von Auszügen aus andern Büchern, die eben so gut in jedem andern stehen könnten. . . . Gewiß, vor Zwanzig oder Dreißig Jahren würde er sich geschämt haben, eine solche Composition einen Roman zu nennen? Was für ein armseliger Wicht ist sein Edua[rd] was für ein mystisches Luftgespenst u. Traumbild seine Ottilie? Und wie sollen wir nicht merken, daß diese Ottilie nur eine neue Auflage, oder vielmehr die Carricatur einer Kopie seiner Mignon, und sein Eduard ein zweiter Don Fernando, aber ein noch viel schlechterer Mensch ist als dieser? (165)

> [Do we not know what a novel is? His book is a farrago, a mishmash of dialogues and lectures on landscaping, architecture, decorating, painting, portraiture, music, mimic art, and God knows on how many arts, and from excerpts from other books that could just as well be part of any other. . . . Certainly, he would have been ashamed to have called such a composition a novel twenty or thirty years ago. What kind of a poor wretch is his Eduard — what kind of a mystical air-spirit and dream-image is his Ottilie? And how are we not supposed to notice that this Ottilie is only a new edition — or rather more the caricature of a copy of his Mignon, and his Eduard a second Don Fernando, only a much worse human being?]

Wieland then briefly condemns the double adultery depicted in the novel and states that such a scene is not worthy of the author of *Werther*, *Tasso* (1790), or *Iphigenie* (1787). He then concludes by asking Böttiger not to relay these opinions any further and to burn the letter as soon as he has read it.[4]

Goethe, of course, was not without enthusiastic proponents within personal correspondences. Charlotte von Schiller thought that *Die Wahlverwandtschaften* demonstrated Goethe's infinite understanding and genius as a writer. She further praised its realistic qualities. Rahel Levin's first impression of the novel was positive, and she commands her sister to read the book and speaks of it as a fortification of the mind (447). The archeologist and philologist Friedrich Gottlieb Welcker (1784–1868) wrote ecstatically of Goethe's new masterpiece to Caroline von Humboldt. He compares the novel to *Werther* and although he finds the themes to be the same, writes of how much more restrained the work of the more mature Goethe is. He judges the effect of the whole to be classical: Goethe exhibits within it a Sophoclean harmony and classical clarity (87). The novel impressed Savigny as harmonious and noble (Letter to Creuzer). Those writing to Goethe himself, of course, were extreme in their praise of his work, as they tried to jockey for favor from Goethe. For example, Zelter writes:

> Es giebt gewisse Sinfonien von Haydn, die durch ihren losen liberalen Gang mein Blut in behagliche Bewegung bringen und den freyen Theilen meines Körpers die Neigung und Richtung geben wohlthätig nach außen zu wirken. . . . So geht mir's wenn ich Ihre Romane lese und so ist mir's geworden, wie ich heute Ihre *Wahlverwandtschaften* las. Das muthwillige geheimnißvolle Spiel mit den Dingen der Welt und den Figuren die darinne angestellt und geleitet werden, kann Ihnen niemals mißlingen, mag auch zwischen durchlaufen was Platz hat, oder sich Platz macht.
>
> Dazu eignet sich endlich noch eine Schreibart welche wie das klare Element beschaffen ist, dessen flinke Bewohner durcheinander schwimmen, blinkelnd oder dunkelnd auf und abfahren, ohne sich zu verirren oder zu verlieren.
>
> Man könnte zum Poeten werden über eine solche Prosa, und ich möchte des Teufels werden daß ich keine solche Zeile schreiben kann. (373)

[There are certain symphonies of Haydn, whose free, broad movements sets my blood pleasantly flowing and my limbs agreeably tending to outward activity. . . . So it is with me when I read your novels; so it was today when I read *Die Wahlverwandtschaften*. That spirited, symbolical playing with the things of this world and the characters you there set up and move about, can never fail of success, whatever else has a place or is made a place for in it. And then the style so well suits — a style composed like that clear element whose nimble denizens flash to and fro, sparkling and darkling, yet never bewildered or lost. One could wax a poet over such a prose — the devil is in it that I cannot so write myself. (Trans. from Mann 1933, 102)]

After Zelter thus praises Goethe's work, he writes of the sensation that the title of the novel has caused among Goethe's friends. He goes on to tell Goethe that they wish to be able to disseminate Goethe's own meaning of the title, but are at a loss as to what that might be. He hints that he too wishes he could have something to say about the title as many regard him as Goethe's spokesman (374). Although the letter, of course, did not influence a large number of Goethe's contemporaries, it is an important piece within the reception history of the novel for two main reasons: first it indicates that even Goethe's closest friends were troubled by the novel's strange title; and second it became influential in the interpretation of the novel over a hundred years later when Thomas Mann quotes it in full in his essay on the novel. One can perhaps further judge how extreme the Goethe cult became by Mann's comments on these lines. He claims that Zelter scarcely does justice to Goethe's writing abilities (176).

Although it is difficult to gauge the impact of private letters on the initial reception of a text, they do show how some of Goethe's best known contemporaries reacted to his novel. In addition, whatever their initial influence may or may not have been, many of these letters played important roles in the subsequent generations of scholarship. A study of the published criticism makes apparent that many of the criticisms voiced in the private correspondences were mirrored in the printed commentaries.

Negative Reviews and Responses

Of the negative reviews that appeared during Goethe's lifetime, two stand out for their influence and the intensity of their criticism: one by August Wilhelm Rehberg (1757–1836) on 1 January 1810 and one by Ernst Joseph Gustav de Valenti (1794–1871) in 1831. Both essays became part of a negative canon of works against Goethe and are representative of the conservative attacks on Goethe as well as on the novel. Although Rehberg and de Valenti approach the novel from somewhat different perspectives (Rehberg as a critic, de Valenti, a clergyman), both ultimately censure the morality of the novel and condemn Goethe as undermining traditional social and religious values. For them, Goethe failed as an artist in his main responsibility to educate and elevate his public.

Rehberg's essay is one of the harshest (and most talked about) published reviews against the novel. Rehberg was a conservative writer, a statesman in Hanover, an opponent of the French Revolution, and one of the first to disseminate Burke's philosophy in Germany.[5] He was the also the childhood friend of Charlotte von Stein's husband. Although the review was published anonymously, his identity did not remain a secret. August Wilhelm Schlegel was aware of the authorship as early as May of the same year. By the end of the nineteenth century, Rehberg's review was still considered one of the most important critiques ever written against Goethe, and one that was still actively addressed (Baumgartner 73; Scherer 352).

Rehberg's essay is an extremely important piece because it is one of the first examples of a long line of conservative opposition to Goethe. For Rehberg, as for many of Goethe's critics who came after him, Goethe was not a serious author, but one who catered to popular, and hence "lower," tastes. Rehberg is therefore extremely critical of the quality of the novel and of Goethe's writing style in general. Because Rehberg gradually builds upon his criticisms of Goethe in order to culminate the review in a condemnation of the novel, I will examine the critique in some detail. Moreover, Rehberg's highly negative assessment of Goethe's other works also establishes the context for his critique of *Die Wahlverwandtschaften*.

In many ways, Rehberg's essay prefigures Goethe's fall from public and intellectual favor that began in the 1820s and continued well into the nineteenth century (Sommerfeld 227; Leppmann 48–65; Mandelkow, *Goethe in Deutschland*, 13–15, 57–84). It is all too often forgotten that although Goethe had a strong circle of supporters who revered him during and after his lifetime, the Goethe cult was not a continuous phenomenon. Indeed, Goethe fell out of favor during the last years of his life, only to be largely ignored for the first decades after his death. Wolfgang Menzel (1798–1873), one of the most influential critics of the 1820s and 1830s, argued that Goethe's work was insubstantial and that Goethe was a "mere author of fashion" (Hohendahl 226). Whereas today Goethe is still often thought of as a spokesperson of traditional patriarchal values, that was by no means the way in which political or religious conservatives viewed him. Goethe was not the favorite of conservative (or for that matter liberal) politicians in the first half of the nineteenth century. Indeed, his novel, *Die Wahl-verwandtschaften,* was repeatedly used by conservatives as evidence that Goethe was attempting to undermine not only conservative and Christian values, but even his own classical aesthetic standards.

Rehberg's tone is often cutting and ironic. Almost half of his review addresses not *Die Wahlverwandtschaften,* but Goethe's status and reputation as a writer. Like Wieland, Rehberg writes that Goethe's early popular success has led him to disregard the quality of his own work. Rehberg's main task throughout the essay is less a criticism of the novel per se than an attack upon the popularity and the "Promethean" myth of Goethe. He attempts to lay bare the reasons behind Goethe's current, and in his mind undeserved, popularity. He treats Goethe not as the revered creator of German literary standards, but as a pop-icon who has gained his popular following by lowering aesthetic standards. Within the review, Rehberg attacks not only Goethe, but the German reading public as well.

Rehberg begins his essay by praising Goethe's abilities to read and reflect the spirit of the German times. However, he then becomes harshly critical of those times and even blames Goethe in part for creating them. For example, he states that if one were to go through Goethe's works one by one, one would see in them the characteristic way of thinking, taste, and sensibility of the German people. Throughout the essay, Rehberg then attempts over and over again to illustrate how bad these German characteristics are. He sees *Die Wahlverwandtschaften* as the culmination of a long process of decline in Goethe's artistic qualities. According to Rehberg, Goethe always gave his readers:

> was ihrem Geschmacke und ihren Gesinnungen angemessen war, und den schwachen Seiten des Charakters schmeichelte. Deswegen ist es sehr geschwind dahin gekommen, daß alles was der Vf. des *Werthers* gab, mit unbegränzter Bewunderung aufgenommen ward. Es scheint aber, daß diese bey dem angebeteten Dichter selbst, Ueberdruß und Widerwillen erzeugt habe. In keines Volks Literatur ist es jemals vorgekommen, daß ein Liebling der Nation das Uebermaß der Verehrung seiner Zeitgenossen mit so derben Aeußerungen der Verachtung erwiedert habe. (101)

> [what was appropriate to their taste and fundamental beliefs, and that which flattered the weak sides of the character. That is why it

has so quickly come to this, that everything that the author of *Werther* produced was accepted with unlimited admiration. It seems, however, that this has produced weariness and aversion in the beloved writer himself. In no other nation's literature has it ever occurred that a darling of the nation has reciprocated the excess of veneration of his contemporaries with such gruff expressions of contempt.]

Rehberg characterizes the Germans as proud because they believe they know how to do everything better than all other nations. Yet, these same "proud" Germans cannot stop grabbing at foreign things or bringing over new foreign elements to Germany. Goethe's German "genius" realized this and gave the public what they wanted. Because "Greekness" was much discussed by the public, he gave the people an Iphigenia. Rehberg ironically notes that Euripides himself would admire Goethe's version of the play should he come back to life. Similarly, Rehberg is critical of Goethe's "Hermann und Dorothee" ("Hermann and Dorothea," 1797). Here Goethe has preserved the "homerische Einfachheit der Sitte" [simplicity of Homeric customs] by adapting them to the lower classes, i.e., demeaning them.

In part, Rehberg implies that the scorn with which Goethe treats his public resides in the quality (or lack thereof) of works that he produces. Voltaire, the great English writers, and the ancients, according to Rehberg, all struggled until their death to earn the praise of the public through the quality of their work. Goethe, in contrast, was content not to excel but to rest upon his laurels and produce works of low quality. Rehberg admits to Goethe's talents and abilities and argues that Goethe's work shows the potential of what he could do had he a different relationship to his adoring public.

Rehberg then turns his pen against *Wilhelm Meisters Lehrjahre*. He laughs at the praise given to the novel by the Romantics[6] (claiming that they were simply trying to become Goethe's disciples), and once again insinuates that the novel's popularity stems from the low tastes of its readers. The character Wilhelm Meister is, according to Rehberg, an unprincipled simpleton. The novel flatters anyone who feels capable of becoming a Wilhelm Meister, especially one who would be all too willing to find a Philine, a countess, and a Natalie with whom to flirt, and above all, one who would want to sleep with a Mariane. Rehberg then applies a heavy dose of sarcasm in "praising" the novel, but in effect leaves his reader with the impression that it is a boring account of uninteresting stories in a pedantic and long-winded style.

Rehberg then turns his attention to *Die Wahlverwandtschaften*. His first complaint (and one similar to many of the private letters) is that Goethe provides so many details of country life that the book is boring. He also intimates, as Wieland does in his later letters, that Goethe provides the details as filler in order to stretch the story into a book-length manuscript. Rehberg then enters the main body of his critique with a scathing character analysis. He finds fault with almost every character. Eduard is a "baronized" Wilhelm Meister, and Charlotte and the Captain are simply boring. He finds Ottilie to be an unoriginal character, one who is reminiscent of both Mignon and an old painting by either Masaccio or Giotto (104). Mittler, in turn, effects nothing, motivates nothing, has no influence, and only appears every now and then from the clouds. The stiff formality of the Schoolmaster's letters ought to make the reader hate healthy reason, while simple masons philosophize like Goethe himself (104). Rehberg further criticizes the dialogue of the novel because he sees no differentiation of language among the noble characters and finds the tone of the whole to be too abstract and metaphysical.

Like most critics of the time, Rehberg believed that the artist has moral and didactic responsibilities towards the public. His chief charge against *Die Wahlverwandtschaften* is its failure to follow the classical tragic formula as advocated by the Enlightenment. The novel fails, in his mind, to use readers' passions to elevate their sensibilities. Rehberg sarcastically claims that Goethe had written the novel in order to mock the propensities and the tastes of the age, including superstition, childish premonitions, belief in coincidences, and landscape gardening. It is clear from Rehberg's tone, however, that he does not really believe that Goethe is critical of his age, but a child of it, if not one of its leading lights. Rehberg claims to see irony, but this claim is only a rhetorical tactic with which to denigrate the novel and provide an opportunity to present his own critique of the times. For example, after describing and mocking the *tableaux vivants* for their attempts to make paintings seem more concrete, Rehberg hopes that next we will hear that a symphony by Haydn will be fixed and baked in a pâté, so that it can be enjoyed with the tongue (105). Similarly, Rehberg writes that the novel contains something for everyone: even scientists (he here probably means Ritter) of the Bavarian Academy will rejoice in the scientific experiments of the Englishman.

Rehberg, however, most shows his disdain for the novel when he suggests an alternative ending. In proposing his own conclusion, he admits that such a book might be less of a true impression of the "Zeitgeist," but it would gain in naturalism, if it were to end thusly:

> Charlotte konnte bewogen werden, in die Scheidung zu willigen. Es ist ja heut zu Tage so leicht Ehen zu trennen, und neue zu knüpfen. Wie manche tanzte gern selbst auf dem Hochzeittage ihrer geschiednen Hälfte! Charlotte hatte gute Gründe im Ueberflusse, sich in die Einsamkeit zurück zu ziehen. . . . Der Baron erhält seinen Willen. Wie könnte Ottilie sich weigern! Nichts in der Welt hatte in ihr den Gedanken erregt, es sey Unrecht, Unfrieden in eine Familie zu bringen, von der man freundschaftlich aufgenommen worden, und niemand hatte versucht in ihr den Gedanken zu beleben, daß man nicht Unrecht thun müsse. . . . Bald aber fühlt auch sie, daß sie sehr unrecht gethan, ein Herz aus der zweyten oder dritten Hand anzunehmen; und daß Eduard eine solche Ehe zehn Jahre früher hätte eingehen müssen. *Sie ist es sich selbst schuldig,* ein solches Unrecht nicht zu leiden. Auch ihr Herz hat Ansprüche. Es knüpft ein Verhältnis mit dem schönlockigten Architecten an, der als Nebenfigur in den *Wahlverwandtschaften* erschienen ist. . . . Soll die poetische Gerechtigkeit bis ans Ende geführt werden, so muß der Baron nunmehr sterben, und die Ottilie an die Reihe kommen, von einem Geliebten bestraft zu werden, der abermals findet, er habe sich einer Ueberjährigen ergeben. (106, emphasis in original)

[Charlotte could be convinced to get a divorce. It is after all nowadays so easy to sever marriages and to form new ones. How many dance willingly even on the wedding day of their estranged spouse! Charlotte had an over-abundance of good reasons to return to solitude. . . . The Baron gets his wish. How could Ottilie deny him. Nothing in the world had aroused in her the thought that it would be an injustice to bring discord into a family from which one had been kindly received. And no one had tried to stimulate the thought in her that one ought not to do wrong. Soon, however, even she feels, that she has done very wrong to take a heart second or third-hand, and that Eduard should have entered into such a marriage ten years ago. *She owes it to herself* not to suffer such an injustice. Her heart, too, has demands. It forms a relationship with the beautifully curly-haired Architect, who appears as a secondary character in the *Die Wahlverwandt-schaften.* . . . Should the poetic justice be carried through to the end, so must the Baron now die, and it is Ottilie's turn to be punished by a lover, who once again discovers that he has given himself to an over-the-hill woman.]

In general, Rehberg's comments on the novel focus on Goethe's style (too detailed and abstract) and the characters (boring, self-indulgent, and immoral). Rehberg criticizes the characters for what would later be called their Romantic tendencies: their propensity to give preference to passion over reason and nature over society. Rehberg's essay, which was one of the first published reviews of the novel, marks the beginning a lively debate between those who saw the novel as aesthetically inferior and immoral and those who argue for its high aesthetic worth and morality. Many of Goethe's contemporaries agreed with Rehberg, while others, as will be discussed in the next section, argued that the novel's outcome was extraordinarily classical. For them, Ottilie's death marks the triumph of mind over body and therefore illustrates the power of Stoic renunciation.

An examination of Rehberg's review demonstrates one of the controversies surrounding the reception of Goethe and his works during his own time. His popularity spoke against him in the eyes of some critics. Rehberg, Wieland, and others believed they saw a willingness on Goethe's part to sacrifice quality and morality in order to sell a lot of books. In their minds, Goethe was not a defender of tradition or of classical values, but a destroyer of them. To them, Goethe, although exhibiting a heightened contempt for the people, was a poet of the people.

Rehberg's review caused quite a stir. In private letters, Goethe's friends and acquaintances called it one-sided and bitter (Böttiger, Letter to Röchlitz; Stein 238), hard and crude (Knebel 411), and a disgrace (Savigny, Letter to Brentano). Jean Paul writes that he was tempted to say a public word against the newspaper for publishing it, even though he himself was not pleased with the way in which adultery was portrayed within the novel (151). What is most striking about the commentaries on Rehberg's piece, however, is that several of the authors agreed in principle with Rehberg's assessment of German taste. Thus the reviews of the time demonstrate the uncertainty with which Germans viewed their own aesthetic abilities. German thinkers during this time were still trying to come to terms with Germany's place within European culture. This confusion is reflected in their assessment of Goethe: to some he is a panderer to lower, German tastes, to others, one of the founding fathers of high German culture, and to still others, a great author who transcended his German "backwardness" to achieve a more European ideal.

Several of the reactions to Rehberg's critique address the issue of German taste and aesthetics. On 14 July 1810, an anonymous reply to Rehberg's review was printed in the *Morgenblatt für gebildete Stände*. It begins by praising Rehberg as someone who understands German literature and the character of the Germans, has a healthy understanding of human beings, and does not lack wit and talent for persiflage. The main fault of Rehberg's review (according to this anonymous author) is that its one-sidedness leads to a judgment that is false and unfair. The author particularly defends Goethe's dramas, *Iphigenie* and *Tasso*, briefly praises *Die Wahlverwandtschaften* and then suggests that Rehberg does not belong to the class that could understand these works. He concludes by conceding one merit to the Rehberg review: that it will cause a reassessment of the practice of blindly imitating or idolizing Goethe and perhaps eventually lead to a more balanced reception of both Goethe and his works.

Böttiger in his anonymously published review (*"Die Wahlverwandtschaften"*) also addresses Rehberg's review and the inferiority of German taste. Like the anonymous critic above, Böttiger argues for the merits of *Iphigenie* and *Tasso*, but in a rather partisan defense of Goethe goes a great deal further. Although he notes that Goethe wove absurd, nonsensical elements into his novel, Böttiger believes that he did so in order to give the Germans something other than politics to talk about (189). Böttiger agrees with many aspects of Rehberg's assessment of German taste, and outlines the reasons why it is not as developed as it could be. He explains that German critics are often professors or businessmen who do not have enough leisure time truly to appreciate aesthetics. Furthermore, he finds that the German reading public is limited in scope. Members of the upper classes, insofar as they read at all, read primarily French texts. The majority of the German reading public is limited to young people of both sexes (192). Nevertheless, Böttiger argues that the Germans do have a small group of knowledgeable critics, a group to which Rehberg would belong were he not so lacking in the imagination and intellect needed to judge a work of literature (192).

Böttiger then focuses his attention more and more on the question of what is "German" in German literature and how one is to assess "German" literary texts, especially ones by Goethe. He disputes Rehberg's version of the development of German literature and goes through strange gyrations and justifications to disprove Rehberg's criticisms. He argues, for example, that not Goethe but Haller and Hagedorn were responsible for bringing the movement of sensibility to Germany, and that works of several earlier authors, including Gellert, Klopstock, and Nicolai, caused even greater sensations than Goethe's texts. Böttiger further disagrees that Goethe's works have anything "German" about them. *Götz* he finds to be so completely Shakespearean in style that it could be taken for a translations of one of Shakespeare's works. Similarly, Werther's weariness with life is so characteristically British that Fanny Burney could just as easily have written it as Goethe (192–93)! Böttiger then defends Goethe by criticizing other authors who are more extreme in exhibiting the characteristics that Rehberg lambastes and excessively praises the "foreign" qualities of Goethe's works. In other words, according to Böttiger, Goethe is deserving of his reputation and popularity due to the non-German qualities of his works. If Goethe is at all to be considered "German," Böttiger argues, it is only because of his protean ability to mimic the manner of any people (193). Finally, Böttiger prophesies that once the German tastes have matured, they will be able to appreciate Goethe's novel and retroactively reassess the criticism written about it (195).

The issue of whether *Die Wahlverwandtschaften* was a typical German product was even discussed outside of Germany. An anonymous French critic of the time echoes many of Rehberg's comments about the Germans ("Französisches"). This critic, too, frames the discussion of *Die Wahlverwandtschaften* within a critique of the German reading public. He claims that German authors do not have any incentive to strive to write good works of literature because their reading public will praise whatever they write (147–48). It is therefore a given, in his mind, that Goethe's novel will be read by the Germans. This review thus attempts to educate the reader about what is wrong with the novel. He begins to criticize the particulars of Goethe's novel, from its title, which should make one immediately mistrust the taste of the author, to its bizarre, superfluous details (148–49).

Of the printed reviews, Rehberg's was the harshest that appeared immediately after the novel's publication. However, beginning in the 1820s, Goethe and his works came under increasing attack by political and religious conservatives. Hohendahl sees the growing dissatisfaction with Goethe during this time as part of a larger "literary-critical conservatism" that "finds in the history of modern literature an aberrant development that, misled by critical Protestantism, tends to contradict church authority on the status and character of transcendence. The conservatives' claim that contemporary literature should be based on Christianity is forced, in the end, to turn even against the neo-humanism of Weimar" (218). Johann Wilhelm Friedrich Pustkuchen (1793–1834), a Lutheran minister, included an attack on *Die Wahlverwandtschaften* in his satiric novel, the "false" *Wilhelm Meisters Wanderjahre* (270–73).[7] Even fiercely nationalist thinkers, such as the journalist and critic Wolfgang Menzel, rejected Goethe as a national symbol for Germany. In his essay, "Göthe und Schiller," he attacked the immorality of *Die Wahlverwandtschaften* as a symptom of French immorality that had seeped its way into Germany after the revolution (368–71, 374).

The most famous of the negative reviews of the 1820s and 1830s was by Ernst Joseph Gustav de Valenti (1831). De Valenti was a protestant theologian, religious writer, and medical doctor. The review was published anonymously in the *Evangelische Kirchen-Zeitung* in 1831 (16–30 July). The editor of this newspaper, Ernst Wilhelm Hengstenberg,[8] was the most important representative of the new Lutheran orthodoxy in the nineteenth century (Mandelkow, *Goethe in Deutschland*, 161). Where the Rehberg review focused on the taste of the German people and the quality of Goethe's works, de Valenti's review centers on moral issues. In both instances, however, Goethe is viewed as too liberal a thinker whose ideas are subversive.

The focus of de Valenti's review is what the role of art should be. Although his views are more extreme than many of the other contemporary critics, he shares the belief that art should have a moral purpose. De Valenti fears that the current artistic trend signals a departure from using art to educate, and his review offers a critique of such art in general by turning to *Die Wahlverwandtschaften* in particular. He especially lambastes the notion that art should be completely free of laws of morality and operate according to its own rules and principles. De Valenti feels justified in offering moral criticisms of aesthetic works because he closely links God with an archetypal notion of the beautiful (das Urschöne, 366). Any work of art, accordingly, that does not treat moral aspects favorably necessarily leads us to a "false" aesthetic and immorality. De Valenti wishes to show the connection between blasphemy and the current "pseudo-art" for two main reasons: to improve and purify our aesthetic tastes and to save our souls in the afterlife (342). He finds Goethe's novel ideally suited to illustrate the impact of immorality within artistic works. The work, he argues, is anti-Christian and represents Goethe's "sacred" creed: that an all-powerful heathen fate rules over both God and human beings (358).[9] In de Valenti's mind, Goethe was a dangerous liberal who through his decadent (and hence poor) art tried to usher in a new era of social and aesthetic freedoms.

De Valenti is highly critical of the novel's chemical theory, which he believes attempts to undermine the social institution of marriage. He interprets the chemical theory to suggest that sexual instinct alone can decide which couples should be forever united. Because marriage vows are not strong enough to keep couples together when they are under the power of "erotischer Sympathie" [erotic sympathy], the book, in effect, erodes the institution of marriage. Erotic desire alone becomes holy and infallible, while marriages not founded upon erotic desire are entered into erroneously. Those characters thwarted by middle-class values from entering into their "true" partnerships (such as Werther or Ottilie) kill themselves in order to await the next world "wo der Wille der Natur die höchsten Triumphe feiert" (345) [where the will of nature celebrates its highest triumphs]. De Valenti further argues that the novel's teaching about the power of erotic sympathy reflects Goethe's own views. He supports this view by referring the reader to Goethe's whole life, his works, and his public. And although de Valenti's reference to Goethe's personal life is not at all specific, it is one of the few instances that a critic in this period mentions biographical details in connection to *Die Wahlverwandtschaften* (346).

The tone of the review becomes increasingly moralistic and demonstrates a strand of religious criticism that continued well into the nineteenth century — although by the end of the century this line of criticism was taken up by Catholic and not Protestant conservatives (Baumgartner). By the time de Valenti gets to the seventh chapter of the novel, he cuts short some of the recapitulation, as he believes that one cannot retell the beginning phases of the break-up of the marriage without engaging in sinfulness oneself or without corrupting the reader. According to his line of argument, it is impossible to mention an immoral act without attracting people towards committing it. He comments that Goethe seems not to notice how favorably he portrays the genesis of the destruction of marriage. With such a portrayal, Goethe falls into the category of the pseudo-art, "welche den Opiumrausch als wahres Wohlseyn und als Normalzustand der kräftig erregten Psyche darstellt" (347) [which portrays the opium-high as true well-being and as the normal condition of the strongly excited soul].

Throughout his review, de Valenti condemns the morality of the characters. As one would expect, he is extraordinarily critical of the Count and the Baroness. He dispenses with Mittler's criticisms of them by pointing out that the ridiculousness of Mittler's character prevents the reader from taking him seriously and is harshly critical of the fact that such a character is the only one who defends marriage (349). The fact that Charlotte likes the Captain even more when he, realizing his passion for Charlotte, begins to avoid her, is an illustration of how the devil uses virtue for his own ends (348). Goethe's portrayal of Ottilie is not spared de Valenti's scorn. That Goethe portrays her as innocent and ultimately as a saint or martyr is simply an indication of the depths to which an artist can sink when he ignores moral precepts in his work. De Valenti further finds the ending of Goethe's novel unbelievable: the common people would never worship Ottilie, the home-wrecker, as a saint. Rather they would judge her much more correctly than any of Goethe's more elevated readers and label her the "Eheteu-fel" [marriage-devil] that she is (362).

The narrowness of de Valenti's aesthetic judgment is perhaps best illustrated by his criticism of Ottilie's death scene. He finds it unbelievable and points the reader to Albrecht von Haller's medi-cal textbooks for a proper description of death by starvation: the delirium, cramps, and fevers of such a person would be obvious to any non-doctor. How is it, de Valenti asks, that the characters in the novel are so surprised by her death (361)?

What is striking about both Rehberg's and de Valenti's reviews is their personal vehemence against Goethe. In both cases, this ve-hemence seems to stem from a conservative fear and distrust of Goethe's ideas. Such conservatives viewed Goethe's *Wahlver-wandtschaften* as the culmination of a long line of works bent on upsetting the hierarchical rules of society. For these critics *Werther* and *Die Wahlverwandtschaften* were organs with which Goethe sought to overturn the rule of reason and religious law. For both Rehberg and de Valenti, Goethe's works were radical and revolu-tionary and as such harmful to society on intellectual, aesthetic, and moral levels.

Although both Rehberg's and de Valenti's reviews tend toward extremes, they do represent the criticisms of the time. Many agreed with Rehberg that the novel was poorly written and that Goethe had imposed upon his reading public. Many others believed, with de Valenti, that the novel was immoral and even dangerous. Men-zel argued that *Die Wahlverwandtschaften,* along with many of Goethe's other works, focused too much on human weaknesses and prejudices (*Die deutsche,* 368–74). Friedrich Schlegel also be-lieved that the world was for once correct in finding *Die Wahlver-wandtschaften* to be a bad and immoral book. In particular, he finds it immoral that the book does not address positive aspects of marriage, but focuses instead on the negative ("Über Liebe," 157). Even several of those critics who ultimately praised the novel found its moral stance too murky for the average reader. For Wessenberg, for example, the moral teaching is buried so deep within the novel that he almost wishes that readers would read Eckermann's inter-pretation, which emphasizes the novel's morality and its ultimate defense of marriage, before reading the novel itself (114).

The anti-Goethe sentiment in the reviews discussed above signaled Goethe's coming fall from public and intellectual favor. As we shall see in the next chapter, in the first fifty years after his death his works were largely ignored and his status as a German icon was called into question. Yet *Die Wahlverwandtschaften* was not without its early proponents. For many, it was not only Goethe's best work, but also a highly moral treatment of marriage — an assessment that Goethe actively sought to disseminate.

Before turning to those reviews that were staunchly supportive of Goethe's novel, it is interesting to note an example of an early American view on *Die Wahlverwandtschaften* (Anonymous "*Elective Affinities*"). Although a later scholar, Blankenagel, found the review to be weak due to its "cramped ethical and religious outlook" (386) — an outlook which Blankenagel argues was shared with "numerous myopic critics in Germany" (388) — the review is surprisingly balanced given the general one-sidedness of the reviews in Germany. The anonymous review begins with an anecdotal overview of the state of the German language and then continues by analyzing Goethe and his novel. He characterizes Goethe as "the well known author of Charlotte and Werter [sic]," "the patriarch" of German literature, and "the father of German sentiment" (53). This reviewer, in linking both *Werther* and *Die Wahlverwandtschaften* as sentimental works of literature, signals the later Anglo-American tendency, still largely evident today, of mischaracterizing Goethe as a Romantic. Because both works are love stories, despite their different styles and the marked differences in tone, the author considers both to be sentimental in style.

The reviewer offers nothing but praise for Goethe's descriptions of nature. Similarly, he is so impressed with Goethe's handling of the scene of the baby's death that he gives the passage in full in German. And although he is ultimately critical of the portrayal of fate within the novel, he admits the power of Goethe's prose. He finds passages throughout the novel to be so absorbing that, if one were reading it at sea during a squall, one would remain oblivious to the commotion.

Despite his overall praise for Goethe's writing abilities, the reviewer is harshly critical of many of the moral and ethical aspects of the novel. Like many of the German critics, he finds fault with the portrayal of baby Otto's features and its inclusion in a work of literature: "There is a mixture of absurdity and indelicacy in this idea which disgraces the work, and which we think, can be tolerated by no nation, that has any pretensions to taste" (55). Similarly, he echoes the main German critics in finding fault with Ottilie's journals (how could such an inexperienced young woman write them?), Goethe's excessive use of details (Goethe is just trying to show off his own knowledge), and the "immoral tendency" and "total want of delicacy" in some parts of the novel. However, the review is much more balanced than those of many German contemporaries. The reviewer, like many German critics, believes that works of art should be ethical, but he does not believe that the ethical criterion is the only one for judging works of art. Thus, he is able to write that in spite of its "glaring" moral defects, "the present work is powerfully attractive, and evidently from the pencil of a master. The style is of finished excellence; remarkably pure" (63). He can never speak of Goethe's genius "without enthusiasm, however much we may be disposed to reprobate his extravagancies" (64).

Shaping the Interpretation

Goethe's novel was not without its supporters in the press. The majority of its supporters, however, operated under the same philosophical rubric as its opponents: art necessarily had a moral and didactic function. Its defenders argued that the novel was extremely moral and that its detractors had simply misunderstood its main message. In strong contrast to those who argued that Goethe had written the novel for popular consumption, Goethe's defenders argued that the novel was so esoteric and complex that it could easily be misinterpreted. Of the reviewers who treated Goethe's novel favorably, many focused on the conflict within the novel between duty and passion. These critics argued that duty and marriage were victorious over nature and the "baser" passions (Abeken, "Ueber Goethes"; Solger; Meißner, *Conversations*, 257 and *Allgemeine*, 382–83; Eckermann). Ottilie for such critics symbolized the victory of human free will over the passions and the "lower" realm of nature (Solger 178–79; Abeken, "Ueber Goethes," 124; Conz, "Noch einige," 253–54). Some reviewers, such as Eckermann, equated the views of the "moral" characters (Charlotte, but especially Mittler) with Goethe's own views (153, 155–56).

Although the novel received several favorable reviews during Goethe's lifetime, two reviews stand out as the most influential in fashioning the novel's reception: Bernhard Rudolf Abeken's and Karl Wilhelm Ferdinand Solger's (1780–1819). These reviews came to be so influential in large part because Goethe actively promoted them (especially in the case of Abeken's essay) as the authorized readings of the novel. Each essay established a canonical reading of *Die Wahlverwandtschaften* that continues to exert an influence even today, especially since both essays often appear in appendices to German editions of Goethe's works. Abeken's essay was central to establishing the tradition of reading the novel primarily as the conflict between nature and duty. This interpretation became the most popular one among Goethe's proponents for generations. Solger's interpretation, which stressed the role of fate within the novel, while instrumental in establishing a canonical interpretation centered on the concept of fate, was not initially as influential as Abeken's essay. What is common to both essays, however, and what also became part of the canonical interpretation of the novel, is unqualified praise for Ottilie.

Before turning to the content of the essays, it is first necessary to understand the context of how they came to be the "authentic" interpretations. What made these essays so influential was perhaps not so much their content, but the fact that Goethe had publicly given his stamp of approval to both. Nor was this stamp of approval his only effort to shape the novel's reception. Even before the novel was published, he tried to influence the public's reaction to it. One of his early attempts to shape the reception was the anonymous advertisement he wrote that suggested the novel's philosophical importance (see Introduction). We also have records of numerous conversations and letters in which he defended the book in light of the criticisms that it was receiving. One of the most important statements in influencing subsequent scholarship (Benjamin 143–44) was a rather early one. In a conversation with Riemer (6/10 December 1809), who complains that the critics fail to understand the conflict of the novel, Goethe explains the reasons behind this misunderstanding:

> Dieser Kampf ist aber hinter die Szene verlegt, und man sieht, daß er vorgegangen sein müsse. Die Menschen betragen sich wie

vornehme Leute, die bei allem innern Zwiespalt doch das äußere Dekorum behaupten.

Der Kampf des Sittlichen eignet sich niemals zu einer ästhetischen Darstellung. Denn entweder siegt das Sittliche, oder es wird überwunden. Im erstern Fall weiß man nicht, was und warum es dargestellt worden; im andern ist es schmählich, das mit anzusehen; denn am Ende muß doch *irgend ein* Moment dem Sinnlichen das Übergewicht über das Sittliche geben, und eben dieses Moment gibt der Zuschauer gerade nicht zu, sondern verlangt ein noch schlagenderes, das der Dritte immer wieder eludiert, je sittlicher er selbst ist.

In solchen Darstellungen muß stets das Sinnliche Herr werden; aber bestraft durch das Schicksal, das heißt durch die sittliche Natur, die sich durch den Tod ihre Freiheit salviert.

So muß der Werther sich erschießen, nachdem er die Sinnlichkeit Herr über sich werden lassen. So muß Ottilie karterieren, und Eduard desgleichen, nachdem sie ihrer Neigung freien Lauf gelassen. Nun feiert erst das Sittliche seinen Triumph. (emphasis in original, *FA* 2, 6:516–17)

[The struggle is however displaced behind the scenes, and one sees that it must have gone on before. The persons conduct themselves like persons of distinction, who for all their inner division still maintain external decorum.

Moral struggles never lend themselves to aesthetic representation. For either morality triumphs or it is defeated. In the first instance, one does not know what was represented or why; in the second, it is ignominious to be its spectator. For in the end, one moment or another must indeed give the sensual the preponderance over the moral, and precisely to this moment the spectator does not accede but demands an even more striking one, which some other, a third person, keeps eluding, the more moral he himself is.

In such representations the sensual must always gain the upper hand, but [be] punished by fate — that is, by moral nature, which salvages its freedom through death.

Thus, Werther must shoot himself after he has allowed sensuality to gain the upper hand over him. Thus, Ottilie must suffer, and Eduard, too, once they have given free reign to their inclination. Only now does morality celebrate its triumph. (Trans. Corngold; Benjamin 312)]

With these defensive and ambiguous statements (Benjamin 312), Goethe tries to accomplish several things. He tries to explain the fact that so many critics viewed the novel as immoral, and he argues that aesthetic concerns prevented him from making the moral struggle too overt. The struggle had to be portrayed behind the scenes and therefore suffered the danger of being overlooked or misunderstood. He further appears to defend the morality of the whole by noting that Ottilie and Eduard suffer for their transgressions.[10] In general, Goethe seems to advocate reading the main theme of the novel as the conflict between passion and duty. This view, as discussed below, also closely corresponds to Abeken's interpretation.

Goethe's campaign to fashion the reception of *Die Wahlverwandtschaften* is further evident in his letters. He wrote to many people about the novel, informing them of a unified "Gestalt," hidden meanings, and the necessity of multiple rereadings. Then, when he saw the negative reaction that it was receiving, he attempted to publish a favorable review he had received in a letter (Letter to Rochlitz, 28 September 1809, Härtl 56; Letter to Eichstädt, 25 November 1809, *FA* 2, 6:513–16; cf. Eichstädt 273–74). When his chosen critic, the novelist and music critic Johann Friedrich Rochlitz, refused to publish his review, Goethe seemed for a time to give up his efforts to shape the critical reception, stating that perhaps it properly belonged to a future time to assess the conflicting opinions on his novel (Letter to Eichstädt, 25 November 1809, *FA* 2, 7:515–16).

By March of the 1810, however, Goethe acting under Riemer's suggestion once again attempted to shape the novel's critical reception. Goethe was so pleased with Abeken's anonymous review of *Die Wahlverwandtschaften* that had appeared in the *Morgenblatt* that Riemer had it reprinted. Whenever Goethe received letters or questions on the novel, he handed out Abeken's review as a means of answering inquiries. He also gave multiple copies to his friends and acquaintances. One recipient was the poet and translator Johann Diederich Gries, who further disseminated these copies as an attempt to proselytize the public, telling Abeken that his essay had become the "interpretatio authentica" because it had officially received the master's stamp of approval (cf. Passow 117).

Abeken was a theologian, philologist, teacher, and director of the Domgymnasium in Osnabrück. He had first had contact with Goethe while a student at Jena and then while a tutor in Charlotte

von Stein's household (1808–10). The "review" had been originally written as personal correspondence to Heinrich Voß. Voß
then sent the letter, with Abeken's permission, to the *Morgenblatt
für gebildete Stände* for publication. (The *Morgenblatt* appeared
daily and was founded by Goethe's publisher.)

Abeken's review, "Ueber Goethes *Wahlverwandtschaften*," corresponds to Goethe's own defense of the novel as expressed to
Riemer. Abeken emphasizes the conflict between duty and passion
and argues that the novel as a whole is moral. He begins by explaining the negative critical reaction. It does not surprise him that
the novel does not appeal to many people. He believes that *Die
Wahlverwandtschaften* has failed to capture the popular imagination because it is too deep. He predicts that many readers will be
put off by the natural principles within the book — especially those
who do not already recognize the power of nature or those to
whom fate has not yet taught that human beings contain within
them a power to overcome natural, passionate forces (122). For
Abeken, as for many of his contemporaries, the main issue in interpreting the novel is to uncover its didactic function. Throughout
the essay, Abeken traces the conflicts between natural necessity and
human freedom. Whereas the more negative reviews examined
particular details and events, Abeken's attempts a broader reading
of the whole. He sets out to discover the underlying philosophy of
the novel — a philosophy that he personally finds morally and
aesthetically uplifting.

For Abeken, the novel has two main didactic functions: first to
illustrate the strength of natural laws; and second to argue that
human beings contain a higher power within themselves with
which to battle these laws. His interpretation of these powers focuses on freedom as a moral force. The novel comes to symbolize
on a microscopic level what human beings are capable of on a
larger scale. Human beings are able to elevate natural drives
through freedom. Charlotte thus symbolizes the victory of reason
and measure over passion. Human tragedies arise, however, when
human beings are not strong enough to overcome the forces of
nature, but are destroyed by them. Ottilie, therefore, becomes a
tragic figure, precisely because she cannot overcome the strength
of her passion. Abeken's discussion of tragedy and his attempt to
frame the conflict between necessity and free will reflects the lively

and ongoing interest in the theory of tragedy at the time. His review is characteristic of this interest in that it concentrates on the role of the emotions and that it extends the analysis to include genres outside of drama.

In analyzing the details of the struggle between natural necessity and human freedom, Abeken's review is noteworthy for its treatment of the polar elements within the novel. While many readers noted the conflict between duty and passion or freedom and necessity, he finds that the entire novel is comprised of opposed relationships. That Eduard and Ottilie have headaches on opposites sides of their heads becomes symptomatic for the differing passions. Eduard's is conscious, because he knows exactly what he is doing, while Ottilie's is not conscious. She is unknowingly carried away by fate, and by the time that she realizes it, it is too late. For Abeken, this is where the tragic element in the novel begins. Like many of the more favorable reviews (Delbrück 120; Conz, "Noch einige," 253; Eckermann 156), Abeken's analyzes Ottilie's ability to conquer nature. Accordingly, he finds that her journal entries show her high stage of development and display the heavenly peacefulness of her soul (124). He further defends the contents of the diary against the charges that she strangely never writes of Eduard (Conz, "Briefe," 97). That she does not reflect on her feelings demonstrates for Abeken her innocence. She is unconsciously swept away by her destiny. His tone while discussing Ottilie nears the ecstatic. For example, in discussing the diary entries, he writes:

Zarte, innige Beziehungen sind überall in den Blättern zerstreut; wer vermöchte sie alle zu enthüllen? und wer wollte sie erläutern? — Das hiesse von der schwellenden Traube den zarten Duft abwischen, mit dem der frische Morgen sie angehaucht, oder den Staub vom Schmetterlingsflügel streifen, um ihn unter dem Mikroskope zu betrachten. (Abeken, 125)

[Tender, inner relationships are scattered throughout the pages; who is able to uncover them all? And who would want to explain them? — That would be like wiping off of a swelling grape the tender fragrance with which fresh morning has breathed upon it — or to brush the dust from the butterfly's wing in order to study it under the microscope.]

In his discussion of the novel's tragic aspects, Abeken emphasizes the uplifting power of tragedy. He believes that this power
occurs when a human being is able to show his or her dignity exactly at that time when he or she is most oppressed by necessity.
Thus, while Ottilie is subjected to natural necessity and fate blindly
leads her forward, she is able to rise above these forces through her
holy thoughts, self-created laws, and higher life. The forces of fate
and nature can annihilate her, but not conquer her. Her ability to
refuse the most basic necessity of food illustrates the power that
she possesses over nature. In Abeken's mind, Ottilie is fully deserving of her saintly status — not because of any religious convictions — but because of her ability to overcome nature's forces. The
"new science" of elective affinities, a science that emphasizes the
immutable physical laws of attraction, may dishearten one until one
sees how Ottilie is able to overcome these laws.

It is not at all surprising that Goethe chose this review for dis-
semination. Abeken is extremely well disposed both towards the
novel and towards Goethe himself. The review glows with praise of
Goethe's artistry, his character development, and the theme of the
whole. Abeken's explanation for the negative reviews also undoubtedly pleased Goethe: the fault lay not in the novel, but in the
reviewers' own lack of understanding.

The reactions to this essay were perhaps predictable. Because
Goethe (two months after its publication) began sending out this
interpretation as the authorized one, his friends and acquaintances
treated it very favorably (Gries; Passow). Others, however, treated
it much more critically. Therese Huber saw it as a collection of
platitudes (Letter to Emil von Herder, 1810), while Böttiger
claimed that Abeken praises the novel as a moral panacea ("Die
Wahlverwandtschaften," 176). Abeken himself reports that Wieland
did not much care for his review (Goethe, 110).

By contrast, Karl Wilhelm Ferdinand Solger's essay (1809) did
not initially play an important a role in the novel's reception. First,
it was never published as a separate piece, but only appeared within
the larger corpus of his collected works. Second, this edition was
published posthumously (edited by Tieck and von Raumer) in
1826 — seventeen years after the publication of the novel. Later
on, however, it did come to influence attitudes toward the novel.

Solger was a professor and noted Romantic philosopher whose early work focused on Greek drama and aesthetics (in 1804 he had translated Sophocles' *Oedipus* and in 1808 he published his interpretation of Greek tragedy). He was known by many of the important thinkers of his time. He had studied with Schelling in Jena, received his position in Berlin through the help of Hegel, and was a close friend of Tieck's. He is most remembered today for his aesthetic writings, and in particular, his notion of Romantic irony. His essay on *Die Wahlverwandtschaften* perhaps most clearly shows a Romantic influence in its emphasis upon the theme of the individual.

Although Goethe did not go to the lengths that he did in Abeken's case, he did state several times that he approved of Solger's interpretation. For example, Goethe told Eckermann on 21 January 1827 that Solger's letters "sind trefflich. In einem derselben schreibt er an Tieck über die *Wahlverwandtschaften,* und diesen muß ich Ihnen vorlesen, denn es ist nicht leicht etwas Besseres über jenen Roman gesagt worden" [are excellent. In one of them, he writes to Tieck about the *Die Wahlverwandtschaften,* and I wish to read it to you; for it would not be easy to say anything better about the novel: *FA* 2, 12:215; cf. *GG,* 3:103; Müller 3 March 1827; Oxenford trans.]. Goethe also discusses Solger's essay and its assessment of Eduard and the Architect and approves most enthusiastically what Solger has said about the latter character. In this same conversation, Goethe also acknowledged the pain he had felt by the novel's initial negative reception: "Es hätte mich damals freuen können, ein so gutes Wort über die *Wahlverwandtschaften* zu hören, während man in jener Zeit und später mir eben nicht viel Angenehmes über jenen Roman erzeigte" [It would have much cheered me to hear so kind a word about the *Wahlverwandtschaften;* for at that time, and afterwards, not many pleasant remarks were vouchsafed me about that novel: *FA* 2, 12:216; Oxenford trans.].

Solger's review differs from most of those of his contemporaries in its sophistication. He first situates the novel within the critical theory and philosophy of its time and then demonstrates its modernity. In particular, he compares and contrasts ancient and modern conceptions of the individual and fate. Thus, although many of Goethe's contemporaries viewed the novel as addressing the issue of fate (Delbrück; Bartholdy; Wagner?; Eckermann), Solger gives a theoretical grounding to his discussion and tries to explain the philosophical differences between classical and modern conceptions.

Solger is clearly impressed with Goethe's novel and calls it "ein unerschöpfliches Kunstwerk" (176) [an inexhaustible work of art]. And while several of Goethe's contemporaries saw the novel as predominantly classical, Solger argues that it is characteristically modern. He begins his essay with a theoretical overview and contrasts the ancient view of fate with the modern one. The ancient view of fate was more universal. Fate affected humanity as a whole rather than human beings in particular. Because society as a whole was more valued than individuals, individuals could only exist to the extent to which they made society's Geschick [destiny] their own. Individuals, who strove against the grain of the whole, were destroyed. To support his claim, Solger cites the evidence of ancient art (tragedy) and historical banishments and ostracisms. He then articulates what this general sense of destiny means in the ancient world. Physically, it refers to the infirmities to which we all are subject, and intellectually it refers to the way in which we all think (177).

Solger then directly juxtaposes the modern view of fate against the ancient one. In the modern world, the individual and not society is at the center stage. The God of the ancient world was absolute and was the same entity for every member of society. The God of the modern world resides within the individual (177–78). The destiny of the modern human being is his/her individuality or character and the expression of this destiny is love and friendship. Only through love and friendship can the image of God within the individual become actual. Solger goes so far as to state that the human being has no other destiny than love. Where ancient individuals were crushed if they attempted to fight against the larger order, the lesson for modern individuals is the opposite. They must value their individuality above the social order.

After thus laying the theoretical groundwork, Solger begins his actual analysis of the novel. The main intent is to show the modern qualities of the novel's treatment of the individual. In particular, he argues that the course of the plot flows from the individual characters. Solger anticipates that many may see nature's function in the novel as contradicting this view, and he even outlines the anticipated critique: the whole book seems to based not upon the actions of individuals, but upon nature. Ottilie's secret inner relationship with Eduard, their opposing headaches, Ottilie's ability to detect metallic ores, the reaction of the pendulum, and the elective affinities all seem to point to the power of nature over human beings.

Solger then answers these objections. An analysis of the role of nature, he argues, demonstrates that it is never at the fore, but always in the background. Without citing any concrete example, he asserts that nature is not the primary cause of any of the events, actions or relationships, but, rather, every single movement in the whole development springs from the characters themselves (201). He even argues that the mutual attraction of the lovers stems not from natural, but from personal forces.

Like many of the other critics, Solger addresses two issues that were actively debated within the reviews: Goethe's use of details and Ottilie's diary entries. Solger defends these aspects of the novel because they support his contention of its modernity. If modern destiny is closely connected to individuals, then the diary entries allow us to contemplate the thoughts of the individual, while the numerous details in the text paint a portrait of their daily lives. The diary reflections therefore provide the opportunity to analyze and examine human individuality. Solger claims that there is no other way to influence human beings but by private conversations and the reflections upon them (183).

Solger foresees that many of Goethe's readers would be repelled by the philosophical reflections and the amount of detail in the novel. One must be prepared to be "gebildet für Goethe und durch ihn" [educated for Goethe and by him], otherwise one would find these aspects of the novel boring. He defends the details of the novel for the same reason that he defends Ottilie's diary entries. The details highlight the individual and are "das sichtbare Kleid der Persönlichkeiten" (180) [the visible dress of personalities]. The details, in short, represent the daily life in which the personality expresses itself. And, as many of the other commentators have noted (Arnim 350; Savigny, Letter to Creuzer; and A. Wagner? 244), these details serve as an exact mirror of the times. Solger praises Goethe's artistry in capturing the times in such a lifelike manner. In this, he compares the novel to ancient epics. After several hundred years one would be able to sketch a perfect picture of daily life from the novel (183).

Like Abeken, Solger sees Ottilie as the most important character in the novel. And like Abeken, the language he uses to describe Ottilie is quite sentimental. The storm of her fate blows her "Knospe" [bud] into the air and disperses "ihren heiligen Blüthenstaub" (179) [her holy pollen]. He emphasizes Ottilie's innocence and grounds it on her lack of consciousness. She remains pure, in his mind, because she never reflects upon her relationship with Eduard. But Solger goes further than many others in praising Ottilie, seeing her good qualities as representative of the "best" in women generally. The notion that she is a product of nature and its victim is expanded to apply to women: "Mit diesen zwei Worten ist alles Schöne und Große ausgesprochen, was von Frauen zu sagen ist" (184) [With these two words, everything beautiful and great that can be said about women is expressed].

Although Goethe gives blanket approval of what Solger has written, it is interesting that he specifically mentions only Solger's treatment of the characters, and not his overarching theory of modernity within the novel. Judging from Goethe's statements as they have come down to us, it appears that he was most pleased by the fact of a positive review rather than by the particulars within it. It is not surprising that the older Goethe would still be sensitive to the reception of his novel twenty years after it first appeared. First, it had received so many negative reviews and attacks throughout the years, often even from those closest to him. Second, he was already beginning to fall out of favor generally with the next generation of literary authors and political thinkers. And although he had struggled to leave behind the legacy of two positive reviews of his novel, the next fifty years marked the novel's low point. *Die Wahlverwandtschaften,* even more than Goethe himself, was largely ignored.

Notes

[1] Härtl's sourcebook is an invaluable source to anyone who would like to gain a complete account of the early reception of *Die Wahlverwandtschaften*. Härtl has gathered and published chronologically all of the known contemporary discussions of the novel.

[2] Werner somewhat changes the original order of the quotation; cf. *FA* 1, 8:502.

[3] This was not an unusual practice. Many of the "reviews" that were published in the journals of the time were originally written as personal letters (Conz "Briefe"; Abeken "Ueber"; Anonymous "Ein Paar"; etc.).

[4] For a discussion of Goethe's relationship with Böttiger, who acted for a time as an intermediary between Goethe and his publishers, see Unseld (73–74; 109; 115–16; 273–74). Unseld labels Böttiger "a dubious figure," who "hawked gossip, scandal, or at least indiscretions to Cotta's newspapers" (274).

[5] For more information on Rehberg, see Scherer (349–53).

[6] Rehberg here satirizes Friedrich Schlegel's "Fragment" which characterizes Goethe's *Wilhelm Meister,* along with the French Revolution and Fichte's philosophy, as the greatest tendencies of the age.

[7] Pustkuchen's *Wilhelm Meisters Wanderjahre* is not technically a parody because part of it was published before Goethe's novel of the same title — causing some confusion for the public (Mandelkow, *Goethe in Deutschland* 62).

[8] The essay is often referred to in secondary literature as being by Hengstenberg. For a discussion of the authorship of this review, see Härtl 1983, 450.

[9] Madame de Staël held a similar view. She writes that the whole novel is lacking in religious feeling, and that the main characters believe more in superstition than in true belief (247).

[10] But Goethe does *not* mention the conclusion of the novel in this context, which hints at a future life of togetherness for Eduard and Ottilie.

Works Cited

[Abeken, Bernhard Rudolf]. Ueber Goethes *Wahlverwandtschaften.* (Fragmente aus einem Briefe). *Morgenblatt für gebildete Stände.* No. 19–21 (22–24 January 1810). Quoted here from Härtl 1983, 121–27. Also reprinted in *HA,* 6:644–51 and Mandelkow, *Goethe im Urteil,* 1:262–74.

———. Letter to Heinrich Voß. 26–30 March 1810. Jena. Quoted here from Härtl 1983, 151–52.

———. *Goethe in meinem Leben.* Ed. Adolf Heuermann. Weimar: Böhlau, 1904. 107–115; 128–35; 228–31; 141. Also reprinted in Härtl 1983, 204–10.

Ancillon, Friedrich. *Philosophie und Poesie* (*=Zur Vermittlung der Extreme in den Meinungen.* Zweiter Theil). Berlin, 1831. Quoted here from Härtl 1983, 376.

Anonymous. Advertisement for the novel in *Intelligenzblatt zum Morgenblatt für gebildete Stände.* 2 December 1809.

Anonymous. "Französisches Urtheil über Goethes *Wahlverwandtschaften.*" *Morgenblatt für gebildete Stände.* No. 71 (23 March 1810). Quoted here from Härtl 1983, 146–50.

Anonymous. "Ein Paar Worte über eine Recension von Goethes *Wahlverwandtschaften* und über eine andere des ersten Buchs der *Wanderjahre Wilhelm Meisters.* (Aus einem Briefe)." *Morgenblatt für gebildete Stände.* No. 168 (14 July 1810). Quoted here from Härtl 1983, 161–63.

Anonymous. "*Elective Affinities;* a Novel by Goëthe." *The American Review of History and Politics and General Repository of Literature and State Papers* 3 (1812): 51–69.

Arnim, Achim von. Letter to Bettina Brentano. 5 November 1809. Berlin. Quoted here from *Achim von Arnim und Bettina Brentano.* Ed. Reinhold Steig. Bern: Herbert Lang, 1970. 350. Also quoted in Härtl 1983, 70–71 and *HA,* 6:657.

[Bartholdy, Jacob Salomon]. "Göthe's *Wahlverwandtschaften.* Ein Roman in 2 Bändchen." *Oesterreichischer Beobachter.* 23 March 1810. Quoted here from Härtl 1983, 144–50.

Baumgartner, Alexander. *Göthe: Sein Leben und seine Werke.* 3 vols. Freiburg: Herder'sche Verlagshandlung, 1882. Quoted here from the second, expanded 1885–86 edition.

Benjamin, Walter. "Goethes *Wahlverwandtschaften*." *Neue deutsche Beiträge* (1924/25). Quoted here from *Walter Benjamin: Gesammelte Schriften* I, i. Ed. Rolf Tiedemann and Hermann Schweppenhäuser. Frankfurt: Suhrkamp. English from *Walter Benjamin: Selected Writings (1913–1926)*. Vol 1. Ed. Marcus Bullock and Michael W. Jennings. Essay trans. Stanley Corngold. Cambridge: Belknap Press, 1996.

Blankenagel, John C. "An Early American Review of *Die Wahlverwandtschaften*." *JEGP* 35 (1936): 383–89.

[Böttiger, Karl August]. "Ueber Göthe's *Wahlverwandtschaften*." *Zeitung für die elegante Welt*. No. 2 (2 January 1810). Leipzig. Quoted here from Härtl 1983, 107–9. Also reprinted in Braun 1885, 232–36.

Böttiger, Karl August. Letter to Johann Friedrich Rochlitz. 28 January 1810. Dresden. Quoted here from the *Goethe-Jahrbuch* 18 (1897): 152. Also reprinted in Härtl 1983, 128.

[Böttiger, Karl August]. "*Die Wahlverwandtschaften;* ein Roman von Göthe." *Bibliothek der redenden und bildenden Künste*. Leipzig, 1810. Quoted here from Härtl 1983, 176–98. Also reprinted in Braun 1885, 265–69.

Braun, Julius W. *Goethe im Urtheile seiner Zeitgenossen: Zeitungskritiken, Berichte, Notizen, Goethe und seine Werke betreffend, aus den Jahren 1772–1812*. 3 vols. Berlin: Friedrich Luckhardt, 1885.

[Conz, Karl Philipp]. "Briefe über den Goethe'schen Roman: *Die Wahlverwandtschaften*." *Morgenblatt für gebildete Stände*. No. 307–10 (25–28 December 1809). Quoted here from Härtl 1983, 90–99. Also reprinted in Braun 1885, 212–15.

———. "Noch einige Bemerkungen über Göthe's *Wahlverwandtschaften*." *Zeitung für die elegante Welt*. No. 242–44 (11–13 December 1817). Quoted here from Härtl 1983, 250–56

[Delbrück, Johann Friedrich Ferdinand]. "*Die Wahlverwandtschaften*. Ein Roman von Goethe." *Jenaische Allgemeine Literatur-Zeitung*. No. 16 and 17 (18 and 19 January 1810). Quoted here from Härtl 1983, 114–21.

Diepenbrock-Grüter, Ludwig von. Diary Entry. 20 November 1826. Lüneburg. Quoted here from *Begegnungen mit Heine. Berichte der Zeitgenossen*. Ed. Michael Werner. Hamburg: Hoffmann und Campe, 1973. 145–46. Also reprinted in Härtl 1983, 323.

Eckermann, Johann Peter. "Bemerkungen über Goethe's *Wahlverwandtschaften*." *Beyträge zur Poesie mit besonderer Hinweisung auf Goethe*. Stuttgart: Cotta, 1824

Eichstädt, Heinrich Karl Abraham. Letter to Johann Friedrich Rochlitz. 25 October 1809. Jena. Quoted here from Härtl 1983, 65. Also reprinted in the *Goethe-Jahrbuch* 20 (1899): 273–74.

Gerlach, Leopold von. Letter to Wilhelm von Gerlach. 14 August 1810. Heidelberg. Quoted here from *Aus den Jahren preussischer Not und Erneuerung: Tagebücher und Briefe der Gebrüder Gerlach und ihres Kreises 1805–1820*. Ed. Hans Joachim Schoeps. Berlin: Haude und Spenersche Verlagsbuchhandlung, 1963. 468–69. Also reprinted in Härtl 1983, 167.

Gerlach, Wilhelm von. Letter to Leopold von Gerlach. 30 June 1810. Berlin. Quoted here from *Aus den Jahren preussischer Not und Erneuerung: Tagebücher und Briefe der Gebrüder Gerlach und ihres Kreises 1805–1820*. Ed. Hans Joachim Schoeps. Berlin: Haude und Spenersche Verlagsbuchhandlung, 1963. 460–62. Also reprinted in Härtl 1983, 160.

Gries, Johann Diederich. Letter to Bernhard Rudolf Abeken. 23 March 1810. Jena. Quoted here from Härtl 1983, 150–51.

Grimm, Ludwig Emil. *Erinnerungen aus meinem Leben (1794–1823)*. Ed. Adolf Stoll. Leipzig, 1913. Quoted here from the 1950 edition, Kassel: Bärenreiter Verlag. Also reprinted in Härtl 1983, 213.

Grimm, Wilhelm. *Briefwechsel zwischen Jacob und Wilhelm Grimm aus der Jugendzeit*. Ed. Herman Grimm and Gustav Hinrichs. Weimar: Böhlau, 1963.

Härtl, Heinz. *Die Wahlverwandtschaften: Eine Dokumentation der Wirkung von Goethes Roman 1808–1832*. Weinheim: Acta humaniora, 1983.

Hohendahl, Peter Uwe. "Literary Criticism in the Epoch of Liberalism, 1820–1870." *A History of German Literary Criticism, 1730–1980*. Ed. Peter Uwe Hohendahl. Lincoln: U of Nebraska P, 1988.

Horn, Franz. *Die schöne Litteratur Deutschlands, während des achtzehnten Jahrhunderts*. Berlin, 1812. Quoted here from Härtl 1983, 225.

Huber, Therese. Letter to Karl August Böttiger. 20 December 1809. Günzburg. Quoted here from Härtl 1983, 86. Also reprinted in the *Goethe-Jahrbuch* 18 (1897): 128 and *HA*, 6:662.

———. Undated letter (ca. 1810) to Emil von Herder. Günzburg. Quoted here from Härtl 1983, 203. Also reprinted in the *Goethe-Jahrbuch* 18 (1897): 130.

Humboldt, Wilhelm von. Letter to Friedrich Gottlieb Welcker. 23 December 1809. Erfurt. Quoted here from Härtl 1983, 88.

25

————. Letter to Caroline von Humboldt. 6 March 1810. Berlin. Quoted here from Härtl 1983, 141. Also reprinted in *HA*, 6:664.

Jacobi, Friedrich Heinrich. Letter to Johann Heinrich Voß. 18 December 1809. Munich. Quoted here from *Aus F. H. Jacobi's Nachlaß*. Vol. 2. Leipzig: Wilhelm Engelmann, 1869. 39–43. Also reprinted in Härtl 1983, 86 and *HA*, 6:662.

————. Letter to Friedrich Köppen. 12 January 1810. Munich. Quoted here from *Aus F. H. Jacobi's Nachlaß*. Vol. 2. Leipzig: Wilhelm Engelmann, 1869. 44–45. Also reprinted in Härtl 1983, 112–13 and *HA*, 6:662–63.

Jean Paul. Letter to Karl Ludwig von Knebel. 24 March 1810. Bayreuth. Quoted here from Härtl 1983, 151.

Knebel, Henriette von. Letter to Karl Ludwig von Knebel. 7 February 1810. Weimar. Quoted here from *Aus Karl Ludwig von Knebels Briefwechsel mit seiner Schwester 1774–1813*. Ed. Heinrich Düntzer. Jena: Friedrich Mauke, 1858. 411. Also reprinted in Härtl 1983, 129.

Köhler, Astrid. *Salonkultur im klassischen Weimar: Geselligkeit als Lebensform und literarisches Konzept*. Stuttgart: M & P Verlag, 1996.

Leppmann, Wolfgang. *The German Image of Goethe*. Oxford: Clarendon Press, 1961.

Levin, Rahel. Letter to Rose Asser. 14 November 1809. Berlin. Quoted here from *Rahel. Ein Buch des Andenkens für ihre Freunde*. Berlin: Duncker and Humblot, 1834. 445–47. Also quoted in Härtl 1983, 73.

Lewes, George Henry. *The Life of Goethe*. 2nd ed. London: Smith, Elder and Co., 1864.

Mandelkow, Karl Robert. *Goethe in Deutschland I: Rezeptionsgeschichte eines Klassikers (1733–1918)*. Munich: C. H. Beck, 1980.

————. *Goethe im Urteil seiner Kritiker: Dokumente zur Wirkungsgeschichte Goethes in Deutschland*. 4 vols. Munich: C. H. Beck, 1975–1984.

Mann, Thomas. *Die neue Rundschau* 36 (1925): 391–401. Quoted here from *Gesammelte Werke in zwölf Bänden*. Vol. 9. Frankfurt: S. Fischer, 1960. 174–86. English from *Past Masters and Other Papers*. "Goethe, Novelist." Trans. H. T. Lowe-Porter. New York: Alfred A. Knopf, 1933. 99–114.

[Meißner, Konrad Benjamin]. "Roman." *Conversations-Lexikon oder Hand-Wörterbuch für die gebildeten Stände*. 2nd ed. Vol. 8. Leipzig-Algenburg, 1817. Quoted here from Härtl 1983, 256–57.

————. "Roman." *Allgemeine deutsche Real-Encyklopädie für die gebildeten Stände. (Conversations-Lexikon).* Bd. 8. 6. Original-Auflage. Leipzig: F. A. Brockhaus, 1824. Cited here from the 1830, 7th ed. Also reprinted in Härtl 1983, 309–310.

Menzel, Wolfgang. "Göthe und Schiller." *Europäische Blätter oder das Interessanteste aus Literatur und Leben für die gebildete Lesewelt.* Ed. Wolfgang Menzel. Zürich, 1824. Quoted here from Härtl 1983, 308–9. Also reprinted in Mandelkow, *Goethe im Urteil* 1:363–67.

————. *Die deutsche Literatur.* 2nd ed. Vol. 3. Stuttgart: Hallberger'sche Verlagshandlung, 1836. 368–74. Also reprinted in Härtl 1983, 330–31.

Passow, Franz. Letter to Ernst Breem. 14 June 1810. Weimar. Quoted here from Passow's *Leben und Briefe.* Ed. Albrecht Wachler. Breslau: Ferdinand Hirt, 1839. Also cited in Härtl 1983, 157–58.

[Pustkuchen, Johann Friedrich Wilhelm]. *Wilhelm Meisters Wanderjahre. Erster Theil.* Published anonymously. Quedlinburg and Leipzig, 1821. Quoted here from Härtl 1983, 270–73. Also reprinted in Mandelkow, *Goethe im Urteil* 316–29.

[Rehberg, August Wilhelm]. Review of *Die Wahlverwandtschaften* in *Allgemeine Literatur-Zeitung.* Nr. 1. (1 January 1810). Halle. Quoted here from Härtl 1983, 101–6. Also reprinted in Mandelkow, *Goethe im Urteil* 1:268–74 and in Braun 1885, 224–32.

Riemer, Friedrich Wilhelm. Diary Entry. 11 August 1810. Teplitz. Quoted here from Härtl 1983, 166.

Savigny, Friedrich Karl von. Letter to Friedrich Creuzer. 25 December 1809. Landshut. Quoted here from Härtl 1983, 89.

————. Letter to Clemens Brentano. 27 February 1810. Landshut. Quoted here from Härtl 1983, 140.

Schelling, Friedrich Wilhelm Joseph. Letter to Pauline Gotter. 12 February 1810. Stuttgart. Quoted here from Härtl 1983, 137.

Scherer, Wilhelm. "Goethe und Frau Rehberg, geb. Höpfner." *Goethe-Jahrbuch* 6 (1885): 345–53.

Schiller, Charlotte von. Letter to Johann Friedrich Cotta. 27 October 1809. Weimar. Quoted here from Härtl 1983, 66.

Schlegel, August Wilhelm. Letter to Julie Schlegel. 10 May 1810. Chaumont. Quoted here from Härtl 1983, 155.

Schlegel, Friedrich. Letter to August Wilhelm Schlegel. 16 January 1810. Vienna. Quoted here from *Krisenjahre der Frühromantik. Briefe aus dem Schlegelkreis.* Ed. Josef Körner. Vol. 2. Vienna, 1937. 100–105. Also reprinted in Härtl 1983, 113.

[Schlegel, Friedrich]. "Über Liebe und Ehe in Beziehung auf Goethe's *Wahlverwandtschaften.*" *Oesterreichischer Beobachter.* Beylage 11 zu Nr. 35 (21 May 1810). Wien. Quoted here from the *Goethe-Jahrbuch* 27 (1906): 252–54. Also reprinted in Härtl 1983, 156–57.

Solger, Karl Wilhelm. "Über die *Wahlverwandtschaften.*" First published in *Solger's nachgelassene Schriften und Briefwechsel.* Ed. Ludwig Tieck and Friedrich von Raumer. Vol. 1. Leipzig 1826: 175–85. Also reprinted in Härtl 1983, 199–202, *HA*, 6:652–57, and Mandelkow, *Goethe im Urteil* 1:257–61.

Sommerfeld, Martin. "Goethes *Wahlverwandtschaften* im 19. Jahrhundert." Jahrbuch d. fr. dt. Hochstifts (1926): 203–50.

Staël-Holstein, Anne Germaine de. *Deutschland.* Trans. into German by Friedrich Buchholz. Berlin, 1814. Quoted here from Härtl 1983, 246–47.

Stein, Charlotte von. Letter to Friedrich von Stein. 7 February 1810. Weimar. Quoted here from *Goethe in vertraulichen Briefen seiner Zeitgenossen: Die Zeit Napoleons 1803–1816.* Ed. Wilhelm Bode. Berlin: Mittler & Sohn, 1921. 238. Also reprinted in Härtl 1983, 129.

Unger, Friederike Helene. Letter to August Wilhelm Schlegel. 20 June 1810. Berlin Quoted here from *Krisenjahre der Frühromantik. Briefe aus dem Schlegelkreis.* Vol. 3. Ed. Josef Körner. Bern: Francke Verlag, 1958. 461. Also reprinted in Härtl 1983, 159.

Unseld, Siegfried. *Goethe and His Publishers.* Trans. Kenneth J. Northcott. Chicago: U of Chicago P, 1996.

Valenti, Ernst Joseph Gustav de. "Ueber Göthes *Walhverwandtschaften.*" *Evangelische Kirchen-Zeitung.* 57–61 (16–30 July 1831). Ed. Ernst Wilhelm Hengstenberg. Berlin. Quoted here from Härtl 1983, 341–75.

Varnhagen von Ense, Rahel Levin. Diary Entry. May 1823. Berlin. Quoted here from Hannah Arendt's *Rahel Varnhagen. Lebensgeschichte einer deutschen Jüdin aus der Romantik.* Munich: R. Piper & Co., 1959. 259–60. Also reprinted in Härtl 1983, 226.

[Wagner, Adolph?]. *"Die Wahlverwandtschaften." Heidelbergische Jahrbücher der Literatur.* 12–13 (1814). Quoted here from Härtl 1983, 230–45.

Wagner, Johann Ernst. Letter to August von Studnitz. 21 November 1809. Meiningen. Quoted here from *Hundert Briefe von Johann Ernst Wagner an Jean Paul Fr. Richter und August von Studnitz.* Ed. A. L. Corin. Liège: Faculté de Philosophie et Lettres, 1942. Also quoted in Härtl 1983, 79.

Welcker, Friedrich Gottlieb. Letter to Caroline von Humboldt. 21 December 1809. Gießen. Quoted here from Härtl 1983, 87–88. Also reprinted in the *Goethe-Jahrbuch* 19 (1898): 199–201.

Werner, Zacharias. Letter to Goethe. 23 April 1811. Rome. Quoted here from Härtl 1983, 216–17. Also reprinted in *HA*, 6:664–65.

Wessenberg, Ignaz Heinrich von. *Ueber den sittlichen Einfluß der Romane. Ein Versuch.* Constanz: W. Wallis, 1826. Also reprinted in Härtl 1983, 323–25.

Wieland, Christoph Martin. Letter to the Countess Elisabeth von Solms-Laubach. 15 June 1810. Weimar. Quoted here from Härtl 1983, 158–59.

———. Letter to Karl August Böttiger. 16 July 1810. Weimar. Quoted here from Härtl 1983, 164–65.

Zelter, Karl Friedrich. Letter to Goethe. 27 October 1809. Berlin. Quoted here from *Briefwechsel zwischen Goethe und Zelter in den Jahren 1796 bis 1832.* Ed. Friedrich Wilhelm Riemer. Berlin: Duncker and Humblot, 1833. Also reprinted in Härtl 1983, 65–66 and *HA*, 6:667.

2: 1832–1918:
From Theory to Fact to Myth

NINETEENTH-CENTURY CRITICISM continued to focus on issues that were similar to those that had characterized the reception of *Die Wahlverwandtschaften* during Goethe's lifetime.
The critics were still mainly interested in determining the question
of the novel's morality, and they also continued the quest to clas-
sify the novel. Definite shifts, however, occurred during this period
that differentiate the later approaches from the earlier ones. In the
first half of the century, the Hegelians examined the moral issues
from a dialectical perspective, while the positivists of the second
half of the century occupied themselves with researching the historical and biographical details behind the novel's composition.
And because Goethe became a popular, nationalist symbol at the
time of positivism, this mode of interpretation dominated, by sheer
bulk, much of the criticism of the nineteenth century. For the
positivists, interpretation became synonymous with the attempt to
gather facts and reconstruct the personal details of Goethe's life at
the time that he wrote the novel. Thus, instead of using evidence
from the novel to argue for its morality or immorality, more and
more critics turned to Goethe's life to make that determination.
They began to discuss in ever greater detail Goethe's relationship
with various women, especially Minna Herzlieb, and they began to
look at the details of his own marriage for "proof" of his marital
convictions and message within the novel. What is perhaps most
striking about the attempt to determine the morality of the novel
by comparing it to events in Goethe's life is the interpretive somer-
saults that critics had to do in order to argue that both Goethe's
life and novel were moral according to the standards of the day. By
the end of the century, Goethe had become such an important
German symbol, that it was almost a given that his life was above
reproach. So great was the power of the image that had been created of him that even those biographers who forced themselves to
admit moral lapses according to nineteenth-century conventions,

were able to excuse his behavior through his very greatness. Men as great as Goethe, they argued were excused from following the same rules of behavior as the rest of mere mortals. Olympians, after all, could act as they please. They set their own standards.

By the end of the nineteenth century and the beginning of the twentieth, the predominant mode of positivistic interpretation was called seriously into question. One of the most important voices against the conflation of biographical facts with the interpretation of fiction was the philosopher Wilhelm Dilthey (1833–1911). In his writings, he repeatedly stresses that it was not simply the experience that shaped a particular work of art, but most importantly, it was the artist's imagination. Nietzsche (1844–1900) also insisted that it was high time "einen Künstler insoweit von seinem Werke zu trennen, daß man ihn selbst nicht gleich ernst nimmt wie sein Werk. . . . Die Einsicht in die *Herkunft* eines Werks geht die Physiologen und Vivisektoren des Geistes an: nie und nimmermehr die ästhetischen Menschen, die Artisten" [4:93; to divorce an artist from his work, and to take *him* less seriously than *it*. . . . To investigate the origins of a work belongs to the physiologists and vivisectionists of the mind, never to men endowed with esthetic sensibility: 235].

Several important interpreters of *Die Wahlverwandtschaften* of the early twentieth century also began turning away from the biographical mode of literary interpretation. As yet, however, they did not follow Nietzsche's exhortation to treat the text itself as an independent entity. In the case of *Die Wahlverwandtschaften,* this approach truly re-emerged with Benjamin's essay. Nevertheless, scholars such as Oskar Walzel and André François-Poncet turned the discussion away from biography and toward the larger context of social history. They both argued that it was not simply the personal development of an individual that influenced the end product of the work, but rather the entire age. Walzel therefore advocated examining the historical and intellectual contexts of a literary work rather than just focusing exclusively upon biographical information. A further move away from positivism was brought about by the burgeoning field of psychoanalysis. Goethe's novel was one of the first works of fiction to be analyzed through psychoanalysis. J. Hárnik published a psychoanalytic interpretation of *Die Wahlverwandtschaften* in the first volume of Freud's journal, *Imago.* (He did not, however, psychoanalyze Goethe but rather his characters.) And while the biographical mode was not abandoned in the early twentieth century, it took on a completely different flavor than that of earlier times. Friedrich Gundolf (1880–1931), one of the most important critics of the age, wrote a biography of Goethe in which he attempted to show the inadequacies of positivistic biographies in capturing the essence of the mythical and heroic aspects of Goethe's life and works. Moreover, where many of the positivistic biographies, such as Bielschowsky's, were meant for popular consumption, Gundolf's was written with a diametrically opposed purpose: to create an image of Goethe not as man of the people, but as an elite author accessible only to the privileged few.

Changes of Fortune

The reception of Goethe and his works throughout the nineteenth century was uneven. In general, one could say that the century began by criticizing Goethe, continued by largely ignoring him, and concluded by apotheosizing him.[1] By the time of his death, he had already begun to fall out of public favor. The previous chapter showed that on the right, political and religious conservatives harshly criticized him for the quality and what they considered the immorality of *Die Wahlverwandtschaften*. Metternich (1773–1859) reflects this sentiment, stating that Goethe had few purely moral and religious concepts, and that his *Wahlverwandtschaften* is an immoral book that leans toward the new religion of the flesh (cited in Hohendahl 220). By the 1820s and 1830s, however, more liberal thinkers had also begun to view Goethe with disfavor. Authors such as Ludwig Börne (1786–1837) and Heinrich Heine (1797–1856) were becoming more and more critical of Goethe because of his seeming indifference to politics. The Young Germans[2] criticized Goethe's works as being apolitical and hence largely irrelevant during this period of turbulent political transitions (Holub 227). Germans in general were turning away from Goethe and toward Schiller as a figure that fit in more with the political and nationalistic times. A measure of Goethe's decline is how he was treated after he died in 1832. The *Literaturblatt*, the literary supplement to the *Morgenblatt*, did not even print an obituary, despite the fact that it was owned by the same publisher that published Goethe's works. Wolfgang Menzel, the editor of the *Morgenblatt* and the most influential literary critic of the day (Beutin 287; Hohendahl 185), so disliked Goethe that he refused to write one. As Leppmann reports, "the name of Menzel carried so much weight at the time, and Goethe's public had by then become so limited, that the editor was only mildly rebuked for his intentional oversight" (48). Moreover, whereas Schiller was honored in the first half of the nineteenth century with an important statue and an enthusiastic celebration on the centenary of his birth, Goethe was not so honored. The centenary of his birth "had been passed over in near silence" (Leppmann 48).[3]

The end of the nineteenth century saw a complete reversal of this attitude. A veritable industry of publications on Goethe appeared, especially biographies written for popular audiences. After the death of his last surviving descendant in 1885, preparations began for turning his house into a museum. The same year, the Goethe Society in Weimar was founded, and its early members were not only scholars from several different disciplines (including Ernst Haeckel [1834–1919], Theodor Mommsen [1817–1903], and Hermann von Helmholtz [1821–1894]), but also writers (including Paul Heyse [1830–1914] and Theodor Storm [1817–88]), politicians, and royalty (including the Emperor of Germany, the King of Sweden, and the Queen of Italy).[4] The popularity of Goethe emerged alongside the rise of German nationalism. He was once again viewed as Germany's primary author and credited by scholars of this generation not only for his artistic accomplishments, but also for his scientific ones. In their fervor, they pronounced Goethe as the inventor of the realistic novel and the precursor to Darwin (Bölsche; Haeckel 66, 75–76, 79).

With a few notable exceptions, during the early part of the nineteenth century *Die Wahlverwandtschaften* was not prominently treated. Scholarly discussions of the novel were mostly short treatments within the context of German literary histories. By 1877, Herman Grimm (1828–1901) reports that "nachdem sie [*Die Wahlverwandtschaften*] fünfzig Jahre lang als das gefürchtetste Werk Goethe's immer von neuem besprochen wurden, heute, vorübergehend, nur noch wenig bekannt" [237; after having been spoken of for fifty years as Goethe's most dangerous work, (the novel) is today passed over and very little known: 469]. Even at the height of the Goethe cult at the end of the nineteenth century and beginning of the twentieth, the novel, according to Arthur Luther in 1905 (150), was scarcely read. Many literary authors also overlooked it in their discussions of Goethe. In 1926 Sommerfeld, in his overview of the novel's reception in the nineteenth century, writes of how the literary figures of the post-classical period, including August Platen (1796–1835), Karl Immermann (1796–1840), Otto Ludwig (1813–65), Adalbert Stifter (1805–68), and Gottfried Keller (1819–90), largely ignored it (231). Georg Gottfried Gervinus (1805–71), in his seminal work *Geschichte der deutschen Dichtung* (History of German Literature, 1842) places the reception of *Die Wahlverwandtschaften* within the context of Goethe's declining popularity. The novel, he says, was poorly received because of the change in politics and artistic style. Young people determine the fate and reputation of poets and their work, and as the younger generation was becoming more and more political, they turned away from Goethe (712). Grimm similarly speculates that the novel was not a critical success because Goethe had written for a public that no longer existed (242). Others (Hebbel; Gervinus; Hettner 157) argued that its time had not yet come — that it was a highly modern, path-breaking work. Conversely, by the beginning of the twentieth century, at least one scholar claimed that the highly modern reader would find the novel completely old-fashioned (Luther 150). Even some of Goethe's main proponents had little to say about it. Thomas Carlyle, probably one of Goethe's biggest supporters, does not even mention *Die Wahlverwandtschaften* in his major works on Goethe. *German Romance,* "Goethe," "Death of Goethe," and "Goethe's Works," include discussions of every major work — and every novel — by Goethe except *Die Wahlverwandtschaften*. Even when Goethe was still alive, Carlyle gave Goethe not his own opinion on the novel, but rather his wife's. He reports that she read the novel "with high admiration; and a sorrow for poor Ottilie. . . . Shallow censurers of the 'Morality' of the Work, who are not altogether wanting here, she withstands with true female zeal" (3 November 1829).

Grillparzer, Eichendorff, and Hebbel

Three important mid-century literary figures, however, did emphasize the novel's importance. Franz Grillparzer (1791–1872), Joseph von Eichendorff (1788–1857), and Friedrich Hebbel (1813–63) found much to praise and criticize in *Die Wahlverwandtschaften*. In addition, both Grillparzer and Hebbel considered the novel a central text in Goethe's corpus. Grillparzer in his journal calls it "ein unendliches Meisterstück" [an infinite masterpiece]. And although he is critical of the space that Goethe devotes to landscaping and architecture, arguing that such incidentals take away from the main action of the work, he nevertheless still finds *Die Wahlverwandtschaften,* due to its "Menschenkenntnis, Weisheit und Empfindung" [knowledge of human beings, wisdom and sensibility], to be a work of literature without parallel. Eichendorff, while finding the effect of the novel, as a whole, harmonic, is critical of the portrayal of the "dissoluter Gefühle" [dissolute emotions] within it. In particular, he is critical of Ottilie's renunciation for moral reasons. He believes that instead of spending all of her time with Eduard until she commits suicide, she should have renounced Eduard by leaving him and never seeing him again. Eichendorff is also morally troubled by Ottilie's status as a Christian saint (469). What is perhaps most interesting, however, in Eichendorff's short treatment of the novel is that he warns against reading a novel in the light of an author's life. He here predicts the very trend that was to predominate by the end of the century and warns against it (470).

Hebbel discusses the novel within the "Vorwort" (Foreword) to his *Maria Magdalene* (1844). He characterizes *Die Wahlverwandtschaften* as a drama and places it alongside *Faust* as the cornerstone of a new dramatic form. The essay is extremely complex and difficult. Like Solger, however, Hebbel argues that Goethe's work is modern in its attempts to emphasize the individual, and like Solger, Hebbel attempts to give a theoretical overview of the history of drama generally, as well as of Goethe's specific place within that history. He argues that to date there have been three great dramatic epochs: that of ancient Greece; that of Shakespeare; and that which Goethe inaugurated but did not complete. Hebbel explains that the central battle within the ancient drama, as demonstrated by Oedipus, was between human beings and fate, where the individual is subordinate to exterior, moral forces. Shakespearean drama, which developed under the influence of Protestantism, freed the individual from the force of fate. Instead, the individual was subjected to extreme dialectical forces from within, whether in the ruthless actions of Shakespeare's more active characters or in the introspection of those like Hamlet.

Hebbel argues that Goethe's *Faust* and *Die Wahlverwandt-schaften* went even further than Shakespeare and placed the dialectical conflict in the center of the drama itself so that the actions of the individual revolve around this conflict:

> Nach Shakespeare hat zuerst Goethe im *Faust* und in den mit Recht dramatisch genannten *Wahlverwandtschaften* wieder zu einem großen Drama den Grundstein gelegt, und zwar hat er getan, oder vielmehr zu tun angefangen, was allein noch übrig blieb, er hat die Dialektik unmittelbar in die Idee selbst hineingeworfen, er hat den Widerspruch, den Shakespeare nur noch im Ich aufzeigt, in dem Zentrum, um das das Ich sich herum bewegt, d.h. in der diesem erfaßbaren Seite desselben, aufzuzeigen. (308)

> [After Shakespeare, Goethe in *Faust* and in *The Elective Affinities* (truly called dramatic) was the first who again laid the foundation for a great new drama. Or rather he began to do the only thing that remained: he placed the problem directly in the Idea. The contradiction which in Shakespeare appears only in the individual he attempted to reveal in that center about which the individual turns, i.e., in such phases of it as are comprehensible to the individual. (87)]

Hebbel does not give examples from the novel to explain what he means here. He appears to believe, however, that Goethe attempted to combine the ancient characteristics of fate with the more modern one of an individual's inner conflict. Ottilie, in this sense, could represent the internal conflict of the individual who faces the outward power of fate. And while the story of Ottilie is quite an individual one, it still fulfills Hebbel's requirement for a (modern) bourgeois tragedy — that it be universally applicable.

As Hebbel continues, he begins to criticize Goethe for only pointing the way to the new dramatic form without clearly establishing it. *Die Wahlverwandtschaften* therefore also represents for Hebbel the shortcomings of Goethe's style. He is particularly critical of how the moral and social concerns are treated within the novel. He explains his position in a passage that would be often cited in the future scholarship on the novel:

Wie Goethe, der durchaus Künstler, großer Künstler, war, in den
Wahlverwandtschaften einen solchen Verstoß gegen die innere
Form begehen konnte, daß er, einem zerstreuten Zergliederer
nicht unähnlich, der, statt eines wirklichen Körpers, ein Automat
auf das anatomische Theater brächte, eine von Haus aus nichtige,
ja unsittliche Ehe, wie die zwischen Eduard und Charlotte, zum
Mittelpunkt seiner Darstellung machte und dies Verhältnis be-
handelte und benutzte, als ob es ein ganz entgegengesetztes, ein
vollkommen berechtigtes wäre, wüßte ich mir nicht zu erklären;
daß er aber auf die Hauptfrage des Romans nicht tiefer einging,
und daß er ebenso im *Faust,* als er zwischen einer ungeheuren
Perspektive und einem mit Katechismus-Figuren bemalten Bretter-Verschlag wählen sollte, den Bretter-Verschlag vorzog und
die *Geburtswehen* der um eine neue Form ringenden Menschheit,
die wir mit Recht im ersten Teil erblickten, im zweiten zu bloßen
Krankheits-Momenten eines später durch einen willkürlichen, nur
notdürftig-psychologisch vermittelten Akt kurierten Individuums
herabsetzte, das ging aus seiner ganz eigen komplizierten Indivi-
dualität hervor, die ich hier nicht zu analysieren brauche, da ich
nur anzudeuten habe, wie weit er gekommen ist. (309)

[Goethe was an artist, a great artist through and through. And I
am unable to explain how he could so offend against logic in *The
Elective Affinities* as to choose for the foundation of his work a
marriage like that between Edward and Charlotte, essentially
worthless, yes even immoral, and treat and use it as if it were of
the opposite nature and perfectly justifiable — not unlike an ab-
sent-minded demonstrator who would bring a puppet to the
anatomical theater instead of a real body. But that he did not go
deeper into the main problem of the novel, that also in *Faust,*
when he came to choose between an unbounded perspective and
a sign-board painted with figures from the catechism he chose
the sign-board; that he thus degraded the birth agonies of a humanity struggling for a new form (which we properly recognize
in the first part) to mere phases of a disease in the second, a disease of an individual, cured later by an act both arbitrary and of
scant psychological motivation — all this was a result of his particularly complex individuality, which I do not need to analyze
here, as I have only to indicate how far he went. (88–89)]

Like many of Goethe's contemporary critics, Hebbel is dissatisfied
with the portrayal of marriage within the novel. Hebbel, however,
frames this dissatisfaction in Hegelian terms. He criticizes Goethe

for not recognizing the direction that human history was taking. It was not taking the dangerous, immoral turn that Goethe had predicted and portrayed through his novel of broken marriages, but rather was heading for a new kind of morality:

> *denn der Mensch dieses Jahrhunderts will nicht, wie man ihm Schuld gibt, neue und unerhörte Institutionen, er will nur ein besseres Fundament für die schon vorhandenen, er will, daß sie sich auf nichts, als auf Sittlichkeit und Notwendigkeit, die identisch sind, stützen und also den äußeren Haken, an dem sie bis jetzt zum Teil befestigt waren, gegen den inneren Schwerpunkt, aus dem sie sich vollständig ableiten lassen, vertauschen sollen.* (Emphasis in original, 310)

> [*For the man of this century does not, as he is accused of, want new and unheard of institutions: he only wants a better foundation for those already existing; he wants to see that they rest on nothing but morality and necessity, which are identical, and that they so exchange the external fixture to which hitherto they have been in part attached for the inner center of gravity from which they can be completely explained.* (89)]

Hebbel criticizes Goethe for being stuck in an older phase of humanity. In his view, dramatic art was bringing about a new phase. He therefore praises *Die Wahlverwandtschaften* to the extent that it seeks to establish a new relationship between fate and the individual, but criticizes its portrayal of social institutions.

Although *Die Wahlverwandtschaften* was not prominently treated by many literary figures, it was addressed by several noted scholars of the period. The most important interpreters of Goethe's novel during the first half of the nineteenth century were the Hegelians. This group played an important role in the reception following Goethe's death because they were the most active critics of Goethe's works during this time. Whereas the Weimar circle of Goethe's admirers (headed by Eckermann) spent most of their time editing and publishing the author's hitherto unpublished works, the Hegelians engaged in (primarily positive) scholarly treatments of it (Mandelkow, *Goethe in Deutschland*, 94).

The Hegelians

The first extended scholarly treatment of the novel after Goethe's death was Heinrich Theodor Rötscher's *Die Wahlverwandtschaften von Goethe in ihrer weltgeschichtlichen Bedeutung, ihrem sittlichen und künstlerischen Werthe nach entwickelt* (Goethe's *Wahlverwandtschaften* in its World-Historical Meaning, explained according to its Moral and Artistic Worth, 1838). Rötscher was a Hegelian, and his work on the novel was much read (Rosenkranz 457; Weiße 85–87; Sommerfeld 233). As the title indicates, Rötscher's book echoes many of the arguments used by Goethe's friends and acquaintances to defend the morality of *Die Wahlverwandtschaften,* and he even directly refers to Solger's positive assessment of it several times throughout his two-hundred page exposition. Like many of the novel's proponents, Rötscher argues that a positive moral lesson emerged from its negative portrayal of marriage and adultery. What is new, however, is his approach. He uses the rubric of the Hegelian dialectic in order to structure his defense. One of his main aims is to resolve the misunderstandings that have arisen from earlier readings of the novel. He believes that once readers have properly analyzed its conflicting strands, a resolution emerges that will elucidate the moral message at the heart of the text. He argues that good works of art, like life itself, are characterized by polar oppositions — that to understand the good, one must view it in opposition to the bad. Accordingly, an artist is not a moral preacher who focuses only upon the good sides of human character, but rather shows both the good and the bad. And while all good art ought ultimately to have a moral center, a good artist never places moral concerns above artistic ones (1–5). The fact that so many critics have argued over the moral message of *Die Wahlverwandtschaften,* shows, according to Rötscher, the greatness of Goethe as an artist. Although Goethe ran the risk of being misunderstood, he refused to sacrifice his artistry (5).

Rötscher finds that the novel simultaneously presents two moral alternatives: either the individual triumphs over nature and exerts his or her moral freedom (Charlotte) or the individual is crushed between the conflicting powers of duty and passion (Ottilie). In either case morality is victorious. In the first instance, morality triumphs directly by transforming the "krankhaften Lebenstoff" [pathological stuff of life] into a healthy force; in the second, morality triumphs indirectly in that the invulnerability of the moral idea and its power arises out of the destruction of the individual (28–29). That which is immoral is destroyed. Charlotte represents the direct triumph of morality; Ottilie represents the indirect. Ottilie symbolizes the tragic triumph of morality because she is destroyed in the process of trying to do the right thing. In his discussion of Ottilie, Rötscher very much follows in the tradition of Abeken, Solger, and Eckermann. For those who defended Goethe's novel against the charges of immorality, Ottilie's character became of central importance. As another similarly minded defender of Goethe's novel points out several years later, if one is to rescue the novel from its reputation of immorality, one has to reconcile Ottilie's love for a married man with her apparent innocence (Lösch 169, 174–78, 181, 184).

Although Rötscher claims in theory to value aesthetic concerns over moral ones, his exposition of the novel primarily addresses its moral message. His use of Hegelian philosophy, moreover, is largely superficial. He uses Hegelian terms, but the tone of his whole treatise is largely moralistic and not philosophical. In other words, Hegel's terms are not used to trace an ever-progressing and changing schema, but to reinforce conservative, Christian values.

Another Hegelian, the theologian and philosophy professor Karl Rosenkranz, also turned to the Hegelian dialectic to analyze the novel.[5] In his *Göthe und seine Werke* (Goethe and His Works, 1847), he first frames his discussion of *Die Wahlverwandtschaften* as part of triad of Goethe's works: *Wilhelm Meisters Lehrjahre* portrays the formation of the individual, *Die Wahlverwandtschaften* the development of the individual through fate, and *Wilhelm Meisters Wanderjahre* the overcoming of fate through renunciation and activity (433). Rosenkranz, like Rötscher, emphasizes the moral message of *Die Wahlverwandtschaften,* and one can see how Goethe's reputation as a defender of conservative values and traditions was being formed.

Rosenkranz's exposition is typical of Goethe's proponents of this time in that he strives as much to counter the earlier negative assessment of the novel as he does to present his own thesis. He believes that his first task is to free the novel from earlier "misinterpretations." In so doing, he sees himself as following in the footsteps of the others, including Eckermann and Rötscher, who have already, in his mind, done a great deal to establish the novel's moral meaning (457). And while Rosenkranz states that any reader of this novel ought to have achieved a certain level of maturity, he also argues that because Goethe handles the moral issues with such delicacy, no one will be harmed by the novel even if it should fall into the hands of less mature readers (458). Thus, while many of Goethe's contemporaries thought the book ought never to be read by young women, Rosenkranz feels such a prohibition is absurd.

What is new in Rosenkranz's analysis is his particular emphasis on love. Many of the commentators who see the novel in terms of a battle between duty and passion do not even address the role of love within the institution of marriage. His analysis therefore signals a slight shift away from the more moralistic readings. For Rosenkranz, a true marriage is not one simply sanctioned by marital vows, but one that combines the social convention with natural love. A tragic situation arises when conventional marriage is not combined with natural love (459–60). Therefore, while marriages for Rosenkranz are generally perfected through children (462), the conception and birth of Charlotte and Eduard's child demonstrates the grave disjunction between nature and convention and marks the characters for tragedy (462–63).

It is clear that both Rötscher and Rosenkranz were fighting against a tradition that viewed the novel as immoral. They were attempting to save the novel for a conservative public and create an image of Goethe as a conservative defender of the institution of marriage. Although their Hegelian approach made the argument from a different perspective, they nevertheless were consciously following in the footsteps of those closest to Goethe (Eckermann, Abeken, etc.).

One of the most important opponents to the Hegelian reading of the novel was the philosopher Christian Hermann Weiße. In his essay, "Ueber Göthe's *Wahlverwandtschaften* und ihre neuesten Beurtheilungen" (On Goethe's *Elective Affinities* and its Most Recent Critiques, 1841), Weiße vehemently disagrees with Rötscher's analysis of the novel. Although he argues that Rötscher's characterization of the novel as an apology for marriage is wrong-headed, Weiße does not therefore read the novel as an immoral work (85–86). Rather, he attempts to demonstrate that its morality addresses a higher sphere than one simply involving marriage. In other words, he believes that Goethe's purpose is not didactic, but philosophical. He argues that Goethe was actually sketching out the philosophical conflict between human and spiritual claims (as opposed to the more common formulation of nature versus duty or passion versus reason). According to Weiße, Rötscher, in focusing the whole discussion on marriage, does nothing more than force Goethe into the role of a pedantic moralist. Weiße therefore clearly breaks with the dominant view that expected works of art to have a moral, didactic function. Weiße also accuses Rötscher both of trivializing Goethe and of intentionally obscuring his argument with the aid of Hegelian terminology.

Weiße himself relies heavily upon Hegelian concepts. He contends that one of the reasons that the public and many of the critics have misunderstood the role of morality in the novel is that they have failed to distinguish between two Hegelian categories of "Geist" (89). The first, belonging to the objective spirit, is associated with conventional morality. According to Weiße, this spirit exhibits its power and has its rights in the earthly realm here and now. The second type of spirit is eternal or absolute and associated with a higher law; in literature it appears as love (such as Antigone's love for her brother). The conflict between these two types of morality, as Hegel had demonstrated through his discussion of Greek drama, is tragic (90) because human beings are necessarily punished for breaking the laws of the land even when they are bid to do so by the higher powers of the absolute spirit. Therefore, although Ottilie and Eduard follow the dictates of the higher power of love, they are rightly punished in this world for breaking its moral codes. That they are promised a life together in the next world, however, signals the ultimate victory of the absolute spirit (91).

In treating the novel as tragic, Weiße consciously follows Solger's earlier arguments on the nature of modern tragedies and their differences with classical ones. Weiße, however, makes a significant departure from Solger — as well as from other earlier commentators — in his discussion of the novel's "Form." He believes that too much of the discussion of the novel to date had dealt only with its content, but that we can learn a great deal about the novel's aesthetic qualities by turning our view to its artistic form (92). Ultimately Weiße argues that the novel's greatest aesthetic deficiency is that its content (that of a tragic story) is at odds with its form (that of a novel) — or, put another way, that Goethe's intention[6] and conception are at odds with his portrayal and execution (87–

88, 97, 100, 101). Although Weiße gives some qualifications to his statement, in essence he believes that only a drama can exhibit the true coherence between form and content. He even speculates at one point how much better *Die Wahlverwandtschaften* could have been had Goethe written it in the form of a play.

Weiße's essay in many ways marks a transition between those critics who concentrated upon the moral/immoral portrayal of marriage in *Die Wahlverwandtschaften* and those who were more interested in its aesthetic qualities, particularly its style and form. With the rise of literary histories during the mid-nineteenth century, more and more scholars, while not completely abandoning questions of morality, focused their discussions increasingly upon style. For such scholars, it became more important to categorize *Die Wahlverwandtschaften* according to its place in literary history than to make judgments about its ethical merits.

The Literary Historians

In addition to the Hegelian interpretations of the novel, other critical readings were developed within the broader context of German literature (as opposed to the more narrow one of Goethe studies). Hegel's influence, however, may be seen even here. His views on the progressing nature of history led to a proliferation of German literary histories, and many tried to reflect those ideas of progress in their assessment of German literature. They thus tried to show how German literature was steadily improving to reach its current "peak" in modernity. One of the most important and influential of these literary histories was Georg Gottfried Gervinus's, *Geschichte der deutschen Dichtung* (History of German Literature, 1842), which in many ways set the standards for such works (Batts 3–4).

Gervinus took a different approach to reading *Die Wahlverwandtschaften* than his immediate predecessors. He generally paints a more balanced picture than either Goethe's staunchest proponents or critics had done. He is able to do so because he does not place questions of the novel's morality at the center of his discussion. Instead, he analyzes the structure and style of the novel. Rather than seeing the novel in terms of classicism, as many of Goethe's earlier supporters had done, or as a Romantic work as several of his detractors had maintained, he views it as a transitional work, one that therefore illustrates the modern direction that German culture was taking. Gervinus argues that *Die Wahlverwandtschaften* signals Goethe's turning away from the Romantic narrative/story [Erzählung] and anticipating the modern style of the novella. Throughout his commentary on the novel, Gervinus praises those aspects that seem more progressive, while criticizing those that he views as more old-fashioned and Romantic.

Gervinus by no means emphasizes *Die Wahlverwandtschaften*. Although he spends some time discussing the importance of Goethe's works (especially *Faust*) for German literature as a whole, he devotes very little to *Die Wahlverwandtschaften* (710–12). Nevertheless, he finds much to praise in it. In particular, he argues that the novel largely transcends the Romantic influences of its day due to its style. Originally, he explains, Goethe planned it as nothing more than a Romantic story to include in *Wilhelm Meisters Wanderjahre*. As the story grew, it became a masterpiece of the new novella form (711). In order to show the development of Goethe's style, Gervinus contrasts *Die Wahlverwandtschaften* with *Werther*, finding the later novel to be written in a completely different spirit. While *Werther* represents a kind of pathology, *Die Wahlverwandtschaften* signals a new epoch in literature. Conversely, Gervinus criticizes *Die Wahlverwandtschaften* where he feels it still follows the older tendencies of the Romantic school. He especially criticizes the wondrous events at the end as indications of Goethe's "descent" into Romanticism.

Gervinus's literary history further marks a new trend in *Wahlverwandtschaften* scholarship in that it situates the novel within the greater context of European literature, comparing it, for instance, with Cervantes's novellas in order to praise *Die Wahlverwandtschaften's* clarity and regularity of execution. He admires Goethe's ability to illustrate the conflicting demands of reason and the daemonic by presenting us with characters who struggle with these oppositional tendencies in their own lives. In general, Gervinus finds that Goethe's ability to create a harmonic mood surpasses that of his literary predecessor, Cervantes.

Another important literary history to treat *Die Wahlverwandtschaften* as a modern work was August Friedrich Christian Vilmar's (1800–1868) *Vorlesungen über die Geschichte der deutschen National-Literatur* (Lectures on the History of German National Literature, 1845). Vilmar was a theologian whose lectures were intended for a primarily non-academic audience (Batts 31). His lectures "had a considerable impact on the public sphere of the day" (Hohendahl 234; 235–36). His book was extremely popular and continued to exert an influence well into the twentieth century. By 1883, it had gone into its twenty-first edition, and the last revised edition appeared in 1936 (Mandelkow, *Goethe in Deutschland,* 311).

Although Vilmar gives *Die Wahlverwandtschaften* only a short treatment, he highly praises Goethe's aesthetic skill. Like Gervinus, he characterizes Goethe as a modern and views the work in terms of a novella. According to Vilmar, Goethe's convincing and realistic "psychische Krankeitsgeschichte der modernen Welt" [story of psychic illness of the modern world] surpasses the artistic perfection of *Wilhelm Meister* (566). Goethe's portrayal of the characters and his "rein objective Darstellung der zerstörendsten Leidenschaften" [purely objective portrayal of the most destructive passions] makes this novel "zu einem noch völlig unerreichten Muster der modernen Novelle (567) [into an as yet completely unrivalled model of the modern novella].

For Vilmar, aesthetic concerns continue to be linked with moral ones. However, while he voices reservations about the morality of the novel, he does not therefore condemn the entire book. He even protests against those who condemn it purely on moral grounds. He defends the aesthetic merits of the novel, which in the end, he believes, have a moral function. He complains that many highly praised books, with all their moral tendencies tell "unwahre Krankeitsgeschichten und noch unwahrere Heilungen" [untrue stories of illness and even more untrue cures]. Such books are more likely to infect the reader with the "Gift" [poison] of passion than is Goethe's novel. In other words, Vilmar argues that books that provide idealized solutions to moral dilemmas are of no benefit to anyone, but only excite their readers and give them false notions about the passions. Vilmar praises Goethe's ability to write the novel in such a way that the reader is captivated but not seduced by the passions (567).

Not all of the literary historians, of course, were in agreement about the merits of *Die Wahlverwandtschaften.* Several years later, Julian Schmidt (1818–86), in his history of Germany literature,

Geschichte der Deutschen Literatur seit Lessing's Tod (History of German Literature since Lessing's Death, 1853), gives a much more critical assessment of the novel than either Gervinus or Vilmar. For Schmidt, as for many of his contemporaries, the realistic novel represented the pinnacle of literary achievement. Much of his criticism, therefore, centers on his assessment of the novel's lack of realism.

Schmidt was the most influential literary historian between the Revolution of 1848 and the founding of the German Empire in 1870 (Mandelkow, *Goethe in Deutschland*, 146). Although he praises certain aspects of the novel, his assessment of it is by and large negative. He criticizes the pacing of the action, the character development, the morality, and, most importantly in his mind, the lack of realism. Admittedly, he considers the first half, due to its portrayal of the growing passion, without parallel in German literature. However, once Eduard leaves the manor, Schmidt argues that the plot seems to stand still. He further criticizes Ottilie's diary entries as a questionable means of character development. In the first place it is unlikely that such entries could have been written by a young woman. Second, Goethe never clearly identifies the unifying themes of the diary — never provides the promised "red thread" that would tie the disparate reflections of the diary together. Third, Schmidt questions whether her journal has any connection with the plot of the novel. As a consequence, he judges the novel to be flawed in that the reader is emotionally unprepared for the suddenness of the catastrophe at the end (170).

Schmidt's character analysis continues in the same vein. Most striking is his criticism that the characters are not passionate enough. Thus, while many commentators praise Charlotte's restraint, Schmidt argues that Charlotte would have been more appealing if her renunciation had cost her more pains. Nor is it Charlotte's inability to love that Schmidt considers a weakness of character, but rather, her inability to *hate* either Eduard or Ottilie (171). Similarly, he finds Ottilie lacking an emotional dimension. The reader would forgive Ottilie's sins against Charlotte, had her passion been portrayed as more powerful and moving (172). Schmidt therefore criticizes Goethe for explaining the passion between Eduard and Ottilie as the result of an external, natural law as opposed to the result of a fierce, personal passion.

Like many earlier critics of the novel, Schmidt argues that the book is immoral, but not because Goethe meant to attack the institution of marriage. To the contrary, Goethe, according to Schmidt, desired to present a defense of marriage and deceived himself into thinking he had succeeded (171). Schmidt highlights several aspects of the novel he considers subversive of marriage, and in particular finds the love-making scene, while masterfully written, disgusting and appalling (172). And where Vilmar praises the objective distance between Goethe and the novel, Schmidt finds Goethe's style to be *too* objective. He criticizes Goethe for presenting facts, but never an opinion or judgment as to how the reader is to interpret them. The novelist should, according to Schmidt, show his own moral views in the novel (173).

Schmidt saves his harshest comments, however, for Goethe's setting the novel in an earlier historical time and thereby ignoring the most important events of his own time: the Napoleonic wars. In this respect, Schmidt resembles the critics of the 1820s and 1830s who found Goethe to be too apolitical.[7] Granting that authors certainly are not required realistically to portray all aspects of the times, he argues that they are required to portray the really important ones (174). He thus demands a new requirement of the artist beyond the moral obligations demanded by earlier critics. A work of art must also reflect political events. It should not "schweben" [sway] in the "Aether der stofflosen Dichtung" [ether of matterless literature], but ought to be based "auf dem festen Boden der Wirklichkeit" (174) [upon the solid ground of reality].[8] That Goethe failed to address Germany's "frightful misfortune," and indeed allowed his character, Eduard, to treat the wars lightly, is an indictment against the book (174–75). Schmidt's commentary shows how much had changed in the reception of the novel since it had been published. A generation before, even Goethe's harshest critics had admitted that the novel was a mirror of the times. Schmidt's criticism demonstrates, however, that the new realism demanded a different perspective. It was not enough to portray the style of aristocratic life; rather, authors must portray contemporary life within the political context of their time.

Schmidt's highly critical approach to the novel quickly became a thing of the past. Later literary histories were much more favorable. By the end of the nineteenth century, Goethe's popularity was immense. Alongside the growth of German nationalism and the quest (especially by Grimm) to make Goethe into a German nationalist symbol, analyses of the novel became more favorable, less critical, and less analytical. Even Schmidt himself, as discussed below, became caught up in the new spirit of the times and eventually reinterpreted the novel in a much more positive light (1890). Wilhelm Scherer's (1841–86) assessment of *Die Wahlverwandtschaften* is therefore more representative of the criticism of the latter part of the nineteenth century.

Scherer's literary history, *Geschichte der deutschen Litteratur* (A History of German Literature, 1883), was immensely influential. It was almost immediately published in translation in both England and America (1886) and appeared in reprinted editions until 1908. Batts explains that the "major novelty of Scherer's work lies in the historical framework that he constructs for German literary history" (58). Scherer posits three "peaks in German literature around 600, 1200, and 1800" (Batts 58). German literature is closely linked to German politics: literary triumphs were simultaneously political ones. Thus, for Scherer the best productions of Wieland, Goethe, Herder, and Schiller were at the same time monuments of Karl August's rule (Scherer 528).

Scherer was one of the most prominent Goethe scholars of this period and a member of the Goethe Society's first executive committee (Leppmann 120). Not surprisingly, he offers almost unqualified praise for *Die Wahlverwandtschaften*. Scherer, for example, judges *Die Wahlverwandtschaften* to be:

> das epische Hauptwerk der ganzen Zeit von Schillers Tod bis zu Goethes Tod. . . . Aber sonst haben gerade die Feinheiten der Composition, die ähnlichen und vorbereitenden Motive, die verwandten Melodieklänge, die strenge innere Begründung der Handlungsweise aus den Charakteren und der Charaktere aus den bildenden Umständen kaum irgendwo ihres gleichen. (681–82)

> [the epic masterpiece of the whole period from Schiller's death to Goethe's. . . . Nowhere do we meet with such subtleties of composition, with such fine adjustment of motives, with such consistency in the development of action from character, and of character from surrounding circumstances. (298–99)]

And where most of Goethe's other proponents felt the need to answer the earlier criticisms, especially the moral condemnations of the novel, Scherer does not address the problematic reception of the novel. Instead, he focuses upon the positive and reiterates the moral arguments of the Hegelians. Where Goethe in *Wilhelm Meister* had treated marriage according to the frivolous views of the eighteenth century, in *Die Wahlverwandtschaften* marriage appears in a much more serious light (682). Scherer further links Goethe's new "seriousness" on the subject of marriage to the new ending to *Stella.*[9]

As Goethe's popularity was growing toward the end of the nineteenth century, more and more was being written about him and his works. By 1877, Grimm notes that hardly a week goes by without something new being published about Goethe (6). One best witnesses the trend to idolize Goethe in the growing number of biographies about him. Not only were numerous biographies published within a short time-span, but the biographies themselves were becoming less critical of Goethe's works as they began to apotheosize his life. New moral readings of the novel also emerged alongside these panegyric treatments of Goethe's life. Even Julian Schmidt's later history of German literature, *Geschichte der Deutschen Litteratur von Leibniz bis auf unsere Zeit* (History of German Literature from Leibniz to the Present Time, 1890), shows a marked softening toward the novel and includes biographical details as part of his interpretation.

Schmidt's later review of the novel (1890) reverses his earlier stance on several of his key statements and perhaps illustrates how much the times had changed in several decades. Most surprisingly, Schmidt now finds the novel and its characters to be much more realistic. Ottilie is no longer the abstract, passionless character he thought her in 1853, but is now a highly moving character who gives the impression of being a real person (382). Whereas earlier, the reader could not sympathize with her because she was not passionate enough, now the reader is moved toward pity due to Goethe's ability to portray her inner world (388). Schmidt justifies this reading of Ottilie by linking her story closely to Goethe's personal emotional state. She represents the pain of Goethe's own renunciation. Indeed, Schmidt now reads the novel largely as a confessional work, and he considers it a moral work because of its correspondence to details in Goethe's life. Because he interprets Goethe's mature life as moral, he also views the novel as moral.

The novel thus reflects Goethe's serious commitment to marriage. Perhaps most striking in Schmidt's reversal is that he no longer criticizes the novel for failing to address the Napoleonic wars and for being out of touch with the times, but instead argues that it represents a transitional historical period (384). The novel, therefore, is realistic in that it portrays a time of change, a change that marks the movement away from an emphasis on the individual to a focus upon social structures (384).

The Rise of Biography

The many literary histories of the nineteenth century addressed Goethe's *Die Wahlverwandtschaften* primarily through text-based analyses: discussion of the plot, structure, character analysis, and main themes. If the morality of the novel was discussed, it was primarily from the perspective of the novel itself and not from the perspective of Goethe's own life. While many of Goethe's biographers still addressed the more formal aspects of the novel, there was an ever-growing trend to link it to Goethe's biography. Biographers, as a consequence, began to discuss Goethe's love affairs, marriage, hobbies, morals, and religion as containing clues to an interpretation of *Die Wahlverwandtschaften*. In particular, the biographers of this period, whether German, American, English or Danish, tended to link Goethe's attraction to Minna Herzlieb to many aspects of the novel. Their scholarship in most cases is almost entirely uncritical. The authors bend over backwards to show that both Goethe's life and its connection to *Die Wahlverwandtschaften* were extremely moral. The language of these texts is often flowery and by today's standards extremely overblown. The biographer Wolff is fairly typical in the language he uses to describe Goethe's relationship to Herzlieb: "In ihrem Auge und Wesen lag etwas Naturdämonisches, dem sich Goethe nicht leicht entziehen konnte" [In her eye and being lay something naturally daemonic from which Goethe could not easily pull away]. Goethe, however, fought his passion with "sittlicher Kraft" [moral power], producing the fruit of *Die Wahlverwandtschaften* (233). The scholarship of many of these biographical treatments further resembled tabloid journalism of today. Friends and relatives of Minna Herzlieb's were interviewed in order to get the real untold story, while she herself was hounded for everything from her picture to possible mementos of her acquaintanceship with Goethe. And because she died in 1865, she witnessed her own life being made into a fiction in the first major Goethe biography written by Lewes.[10] The fact that she suffered from mental illness and was in and out of mental institutions did not stop authors from either seeking her out or writing about her in their efforts to understand Goethe's novel.

Over a dozen Goethe biographies (many simply titled *Goethe*) were written between 1895–1916 (four in 1895 alone), including those by Albert Bielschowsky (1895), Richard Meyer (1895), Karl Heinemann (1895), Eugen Wolff (1895), Georg Witkowski (1899), Eduard Engel (1909), Georg Brandes (1915), and Friedrich Gundolf (1916). The first major biographer was an Englishman, George Lewes (1855), who sought to expand Goethe's audience abroad. By the end of the century, most of the biographies were written by Germans (although several were also translated into English) in a very nationalistic spirit, with the object of making Goethe into a German national hero — and in some cases a mythic superhero. *The* question for every educated German, as Engel would have it, was what his or her relationship was to the greatest man of "our people" (1:1). Seen within the context of the predominance of such biographical readings of Goethe's works at the end of the century, it is no surprise that Walter Benjamin vehemently reacts against this approach in his seminal essay on *Die Wahlverwandtschaften*. There, Benjamin complains that not only is Goethe's life itself treated as a work of art, but it has become one not even distinguished from the actual works (160). Indeed, as the language quoted above about Minna Herzlieb demonstrates, some commentators were trying to make a novel (and a pot boiler at that) out of Goethe's life.

Lewes and the Beginning of Biographical Criticism

The first comprehensive biography — and one of the most influential ever written on Goethe — was by George Henry Lewes. The book first appeared in 1855 and was dedicated to Carlyle, "who first taught England to appreciate Goethe." By 1900 it had gone through eighteen English editions and was translated into German (three times), Italian, and Polish. In the twentieth century, it was still considered one of the best introductions to Goethe (Leppmann 73). Lewes's study marks a new epoch in the criticism of *Die*

Wahlverwandtschaften. Although Lewes's analysis does not primarily focus upon the autobiographical aspects of the novel, his is the first openly to link events and people from Goethe's life to *Die Wahlverwandtschaften*. He justifies this approach by pointing to Goethe's own statement that the novel contains a deep passionate wound. He also believes that the biographical facts establish, as in *Werther,* a close a connection between life and art (504). Goethe thus "dramatises the two halves of his character" by representing himself through two characters within the novel (504): the "impulsive" Eduard and the "reasonable strong-willed" Captain (508). In addition, as far as Lewes is concerned, Minna Herzlieb, the adopted daughter of the Jena bookseller, Frommann, *is* Ottilie.

In dealing with the issue of morality within the novel, Lewes seems surprisingly modern — especially in light of the direction that most Goethe biographies were to take in the subsequent years. He argues that the book does not contain a defense (or for that matter) a critique of a universal moral code. Instead, he suggests that each person who reads the novel will approach it according to his or her own individual perspective and therefore come up with separate conclusions. The novel presents a "dilemma to the moral judgment, on which two parties will pronounce two opposite opinions" (505). Those who condemn the novel "look at human life, and consequently at Art, from the abstract point of view, [and,] disregarding fact and necessity, treat human nature like a chess-board." In contrast, those who praise the novel "look at life as it *is,* not as it might be . . . accept its wondrous complexity of impulses and demand that Art should represent reality — [and] consider this situation as terribly true, and although tragic, by no means immoral" (505). Rather than siding with either camp, Lewes explains that both "have drawn certain general conclusions from an individual case" and that "neither conclusion is correct — except as the private interpretation of the reader" (506). While he agrees with Hegel that "every work of Art has its moral," to Lewes, the *"moral depends upon on him that draws it"* (506). There is therefore no single correct interpretation of the novel, but several. Goethe was an "Artist" and not an "Advocate," and therefore it is a mark of his high artistry that a clear moral message does not emerge.

While Lewes praises Goethe's artistry in creating a "true picture" of human life, his ultimate assessment of the novel is somewhat negative. He is critical of the details presented in the novel and erroneously believes that their density is not troubling to German readers (see chapter 1). While French and English readers may feel "wearied by the many small details which encumber the march of the story . . . no such weariness is felt by German readers, who enjoy the details, and the purpose which they are supposed to serve" (509). More amusing, however, is his friend's opinion that the details "are artistic devices for impressing the reader with a sense of the slow movement of life" (509). Lewes himself believes that the details are "out of all proportion, and somewhat tedious" (509). Finally, in comparing *Die Wahlverwandtschaften* with the earlier works of Goethe's classical period, he finds it "often weak, cold, mechanical in the construction of its sentences, and somewhat lifeless in the abstractness of its diction" (510).

The Political Goethe: Grimm

Herman Grimm's (1828–1901) *Goethe Vorlesungen* (1877; *The Life and Times of Goethe,* 1880) was the next important Goethe biography, and one of the central factors in Germany's rediscovery of Goethe (Leppmann 77; Mandelkow, *Goethe in Deutschland,* 206). Before I turn to Grimm's specific discussion of *Die Wahlverwandtschaften,* it is important to get a sense of his general approach to Goethe studies. His book indeed seems to have set the tone for many of the future discussions of both Goethe and *Die Wahlverwandtschaften.*

Grimm's unbounded praise of Goethe may be partly explained by his background. The eldest son of Wilhelm Grimm and a professor of art history in Berlin, he had intimate connections with Goethe's circle and became a type of spokesperson for Goethe's cause. His wife was Bettina von Arnim's youngest daughter, and he personally knew many of Goethe's friends and acquaintances, including Goethe's grandsons, Marianne von Willemer, Clara Schumann, and Alexander von Humboldt (Leppmann 77; Mandelkow, *Goethe in Deutschland,* 206). Where Goethe had fallen out of favor with the Young Germans and the later realists for not being political enough, Grimm saw Goethe's intellectual contributions as essential to the development of the German nation-state. Thus,

"Goethe hat unsere Sprache und Literatur geschaffen" [1:2; Goethe has created our language and literature: 2] and out of this creation, sprang political nationalism:

> Aus dieser Einheit der Sprache ist bei uns die wahre Gemeinsamkeit der höheren geistigen Genüsse erst entsprungen, und ohne sie wäre unsere politische Einheit niemals erlangt worden, die einzig und allein der unablässig vordringenden Thätigkeit derjenigen bei uns verdankt wird, die wir im höchsten Sinne die "Gebildeten" nennen, und denen Goethe zuerst die gemeinsame Richtung gab. (1:4)

> [Out of this unity of the language arose among us the true fellowship in higher intellectual enjoyment to which we are solely indebted for our political unity, — a unity which could never have been achieved without the unceasing activity of those whom we, in the highest sense, call "the educated," and to whom Goethe first gave the common direction. (4)]

In particular, Grimm wishes to combat the charges that Goethe was not politically active in his day. Through a sleight of hand, he reinterprets Goethe's political passivity as his way of preparing the way for the future German empire. Grimm further defends Goethe against the charges that he was a conservative reactionary:

> Goethe, dessen Natur jede Agitation fremd war, der, in seinen letzten Jahren zumal, wo nach seiner Meinung am meisten gefragt wurde, den Anschein einer behaglich reactionären Denkungsart hatte, nimmt als Politiker und Historiker jetzt eine andere Position ein. Wir gewahren in ihm einen von denen, die unsere heutige Freiheit am sichersten vorausgewußt und für sie vorgearbeitet haben. Wir lesen mit Staunen, wie er die revolutionäre Bewegung der zweiten Hälfte des 19. Jahrhunderts sicher profezeite. Wir verstehen, warum er die abwartende Ruhe der eignen Epoche, in die seine letzte Jahre fielen, für ein unabänderliches Geschick ansah. Wir sehen, wie er die freie Zukunft seines Landes fest im Auge hielt und seine Werke in der Stille für diese Zeiten ausrüstete. Goethe's Arbeit hat den Boden schaffen helfen, auf dem wir heute säen und ärnten. Er gehört zu den vornehmsten Gründern der Deutschen Freiheit. Ohne ihn würden uns bei all unsern Siegen die besten Gedanken fehlen, diese Siege auszunutzen. (1:9)

[Goethe, to whose nature every form of agitation was foreign, and who — especially in his later years, when his opinion was most frequently asked — had the appearance and seemed to have the style of thinking of a comfortable conservative, as statesman and historian now takes a new position. We perceive in him one of those who most confidently foresaw our present freedom, and prepared the ground for it. We read with astonishment how accurately he prophesied the revolutionary agitation of the latter half of the nineteenth century. We understand how he came to look upon the dead calm in which his last years fell as an unavoidable necessity; we see how he held steadfastly in view the free future of his country, and quietly gave to his works the material needed for these days. Goethe's labor helped to create the soil on which we today sow and reap; he belongs among the foremost founders of German freedom; without him, in spite of all our conquests, we should be wanting in the ideas which enable us to derive the noblest benefits from them. (8)]

Grimm does not even claim to give an objective account of Goethe's life, but states overtly that he wishes to reconstruct Goethe's image in a very positive light. The "gesund, schön und kräftig" [healthy, handsome and vigorous] Goethe is accordingly Germany's Homer and Shakespeare, whose image will reign over Germany for centuries (1:9).

Grimm's enthusiasm for Goethe is evident in his analysis of *Die Wahlverwandtschaften*. His biographical study of the novel is different in scope than Lewes's earlier treatment. First, Grimm's biographical speculations play a much more prominent role in his investigation. Second, although Lewes treats Goethe's scientific writings themselves "with what proportionately may seem great length" (viii), he does not directly discuss *Die Wahlverwandtschaften* in terms of Goethe's science. Grimm, by contrast, directly approaches the novel in terms of Goethe's natural philosophy.

Grimm views the novel very much as a confessional work. Like Lewes, he justifies a biographical reading by turning to Goethe's statements about an open wound which required healing (463). However, Grimm does not believe, as Lewes had, that Goethe represented himself as either one of the male characters. Instead, he offers the original and rather radical argument that Goethe's alter ego in the novel is Ottilie. He does so by linking the entire story to Goethe's relationship with Charlotte von Stein. Goethe's encounter with Minna Herzlieb, in Grimm's account, was simply a fresh impetus that finally enabled Goethe to write the story that he had long before created. Before presenting his own particular interpretation, Grimm first dismisses other possible interpretations involving Stein. He rejects the "natural" supposition that Goethe investigates in fiction what would have occurred had he married Stein after the death of her husband. Grimm believes that Goethe intentionally sought to give this impression about his novel because he wished to mislead the critics. The "real purpose" of the novel was for Goethe to relive his earlier relationship with Stein and thereby expiate his guilty feelings for putting a strain on her marriage.

Grimm begins his argument with Goethe's reference to the biblical definition of adultery: "das was der Roman wolle, sei ja so deutlich: er bilde nur eine Illustration des wortes Christi: 'Wer ein Weib ansiehet, ihrer zu begehren, der hat schon die Ehe gebrochen mit ihr'" [2:331; What the romance means is very clear. It is only an illustration of Christ's words, "Whosoever looketh on a woman to lust after her hath committed adultery with her already in his heart": 465]. Instead of applying these words, as most commentators who quote them do, to the night of spiritual adultery, Grimm applies them to Goethe's relationship with Stein. Therefore, where numerous earlier commentators argued that the novel lectures its readers, Grimm argues that Goethe's point was to lecture himself against acting like Ottilie in ruining a marriage (465).

Grimm, in the end, does not differ that much from the defenders of the novel who argue that Mittler's words contain the moral of the whole. Unlike earlier critics, however, he contends that Goethe's new-found morality stems from the new view of the world derived from his scientific studies. It is not surprising that Grimm places such emphasis upon Goethe's natural studies given that one of Germany's foremost scientists, Ernst Haeckel, was forcefully arguing that Goethe had anticipated Darwinian evolution. Grimm capitalized on this claim and also placed particular emphasis upon Goethe's study of the intermaxillary bone. (Goethe was one of the first to argue that this bone exists in human skulls.) The existence of this bone, Grimm argued, had convinced Goethe that human beings were part of the whole economy of nature.

Like many other commentators, Grimm sees the main battle within the novel as that between freedom and necessity. Earlier commentators, however, link this battle either to Kantian morality or to ancient conceptions of tragedy. Grimm, in contrast, directly links this idea to Goethe's natural philosophy. He first explains what necessity means in nature. He compares natural necessity to being bound to a particular economy or budget: "Für die physische formulirt sich das Gesetz des Nothwendigen dahin, daß die schaffende Natur sich gleichsam ihr festes Budget machte, dessen Gränzen sie nicht überschreitet, so daß wo sie ihren Gestalten auf der einen Seite ein plus giebt, diesem ein minus auf der andern nothwendiger Weise entsprechen müsse" [2:227; In the physical world, the law of Necessity means that creative Nature has, so to say, a fixed budget of expenditure, the limits of which she never oversteps; so that if on one side in some of her forms there is a *plus,* it is counterbalanced in others by a *minus:* 461]. Similarly, the actions of the human characters in the novel are viewed according to values:

> [Goethe] sucht die "Nothwendigkeit" des sich Ereignenden dadurch zu erklären, daß er jeder Figur gleichsam einen doppelten Werth verleiht. Er läßt jeden Mitspieler einmal als naturhistorisches willenloses Stück Schöpfung agiren, wie einen Würfel, von höheren dämonischen Mächten auf den Tisch geworfen, der selber nicht mit zu entscheiden hat, wieviel Augen fallen. (2:235)

> [(Goethe) endeavors to make plain the necessity of everything which happens by lending, as it were, a double value to each character in the romance. In the first place he represents each as an organic part of creation, acting instinctively according to fixed laws, as the die thrown on the table by higher spiritual powers has no choice how many spots shall turn up. (468)]

Grimm then differentiates human beings from the rest of nature. In addition to being subjected to natural laws, they are also capable of free actions and choices. He attributes the condemnation of the novel by many of its early critics in part to the fact that though they recognized the role of necessity, they failed to see the role of freedom in the novel. Such critics therefore gave the novel a much more fatalistic meaning than Goethe had intended.

The Heroic Goethe: Bielschowsky

While Grimm's biography set the panegyric tone of many works on Goethe during the late nineteenth century, his was not the most popular biography of the time. Albert Bielschowsky's influential biography, *Goethe: Sein Leben und seine Werke* (1895; *The Life of Goethe*, 1905) enjoyed phenomenal success among the general reading public. By 1922 it was in its 42nd edition. Bielschowsky was celebrated as the "German Lewes" and his biography informed an entire generation of German readers (Mandelkow, *Goethe in Deutschland*, 264–65). In his preface to the American translation, William Cooper, the translator, calls Bielschowsky's biography the "standard" one and characterizes its author as "thoroughly saturated with the spirit of the poet. One feels almost as if Goethe had sat at Bielschowsky's elbow and dictated to him" (iii, vi). This biography will further "have its permanent place beside the poet's own writings" (vi).

This biography continued the trend that Grimm had begun to establish Goethe as the national hero of the German nation. However, the language of Bielschowsky's biography is even more overblown and sentimental than Grimm's and tries to make a greater emotional appeal to its readers. In the opening pages of his work, Bielschowsky depicts Goethe as superhuman, an "Übermensch" (1:4):

> Goethe hatte von allem Menschlichen eine Dosis empfangen und war darum der "menschlichste aller Menschen." . . . Es mag Menschen gegeben haben, die einen schärferen Verstand, andere, die eine stärkere Energie, andere, die eine tiefere Empfindung, eine lebendigere Phantasie hatten, aber es hat ganz gewiß nie einen Menschen gegeben, in dem alle diese Seelenkräfte in gleich großem Maßstabe wie bei Goethe vereint gewesen wären. (1:1–2)

> [Goethe was the most human of all men, because he had been endowed with a portion of everything human. . . . There may have been others of clearer understanding, of greater energy, of deeper feelings, or of more vivid imagination, but it is quite certain that there never was an individual in whom all these faculties were united in such striking proportion. (1:1–2)]

For Bielschowsky, however, Goethe's most important work was his life. Thus Bielschowsky radically changes the thrust of earlier biographies. Whereas biographers such as Grimm turned to Goethe's life in order to help interpret his works, Bielschowsky turns to Goethe's life itself as an object of interpretation. He does so because he treats Goethe's life as an aesthetic object and justifies this approach using psychoanalytic terms. Bielschowsky admits the life was not created consciously. However, he also notes that unconscious impulses were also present in Goethe's literary compositions (1:6). Because Bielschowsky believes that Goethe's life and works spring from the same unconscious desires, both are open to aesthetic analysis.

Bielschowsky focuses the discussion of *Die Wahlverwandtschaften* upon Goethe's relationship with Minna Herzlieb. Unlike the earlier defenders of Goethe's novel, Bielschowsky's turns explicitly to Goethe's own life to argue for the novel's morality — a morality that Goethe propounded, according to Bielschowsky, to counter Friedrich Schlegel's and the Romantic movement's more loose interpretation of marriage.

As a means of providing background information to the novel, Bielschowsky goes into great detail about Goethe's relationship to Herzlieb and her family. We are told about Goethe's growing affection for Herzlieb, his struggles to stay away from her, and the competitions among Goethe, Werner, Riemer, and Knebel to write sonnets in honor of her and the other women in her circle. The affair, according to Bielschowsky, "gab es einer großen tiefsinnigen Dichtung den Lebensodem" [2:261; breathed the breath of life into a great work of deep significance: 2:352]. Bielschowsky's statements about the *Die Wahlverwandtschaften* echo Goethe's own statements in *Dichtung und Wahrheit* about the composition of *Werther*. *Die Wahlverwandtschaften* thus becomes a confessional work that Goethe wrote both to punish himself and to warn himself from straying in the future. Goethe was castigating himself because he had let his passion for Herzlieb carry him away, and in order to punish himself, Bielschowsky argues, he even caricatured the "weak" side of his own personality in the character of Eduard (2:293–94).

Goethe's life and works, therefore, are seen in a morally didactic light. In discussing Goethe's moral life in connection to the novel, Bielschowsky paints Goethe in the light of a Christ figure: "Er hat gekämpft und gesiegt. Er hat sich getötet und ist zum Leben aufgestiegen. . . . Was er gelernt, suchte er zu lehren" [2:294; He fought the good fight and came off the conqueror. He killed the self and rose to life. . . . What he learned he sought to teach others: 2:387].

This attempt to link Goethe's life to the moral teaching of the novel pervades Bielschowsky's interpretation. He argues that Mittler's words reflect Goethe's deepest convictions (2:292) and even speculates that they are meant as a sermon against Schlegel's "frivolous" words on group marriages in the *Athenäum* (Schlegel suggests marriage à quatre): "Auf diesen frivolen, in philosophelndem Dünkel sich spreizenden Wortschwall erteilen *Die Wahlverwandtschaften* die gründliche, in Granit gegrabene Antwort" [2:293; To this frivolous, swaggering verbiage, puffed up with philosophical conceit, *Die Wahlverwandtschaften* gives a sound answer engraved in a shaft of granite: 2:386].

Given Bielschowsky's highly moral reading of Goethe's life, it is no surprise that he holds the novel to be the fight for the sacredness of marriage (2:292) and the symbolic corroboration of Kant's categorical imperative (2:291). The final didactic message is for Bielschowsky equally clear: the novel teaches that whoever does not value moral laws must perish (2:291). In his moralistic interpretation, baby Otto "ist aus der Lüge geboren. . . . Es ist als Geschöpf der Lüge zum Tode verurteilt. Denn nur die Wahrheit ist wesenhaft. Die Schuld an seinem Tode muß auf die fallen, die ihre Schuld an seiner innerlich unwahren Existenz nicht durch Selbstüberwindung gesühnt haben. Das sind Ottilie und Eduard" [2:276; is born of deception. . . . As a creature of deception [he] is doomed to die; for only truth has real life. The guilt of its death must fall upon those who are to blame for its inwardly untrue existence and have not atoned for their guilt by overcoming self, that is, Eduard and Ottilie: 2:367]. Notably, this passage was one that Benjamin harshly attacked in his essay several years later.

Other Biographical Approaches

While Grimm and Bielschowsky were among the more influential biographers of the time, many others similarly examined *Die Wahlverwandtschaften* in light of Goethe's life. There were, of course, many variations in the approaches. In his popular biography, *Goethe* (1895), Karl Heinemann, like many others, argues that

Goethe's attraction to Minna Herzlieb is the impetus behind the novel's composition. Although earlier commentators did not mention Goethe's personal circumstances in connection to the novel, Heinemann argues that the "false interpretation" of the novel (i.e., its immorality) is due more to circumstances surrounding Goethe's own marriage than to the textual details of the novel itself. Because the public knew that Goethe had long lived with Vulpius without marrying her, they "overlooked" the fact that the novel's conclusion supports the indissolubility of marriage, and believed it instead to argue the opposite (284). According to Heinemann, however, Goethe's intention was to show the public how seriously he took marriage in light of his new relationship with Vulpius. Heinemann argues that many of Goethe's earlier works showed the German public how inviolable and holy he thought marriage to be (284–85) and that *Die Wahlverwandtschaften* was similarly a defense of marriage. Heinemann therefore follows the long line of Goethe defenders who argue that the novel has a morally didactic purpose.

Witkowski, too, begins his commentary (1899) on the novel by drawing comparisons between Ottilie and Minna Herzlieb (379) and, perhaps following Bielschowsky's lead, revisits the account of the sonnet competition with Werner. Witkowski, however, places this episode, as well as the entire novel, within the framework of Romantic influences: the sonnet form was a favorite of the Romantics (379), the novel's discussion of divorces and partner exchanges stemmed directly from the practices of the Romantics (381–82), and the novel's portrayal of science, especially that of magnetism, was a reflection of Romantic interests (382, 384, 388). He argues that Goethe differed in one very important respect from the Romantics. Whereas Goethe practiced renunciation when faced with passionate entanglements, the Romantics did not (381).

Goethe's growing apotheosis was not only the work of German authors. Therefore, while German nationalism certainly played a role in creating a heroic image of Goethe, it was not the only source. Several non-German scholars also wrote enthusiastically about Goethe and his works and argued that he was one of the greatest artists who had ever lived. Many of these biographies mythologize both Goethe's life and works. For example, in *Goethe: His Life and Works* (1886), George Calvert continues to focus on Minna Herzlieb's "inspirational" role in *Die Wahlverwandtschaf-*

ten. We actually "owe" the book to Herzlieb. (192). The novel is "unsurpassed among prose fictions for aesthetic merits [and] may be regarded as a thrilling protest against conjugal infidelity" (46). While Calvert notes that "scarcely a book of Goethe's has been more subject to ignorant detraction, to shallow misinterpretation than the *Wahlverwandtschaften*" (46), he spends more time defending not the novel against the criticisms of immorality, but Goethe's life itself. So Calvert not only conflates Goethe's life and works, but analyzes the morality of both. He chauvinistically defends Goethe's manliness and suggests that he does not have to adhere to the same standards as others. If we "smile now while reading of the affair" between Goethe and the young woman, nevertheless Goethe's "nature demanded that he should ever carry about with him in his brain some image of womanhood to cheer him and agitate him. . . . But Goethe seems to have the marrow of the Patriarchs, the type of whom is still extant, Sir Samuel Baker telling of a Sheik in Abyssinia who leaped alertly down from the white camel to greet him, and who, now in his eightieth year, had just taken another wife, aged fourteen" (193).

One of the most extreme biographical accounts due to its sensational tone is Denton Snider's *Goethe's Life-Poem* (1915). Snider seems to want to excite interest in his American audience by injecting his prose with as many emotional images as possible.[11] In his chapter on *Die Wahlverwandtschaften,* no distinction is made between Goethe's life and work: "Grip this book at its center and we shall find love ensconced there as the subtle demi-urge who is undermining legal marriage and thus producing a tragic conflict. . . . Would he [Goethe] have touched pen to paper unless he could have recorded himself at an ultimate crisis of his own destiny?" (524) Minna Herzlieb is again at the center of this "crisis." The novel becomes, as a result, not a work of art standing on its own merits, but a public diary or "confession" — a confession that ultimately argues for the institution of marriage (528–29).

Not all biographical approaches emphasized moral interpretations. Although he still excessively praises Goethe, the influential Danish scholar, Georg Brandes, argues for a less moralistic interpretation of *Die Wahlverwandtschaften.* Brandes writes his work expressly with the intent to broaden Goethe's audience beyond the boundaries of German-speaking countries, and he sets out to create a superhuman image. Goethe was accordingly "the greatest poet of the last three centuries," "the incarnation of humanity at its loftiest," and "more superbly endowed than any of his predecessors for several centuries back" (1:xii). He was the German Michelangelo, Dante, Galileo, Voltaire, Shakespeare, Newton, Darwin, and Linnaeus (1:xiv–xv). In his introduction, he summarizes the German reception of Goethe. After a "relatively long period during which [Goethe] was misunderstood and wrongly interpreted, he has become the national Germanic god" (1:xiv). And although Brandes clearly wants to separate Goethe from German politics, he still quite closely ties the two together. Indeed, Goethe becomes the litmus test of German political trends. German politics are good to the extent that they have followed Goethe's model, bad to the extent that they have fallen away from him. Brandes explains:

> If Germany at this moment is one of the most powerful countries on the earth, Goethe has had his part as a teacher and educator in this development. If, on the other hand, Germany in its power has fallen a hopeless prey to arrogance and haughtiness, it simply means a defection from Goethe. (1:xxx)

Brandes clearly wants to promote Goethe's popularity in Europe and America despite the German propensity to use him as an icon for nationalistic purposes. He laments that, outside of Germany, the rest of Europe and America either ignore Goethe and his works or are too critical of him. Yet, Brandes argues, for "Europe and America he should typify not merely the deepest and broadest poetic phenomenon but also the most superbly endowed human being in general that has concerned himself with literature since the days of the Renaissance" (1:xv).

Brandes's extremely favorable treatment of *Die Wahlverwandtschaften* begins with the now almost formulaic construction of linking it to Goethe's attraction to Minna Herzlieb (2:270–71). But he soon drops this thread and concentrates instead, as many earlier commentators had done, on the conflict between human free will and natural forces. Brandes differs markedly from the earlier commentators in that he views nature as the predominate force in the novel (2:272), and yet does not condemn the novel for its immorality. In fact, Brandes does not read the novel as having a didactic function at all. Instead, he focuses upon Goethe's ability to portray life as it is. Thus where many critics condemned the novel for teaching that natural forces were stronger than human will, Brandes does not see this characterization as immoral. In his view, it is simply the way things are. The novel is therefore neither a defense of the institution of marriage, nor an assault upon its foundations. Rather, it depicts one of the numerous possibilities within marriage. In the novel, Goethe "visualized the seamy side of domestic life, portrayed the passions as dark powers, and set forth marriage as an institution which constitutes for some an easy and useful cloak for their feelings, for others a strait-jacket" (2:295).

The biographical approach to criticism was not confined to biographies. One can further document the influence and predominance of this approach at the time by turning to several articles on *Die Wahlverwandtschaften*. Many articles at the end of the nineteenth century exclusively examined Minna Herzlieb's connection to the novel. Within these articles, not only was Goethe's life being confounded with fiction, but so was Minna Herzlieb's. Both Adolph Stahr and F. K. M. [Friedrich Karl Meyer] attempt through biographical studies of Herzlieb to prove without a shadow of a doubt that she is almost indistinguishable from Ottilie. They discuss her appearance and her personality (citing letters of her friends and acquaintances, and in the case of the latter critic, a personal meeting a year before her death). Perhaps recognizing the inappropriateness of digging into the details (and then publishing, albeit posthumously, the sad story of Herzlieb's unhappy marriage and frequent bouts with insanity), both seek to justify their intrusive approach. F. K. M. argues that in every period of Goethe's life there was a woman who influenced his artistry, who then could be found mirrored in his works. Because Goethe had remained silent about the source of his inspiration of Ottilie, this opened up a twofold "obligation" to the biographer: he had first to discover who the woman was; and second, he had to uncover the reasons behind Goethe's silence (623). Stahr similarly writes that fully understanding the Herzlieb-Ottilie connection is of central importance for the aesthetic and psychological understanding of the novel (665).

Another article that overtly admits the influence of the predominant biographical approaches is Wilhelm Bölsche's (1861–1939) essay, "Goethes *Wahlverwandtschaften* im Lichte moderner Naturwissenschaft" (Goethe's *Elective Affinities* in Light of Modern Science, 1889). Bölsche, however, does not focus on the

Minna Herzlieb episode but looks to the new information that had emerged regarding Goethe's scientific interests. He therefore argues that Goethe's interest in science ought to be the source for reading the novel in a new light (171).[12] In contrast to earlier critics (such as Julian Schmidt, 1853), who argued that the novel was weak and unappealing because it was not written in the "superior" style of realism, Bölsche believes that knowledge of Goethe's scientific interests revises this assessment. As a consequence, Bölsche argues not only that the novel is therefore realistic due to its portrayal of natural forces and psychology, but that it should be seen as a predecessor to such realistic works as the novels of George Eliot and Balzac (170, 172–73). In an open nod toward German patriotism — but also citing the necessity for literary "Ehrlichkeit" [honesty] — Bölsche argues that *Die Wahlverwandtschaften* was the pioneering work of literary realism (170–71).[13] In other words, it becomes of central importance for Bölsche to establish Goethe as a leading figure in the sphere of European culture.

The Backlash

A notable exception in the growing positive assessment of Goethe and his works was a biography by the Jesuit priest, Alexander Baumgartner. Baumgartner wrote his biography, *Göthe: Sein Leben und seine Werke* (Goethe: His Life and Works, 1882), expressly to counter the growing influence of the Goethe cult. In his introduction, Baumgartner is explicit about his disapproval of Goethe scholarship: it is not critical enough, but engages in excessive veneration that borders on religious veneration (1:vi). Baumgartner complains that it is taken for granted that Goethe was an ideal human being and that even his faults and mistakes are idolized (1:vi).

Baumgartner is extremely zealous in his negative characterizations of Goethe and his interpreters because so much is at stake for him. Like de Valenti fifty years earlier, he concentrates on Goethe's works as being destructive to religious and conservative values. Baumgartner, however, goes beyond de Valenti's attack on the immorality of the novel and the didactic purpose of art to argue that Goethe has been an influential force in bringing about the negative aspects of modernism. Goethe, in Baumgartner's view, is the quintessential modern: he is anti-Christian, a Darwinian, a materialist, and the high priest of love (1:ix). In particular, Baumgartner is reacting against two tendencies that he saw in German culture at the time. First, he is extremely troubled by the propensity (openly advocated by David Strauss) to replace a Christian education and biblical learning with a study of Goethe and the other German classical authors (1:ix–x); and second, he views with alarm the growing association between Goethe and Darwinism. In his mind, both tendencies were threatening Christianity (1:x, xiii). He viewed Goethe and his works as a Trojan horse that would infiltrate our lives and make modern values victorious (1:xiii). This Goethean threat, although most acutely felt in Germany, was, thanks to Carlyle, Emerson, and Calvert, spreading throughout Western Europe and America (1:xii–xiii). Goethe was fast becoming "eines der mächtigsten Idole der modernen Welt" (1:xiii) [one of the most powerful idols of the modern world].

Baumgartner's treatment of *Die Wahlverwandtschaften* is almost entirely negative. He follows most of the other biographers in linking it with Goethe's attraction to Minna Herzlieb. But unlike Grimm, Bielschowsky, and many others, he is extremely critical of Goethe. Quoting a passage from Lessing's *Laokoon* (that an older person who loves a younger one is a disgusting object) he implies that Goethe is this disgusting object (3:62). Eduard and Goethe become the same person: both are married men who love a younger woman (3:75). And because Goethe is himself carried away by his passion, he is not capable of writing about it with the proper distance. Baumgartner characterizes Goethe's passionate portrayal of the characters and their situation as "eine vollständige Schule ehebrecherischer Liebe" (3:76) [a complete school of adulterous love].

In general, Baumgartner finds that Goethe has turned away from all the noble and uplifting tendencies of his day and limited this novel (as well as *Werther* and *Wilhelm Meister*) to the narrow sphere "des Krankhaften, des Ungesunden, selbstgemachter Phantasieleiden, moralischer Verirrung" (3:65) [of the sick, the unhealthy, the self-created fantasy of suffering, the morally aberrant]. *Die Wahlverwandtschaften* is nothing more than a pathological analysis (3:67). Baumgartner also reviews several of the earlier condemnations of the novel (Rehberg's in most detail) and argues that the novel still ought to be considered as immoral (3:73). He questions several times whether anyone at Goethe's advanced age of

sixty should be writing love stories at all (3:62, 3:66) and de-
nounces him for spending two years working on a novel. Instead of
focusing his interests on the heart of a young girl, Baumgartner
thinks that Goethe ought to have been more interested in philosophy, religious systems, politics, and the arts and sciences (3:66).

Given Baumgartner's perspective as a Jesuit priest, it should
come as no surprise that he criticizes the religious references and
symbolism, especially the Catholic ones, in the novel. He finds that
those who have previously praised Goethe's "Catholic" symbols
had confused true Catholicism with the Romantic renditions of it.
Such critics had forgotten that there is a difference between the
Catholic faith and Protestant romanticism (3:81). Ottilie's penance
is not that of a Christian, but of an overstrained female (3:71).
Similarly Goethe's rendition of renunciation is not meant in the
Christian sense of renouncing all worldly goods in this life in order
to achieve a higher life in the next one. Rather, Goethe momentarily renounces passion only to build the excitement of its enjoyment
later (3:77–78). He further finds that Ottilie's suicide and subsequent saintly status destroy and undermine the Christian perspective. Goethe's Madonna is "eine Art nervös-magnetischen
Mediums" [a kind of nervous, magnetic medium] and his gothic
chapel is nothing more than a "gothischer Schnickschnack" (3:82,
3:83) [a worthless, gothic thing].

Although the major portion of his treatment of the novel is
negative, Baumgartner does praise the style of Goethe's writing.
He defends Goethe's use of details and specifically argues against
Lewes's attack on them. These details, according to Baumgartner,
create the world of the story. He also praises Ottilie's diaries,
viewing them as a kind of modern version of the Greek chorus.
The fact that the novel is so well written, however, is for Baumgartner intimately connected with its immorality. Although the
book contains some moral messages throughout, Goethe ultimately portrays the passions in such a way as to excite them (3:74–
75). The "poison" is thus wrapped in sweetness (3:79).

New Scholarly Directions

Baumgartner's work was a backlash against the growing German
obsession with Goethe and the attempt to deify him. A different
kind of backlash, however, was also developing, even among schol-

ars more positively predisposed to Goethe. Scholars were becoming critical of the predominance of biographical approaches to the novel. Walter Benjamin has become the most famous of the critics to argue against the tendencies of biographies to treat Goethe's works and life as inseparable. Already in 1906, however, Oskar F. Walzel was arguing against this tendency. His article attempts to free *Die Wahlverwandtschaften* from the isolating perspective of biography and place it instead within a greater historical context (168). Instead of examining Goethe's life at the time of the novel's composition, Walzel examines the historical events and intellectual tendencies that were current at the time. In particular, he traces certain aspects of the novel to the German Romantics and their approach to science, literature, and morality.

Walzel does not entirely free himself from the biographical method of which he is so critical. Although he explicitly wishes to go beyond biographical details in his study of the novel, he does rely upon Goethe's own statements about the novel and the Romantics in his interpretation of it. And although he argues that knowledge about Minna Herzlieb does not add much to our comprehension of the novel, he does still turn to Goethe's relationship with various women (Buff, Stein, Herzlieb) to argue for Goethe's morality and for the morality of the novel (183). In the process, he bends over backwards to give the biographical details from Goethe's life a moral spin. He therefore turns to such details as the fact that Goethe left Wetzlar and had a pure relationship with Stein to demonstrate Goethe's inherent respect for marriage (182–83). He also argues that Goethe's sense of guilt over Minna Herzlieb actually shows his respect for marriage (183).

In his exposition of the novel, Walzel closely follows the earlier arguments of Abeken and Eckermann. The primary question for Walzel still remains the morality of the novel. What is new in his treatment, however, is his attempt to contextualize the novel within the historical framework of Romanticism. In so doing, he attempts to broaden the critical sphere to show that works do not arise in isolation within the author's mind, but in reaction to specific events and works of literature. In order to establish the various influences upon Goethe, Walzel quotes from personal letters, literary works, journals, and scientific treatises. He discusses the lifestyles of the Romantics and compares them to the various characters in the novel, analyzes the connection between Romantic scientific theories and the scientific references in the novel, and attempts to trace the ethical theories of the novel back to Kant's principles. Like Bölsche and Brahm, he sets out to use these historical occurrences to demonstrate Goethe's "modern" style, i.e., his realism (189).

A few years after Walzel's article and much in the same spirit, a young Frenchman, André François-Poncet, published his dissertation, *Les Affinités Électives* (1910). This book was extremely influential in the novel's reception throughout much of the twentieth century (Reiss 218). François-Poncet, like Walzel, rejects the importance that biographers since Lewes had placed upon Minna Herzlieb's role in the composition of the novel (xvii–xviii). Although François-Poncet is critical of Walzel's ultimate conclusions regarding the role of Romantic influences upon the novel, he does credit Walzel as being the first to attempt to understand the novel within its more general "milieu" as opposed to tying it exclusively to Goethe's life (236). And like Walzel, François-Poncet believes that the key to interpreting the novel lies in viewing it within the social and historical context of its day. François-Poncet, however, attempts to broaden the context beyond Goethe's relationship to the German Romantics. He delves into much more detail about Goethe's scientific, landscaping, pedagogical, and aesthetic interests than any previous scholar had done in connection with the novel. And while his carefully researched book offers many new insights, it still shares some of the traces of the earlier biographical approaches. He does not reject, but embraces throughout his discussion, the idea that one ought to know as much about Goethe's personal life and loves at the time that he wrote the novel. Unlike many of his predecessors, however, François-Poncet attempts to show that the novel operates on a variety of levels. Therefore, he does not attempt to show the influence of one particular event or person upon a particular aspect of the novel, but argues that it ought to be read in light of several simultaneous events in Goethe's life. For example, Ottilie owes her existence not simply to Minna Herzlieb, but to a variety of women (29–38); the layout of the manor and park is a conglomeration of several landed estates (109–16); and the pedagogical theories espoused by the School Master and Ottilie have several sources (138–55).

The first chapter of François-Poncet's book extensively explores the "sources" for the novel. He begins by focusing upon the scientific influences, from Bergman's theories to Romantic experiments and philosophy (5–12). He then examines the various possible psychological sources, by which he means, more or less, the possible texts or events that may have inspired aspects of *Die Wahlverwandtschaften*. His search for the sources begins by analyzing other works of literature that Goethe read around the time of the novel's composition (12–14). He then canvasses the personal histories of Goethe's friends and acquaintances (16–24). Most particularly, he recounts the various marriages and divorces (Theresa Forster/Huber, Sophie Mereau/Brentano, Caroline Schlegel/ Schelling, etc.) of the Romantic circle. And despite his criticisms of the biographical method, he does not shy away from including facts from Goethe's life in his speculations regarding the novel (25–38). He surmises, for example, that Goethe's concern over his own bastard son and the political events of the Napoleonic wars directly influenced his own ideas of marriage that he then reflected back into the novel. Although he mentions Herzlieb as one of the inspirations of the novel, one of François-Poncet's goals is to free the scholarship from the exclusivity of the Herzlieb approach. He therefore takes on the strongest evidence of Goethe's passion, the sonnets that had been ostensibly dedicated to her, and demonstrates that many of them were not written for Herzlieb, but to Bettina Brentano (29–38). The result of this chapter is that despite the fact that François-Poncet openly advocates turning away from biographical sources, he has painted a more complete picture of Goethe's life around the time of the novel's composition than had the many biographies. His is superior to the earlier approaches in that he does not attempt to reduce the facts to simple conclusions, but attempts to keep several interpretive possibilities open.

As a whole, François-Poncet argues that the novel is not primarily an aesthetic piece or a literary creation, but rather a philosophical exercise: Goethe attempts through the novel to let us see his own opinions and to inspire deep, philosophical thoughts in the reader (180–81). Therefore, while François-Poncet criticizes such things as the aphorisms in Ottilie's diary on aesthetic grounds (it is unbelievable that she would be capable of writing such pieces), he defends them upon philosophical grounds in that they inspire reflection (173–83). The novel for him is a highly moral one in which Ottilie's actions prove that the spirit is more powerful than the body (194). Her death is not the horrible end of a person's life, but the beginning of a higher and more pure existence (203–4). In judging the novel as tragic, he largely follows the tradition begun by Solger (218–19). And despite François-Poncet's insistence that he has broadened the discussion to include such concepts as fate and a more ancient understanding of tragedy, his conclusion echoes most of his predecessors who have been favorably disposed to the novel. The ultimate "message" of the novel is that human freedom can triumph over nature and fate (230).

A much clearer break with the biographical method occurs in J. Hárnik's article (1912), "Psychoanalytisches aus und über Goethes *Wahlverwandtschaften*." Not since the Hegelians had anyone extensively and overtly turned to an outside theory as a means of analyzing the novel. Hárnik's article, moreover, much more resembles a modern scholarly article in that it directly cites from the theory with which it attempts to analyze the text. This article, which appeared in the first volume of Freud's edited *Imago*, completely ignores Goethe's life in its interpretation of *Die Wahlverwandtschaften*. Instead, Hárnik turns to psychoanalytic theory and psychoanalyzes not Goethe, but the characters within the novel. In fact, Hárnik's main goal is not to interpret the novel, but to prove the strength and validity of psychoanalysis by showing the congruence between Freud's theories and the events in the novel (510–11). In his justification of his approach, he shows himself to be very much a part of the group that privileges Goethe above other authors and thinkers. According to Hárnik, not all literature is worthy or appropriate for the "science" of psychoanalysis. He justifies turning to Goethe's novel on the grounds that Goethe is much more than a literary figure. We should follow Ernst Haeckel's lead and consider Goethe as Haeckel does, namely as the greatest predecessor of the "modern heroes" of the natural sciences (510). Are we to consider the poet a great thinker only in biology and not in matters of psychology (511)? In other words, Hárnik argues that Goethe prefigured not only the science of evolution, but also the science of psychoanalysis. That aspects of Goethe's novel correspond with Freudian theory is proof in Hárnik's mind both that Goethe anticipated psychoanalysis and that psychoanalysis is right.

Hárnik focuses upon two main events in the novel: Ottilie and Eduard's growing passion and the death of the child. In neither case does he offer a great deal of analysis, but mainly juxtaposes Freudian quotations against lengthy quotations from the novel. In the first instance, Hárnik cites from Freud's *Traumdeutung* (Interpretation of Dreams, 1900) and *Drei Abhandlungen zur Sexualtheorie* (Three Essays on the Theory of Sexuality, 1905) and briefly summarizes Freud's "classic" representation of the development of sexual desires. Accordingly, adolescence generally marks the transition from an incestuous desire for one's parent of the opposite sex to the overcoming of these desires and indeed to the liberation from parental authority (507). Further, as it is not uncommon for the initial desire to exert an influence, a young man will very often seek an image reminiscent of his mother, while a young woman that of her father. Hárnik argues that Ottilie's infantile desire for a father figure explains many of her and Eduard's actions. Their love truly develops only after Ottilie has removed the pictorial image of her father — of her childhood ideal — from her neck. Hárnik places special emphasis on the fact that she removes the locket at Eduard's request. Although Eduard claims to have a concern for her safety (the locket with her father's picture may catch on something during their walks and cause injury to Ottilie), Hárnik views Eduard's request as a rationalization of unconscious wish-impulses (509). What Eduard really wants is to divide Ottilie from her idealized image of her father. The fact that Ottilie gives up the image (and later even the chain from which it hung) indicates that Eduard has replaced her father as the ideal (510).

Hárnik goes into even more detail to demonstrate how Ottilie's actions around the time of the baby's death support Freudian theories. Citing Freud's opinion that many accidents are intentional acts, Hárnik dismisses the idea that the child's death was purely an accident. He offers instead two simultaneous scenarios that explain Ottilie's actions. First, the "accident" of drowning the child is an expression of Ottilie's secret desires. The child is the last obstacle between her and Eduard, and by killing the child, Ottilie clears the path for the fulfillment of her desires (514). All the other characters to a greater and lesser extent are also relieved by its death. Because Ottilie is the one who actually has acted to accomplish this wish, she knows on some level that she has murdered the child and is overcome by guilt (516). Second, Hárnik also links Ottilie's actions to a completely different desire: that of becoming a mother herself and bearing Eduard's child. He sees evidence for this in the symbolic association of pulling the child out of the water — an association Hárnik closely links to the process of birth in dream interpretation (516–17). He cites as further evidence to support this theory the scene in which Ottilie mimics breastfeeding in her attempts to revive the child by placing it against her naked breast and her motherly care for the child during the earlier part of the novel (517).

Finally, Hárnik, following the lead of earlier interpreters, comments on the role of fate in the novel. In a manner similar to Rosenkranz's assertion (464, 466) that the characters create their own fates, Hárnik seeks a scientific explanation for this interpretation. For him, words such as "Schicksal" [fate] or "Verhängnis" [destiny] are without doubt the terms for the powers within the human soul (515). To support this claim, he cites Charlotte's speech to the Captain after her baby has died: "Doch was sag ich! Eigentlich will das Schicksal meinen eigenen Wunsch, meinen eigenen Vorsatz, gegen die ich unbedachtsam gehandelt, wieder in den Weg bringen. Habe ich nicht selbst schon Ottilien und Eduarden als das schicklichste Paar zusammengedacht" [FA 1, 8:497–98; But what am I saying! In fact, fate is trying to carry out my own wishes and intentions, which I have counteracted in my thoughtlessness. Didn't I always imagine Ottilie and Eduard as a most charming match?: 11:24)]. Hárnik thus seeks to demystify fate and place it within the context of strong human desires.

Gundolf and the "Inner" Biography

Another example of the backlash against approaches that focused upon biographical facts came from Friedrich Gundolf (1880–1931), one of the most important and influential Goethe scholars of this period. Gundolf was a disciple of Stefan George, and his controversial book, *Goethe* (1916), marks a decided break with earlier treatments of Goethe's life. Gundolf too links Goethe's life and works, but does so from a completely different perspective and with a radically different emphasis. For Gundolf, Goethe's life is most evident not in the events and encounters that formed it, but in the works that he created. He wishes to portray not Goethe's life per se but his "Gestalt" — a Gestalt that is best witnessed through his creative productions (1): "Der Künstler existiert nur insofern er sich im Kunstwerk ausdrückt. . . . [Kunst] ist eine primäre Form des Lebens" (2) [The artist exists only insofar that he expresses himself in the artwork. . . . art is a primary form of life]. There is therefore no need to explain Goethe's works from the context of biographical details or to search behind his works in order to understand his life, "denn [seine Werke] selbst sind sein Leben" (4) [for his works are his life]. Where previous biographers attempted to understand Goethe's works by studying his life, Gundolf claims to understand his life by studying his works. The degree to which Gundolf linked Goethe's life and works can be evidenced in his discussion of Goethe's classicism. While earlier critics spoke of particular works as "classical," Gundolf argues that Goethe's life, too, was "classical." "Classic," however, is no longer understood in terms of the style, characterization, or treatment of ancient conceptions of fate, but in Gundolf's terms as a superhuman melding of art and life (4, 12–14).

In seeking to write the "inner" biography of Goethe, Gundolf is still very much a part of the nationalistic tradition that sought to elevate Goethe's standing and make him into a superhuman German figure. According to Gundolf, Goethe is a kind of personification of the German "Geist." Indeed, one could say that Gundolf consciously attempts to privilege Goethe even more than earlier critics. He claims that Goethe is too great a figure to be understood by the masses. Rather, he can be understood only by the intellectual elite who are also the only ones capable of understanding the greatness of his works. Gundolf's extreme elitism is evident in his assessment of other biographies. He is harshly critical of those who attempt to explain Goethe's works by examining the daily details of his life. In his mind, such scholars are philistines who attempt to drag down the great artist, whom they cannot understand, to their own level (2). In essence, he argues that since they are incapable of understanding Goethe's ideas, they talk about only those things that they understand: the mundane aspects of his life. Gundolf claims in his biography to do what they failed to do: address Goethe's creative, mythic spirit.

Gundolf overtly declares war against the biographers, whom he accuses of psychological relativism (6). He argues that Goethe's works cannot be analyzed like an equation where one particular event in his life can be directly linked to an aspect of his creative production. In particular, he rejects any approach that views Goethe's literary productions as confessional acts — as the outgrowth of psychological impulses of guilt (6). He argues that this approach is a much too simplistic one that does not address Goethe's creative essence, but instead uses Goethe as a guinea pig for the latest methodological trends (6–8).

Gundolf differentiates himself from many of the other biographers by emphasizing the intellectual rather than the biographical context of *Die Wahlverwandtschaften*. Throughout his chapter on the novel, he compares it in style and content to *Werther* and the *Wilhelm Meister* novels. Whereas *Werther* is the expression of a former passion and *Wilhelm Meisters Lehrjahre* is a panorama of the classes and kinds of education, *Die Wahlverwandtschaften* speaks of "überpersönlichen Mächten und ihrer Wirkung auf das seelische, sittliche, gesellschaftliche Leben des einzelnen Menschen" (551) [superhuman powers and their effect on the spiritual, moral, social life of the individual human being]. *Werther* is about the human soul and *Wilhelm Meister* is about social institutions. *Die Wahlverwandtschaften* is, in contrast, about natural laws and processes. Because it is about these impersonal powers, this novel, unlike Goethe's earlier ones, does not have a hero from which the plot emanates. For Gundolf, the focus of the novel is not the activities of the characters, but how they function within a world that operates according to natural processes (557). The characters are not psychological beings subject to traditional character analyses, but cosmic beings who themselves become witnesses to the larger cosmic processes around them (559–60).

Despite Gundolf's emphasis upon intellectual and philosophical issues, he nevertheless begins his discussion of *Die Wahlverwandtschaften* where the other biographers began theirs: with Minna Herzlieb. And although he is careful not to equate Ottilie with Herzlieb, he does credit her, as the others do, as the inspirational source of the novel (550, 571). Had Goethe never met Herzlieb, the novel may never have been written (569, 570). For Gundolf, however, the most salient issue is not the love story, but what

Goethe created out of the experience. He is interested in the relationship between Herzlieb and Goethe only to the extent that he can see a direct connection to the novel. Unlike his earlier love affairs, Gundolf claims that Goethe entered into his passion for Herzlieb with the foreknowledge of the necessity of renunciation. His love for her was not the burning passionate love that he had felt for Lili or Lotte, and which resulted in more passionate prose, but rather a fatherly type of affection (550). The resulting novel is therefore more subdued and less passionate than either *Werther* or *Wilhelm Meisters Lehrjahre*.

Gundolf makes several bold breaks with the traditional readings of the novel. Most strikingly, he claims that it is not about marriage nor is marriage its main problem. It is not a social or psychological examination of a particular problem or a study of a particular society. And as Gundolf wishes to elevate Goethe's life into something larger than human, so too does he seek to elevate the novel into a much larger work than the treatment of a societal issue such as marriage. For Gundolf, the novel is a cosmic work in which marriage was the smallest space in which Goethe could display the rule of natural and fateful powers upon human beings (565–66). Marriage, however, is but one means to explore the multifaceted human experience that Goethe explores in the novel (566–67). Gundolf finds that the novel is about mystery, sacrament, nature, and fate and not simply about a societal contract or a cultural institution (567).

In another striking departure, Gundolf claims that the novel's morality has nothing to do with Christianity or even with the Kantian imperative. He also dismisses the claims that the novel is at all immoral. It is not a defense of adultery or a glorification of marriage. Nor is it a moral discussion using psychological sources for support (564). It has nothing to do with these concerns because Gundolf believes that Goethe's conception of law lies outside of such concerns. He claims that the main issue is the conflict between law and desire — though by this Gundolf does not mean, as most of the earlier commentators do, the struggle between social conventions and passion. Goethe, according to Gundolf, is concerned with neither social nor religious laws, but with certain impersonal forces that are natural in that they pervade everyone's lives. And although Gundolf argues that the novel's emphasis upon natural law does not eliminate the possibility of freedom and is not fatalistic, aspects of determinism pervade his discussion. Human beings do not lead completely determined lives because they indeed choose particular paths in their lives. Once a path has been chosen, however, they are then subject to outside forces beyond their control (563). And while Gundolf emphasizes the dynamic qualities of Goethe's conception of the law, it too, in the end, seems largely predetermined. Gundolf argues that laws for Goethe are not mathematically static, nor are they at all related to mechanical causation (553). Rather, laws emerge in Goethe's novel according to an organic model of plant growth, where the seed potentially contains the entire plant and where growth is an unfolding and not the result of mechanical cause and effect. While not subject to mechanical laws, the plant nevertheless largely grows in a predetermined pattern. Gundolf refers the reader to Goethe's poem, "Urworte Orphisch" (Primal Words Orphic, 1817–18), to help characterize the notion of fate in the novel. In the "Dämon" stanza, everyone is born with aspects of their lives that are predetermined and cannot be changed. Gundolf argues that Goethe's artistry lies in the way in which he is able to portray the unfolding of each character's inner laws. Once the characters make a particular choice, their fates develop along the lines of a plant's development from seed to adult (554). These individual laws become the center of the novel, and those commentators who complain of a lack of movement or activity in the novel have missed this important fact (556–57).

Gundolf further argues against the complaint of many scholars that the novel contains too many superfluous details. He praises the economy of the whole and argues that every detail is connected to the novel in some important way (562). In particular, Gundolf praises the repetition and the subsequent intensification of the certain symbols or occurrences. He points to Eduard's relationship to the glass as a good example of this tendency. Eduard initially believes it to bring him luck, but it ultimately comes to symbolize his unlucky fate (561). Gundolf believes that this measured style produces not only Goethe's most pure and perfect prose (574), but also the best prose in the German language (576).

Although Gundolf states that Ottilie is neither the main character nor problem of the novel (569), he nevertheless, like most of his predecessors, portrays Ottilie as the highest character in the novel. The reasons behind his assessment, however, are closely related to his view of the personal law. He views her as an elevated character, not because of the triumph of moral law over natural forces, but because she heroically fulfills her own law by consciously offering herself up as its victim. Gundolf explains this by giving a gender-determined analysis of the heroic role of men and women. Whereas he grants men the opportunity to perform heroic deeds, women may do so only passively. He considers actions to be unnatural for women (572). In those instances when a woman cannot "fulfill" her "fate" as a mother or lover, then she can only fulfill her law as a saint (572). Ottilie is the most heroic of Goethe's heroines because she is the first to offer herself up willingly (573). She does so, moreover, at that point at which she realizes that she can never be a mother (574).

Although Gundolf's work began to challenge many of the positivistic and moralistic interpretations of the novel, a much more radical and original challenge appeared a few years later when Walter Benjamin published his essay on *Die Wahlverwandtschaften*. In the next chapter, I will discuss his criticisms of the biographical school as well as his attempts to found a new critical approach — attempts that were brought most fully to fruit in the last twenty years of the twentieth century.

Notes

[1] For excellent discussions of Goethe's reception generally, see Leppmann and Mandelkow (*Goethe in Deutschland*). Mandelkow discusses some of the exceptions to the above characterization.

[2] The Young Germans were by no means a cohesive group, and while their reception of Goethe varied widely and changed over time, one could generally say that they tended to be critical of Goethe. For a more detailed discussion, see Mandelkow (*Goethe in Deutschland* 77–84; 101–120); Hohendahl (204–6, 222–28); and Beutin (272).

[3] Mandelkow tempers this assessment by pointing out the that Germans had weightier issues to face in the aftermath of the 1848 Revolution than celebrating Goethe's birth (*Goethe in Deutschland* 146).

[4] For a discussion of the Goethe Society, see Leppmann (118–38) and Mandelkow (*Goethe in Deutschland* 224–32).

[5] Mandelkow counts Rosenkranz as the most important Goethe interpreter from the Old-Hegelian school. For Rosenkranz, there was a complete affinity between Hegel's philosophy and Goethe's poetry (Mandelkow *Goethe in Deutschland* 95).

[6] Weiße remains vague as to how he knows what Goethe's intentions for the novel were.

[7] For a discussion of Schmidt and realism, see Hohendahl (255–79).

[8] For a discussion of Schmidt's politics and involvement with the Revolution of 1848, see Hohendahl (255–57). For example, Hohendahl writes that in the "*Grenzboten* in 1850, Julian Schmidt represents the standpoint that the revolution had been not merely political but simultaneously a literary revolution. He distinguishes between the literature of the restoration (which he accuses of emptiness), the emphatic literature of the years of the revolution, and the postrevolutionary literature whose program he would like to propose" (255–56).

[9] In the 1776 version, the play ends in a ménage à trois: an older woman and a younger woman agree to share the man: "Eine Wohnung, Ein Bett, und Ein Grab" [one house, one bed and one grave]. In the 1806 version, the husband and the younger woman kill themselves.

[10] Minna Herzlieb was troubled by many biographers for information about her relationship with Goethe (Stahr 675; F. K. M. 632–33). She also endured — without ever correcting (Stahr 675) — numerous factual errors, including several by Lewes.

[11] For a similar treatment of the novel, see also Thomas, who describes *Die Wahlverwandtschaften* as a "tale of morbid despair ending in voluntary death. . . . It is harmonious in tone and tinged toward the end, with the somber hue of tragic fatality" (297). The structure of the book is likened to a "mountain stream" that "widens out as it reaches the plain, flows along pleasantly for a while, and then gathers itself together for the inevitable plunge over the precipice" (297).

[12] Otto Brahm makes a similar argument. In a short essay, he outlines the Romantic experiments that were at the base of the magnetic experiments in *Die Wahlverwandtschaften*. He does so in part to demonstrate the realistic and hence modern aspects of the novel (197).

[13] Similarly, Bölsche argues (following Haeckel) that Goethe's scientific ideas preceded Darwinian ones (171). Bölsche was a disciple of Haeckel's and supervised the publication of Goethe's scientific work in Karl Heinemann's edited edition of Goethe's works (Mandelkow, *Goethe im Urteil* 3:516).

Works Cited

Batts, Michael S. *A History of Histories of German Literature, 1835–1914.* Montreal: McGill-Queen's UP, 1993.

Baumgartner, Alexander. *Göthe: Sein Leben und seine Werke.* 3 vols. Freiburg: Herder'sche Verlagshandlung, 1882. Quoted here from the second, expanded 1885–86 edition.

Benjamin, Walter. "Goethes *Wahlverwandtschaften.*" *Neue deutsche Beiträge* (1924/25). Quoted here from *Walter Benjamin: Gesammelte Schriften* I, i. Ed. Rolf Tiedemann and Hermann Schweppenhäuser. Frankfurt: Suhrkamp. English from *Walter Benjamin: Selected Writings (1913–1926).* Vol. 1. Ed. Marcus Bullock and Michael W. Jennings. Essay trans. Stanley Corngold. Cambridge: Belknap Press, 1996.

Beutin, Wolfgang et al. *A History of German Literature: From the Beginnings to the Present Day.* Trans. Clare Krojzl. New York: Routledge, 1993.

Bielschowsky, Albert. *Goethe: Sein Leben und seine Werke.* 2 vols. Quoted here from the 23rd ed., 1911. Munich: C. H. Beck. English from the 1911 translation *The Life of Goethe.* Trans. William Cooper. New York: G. P. Putnam's Sons.

Bölsche, Wilhelm. "Goethes *Wahlverwandtschaften* im Lichte moderner Naturwissenschaft." *Die Gesellschaft* 5 (1889): 1330–40. Quoted here from Mandelkow, *Goethe im Urteil* 3:170–78.

Brahm, Otto. "Eine Episode in Goethes *Wahlverwandtschaften.*" *Zeitschrift für deutsches Altertum und deutsche Literatur* 26 (1882): 194–97.

Brandes, Georg. *Wolfgang Goethe.* 2 vols. Copenhagen: Gyldental, 1915. Quoted here from the 1925 English edition. Trans. Allen W. Porterfield. New York: Frank-Maurice.

Braun, Julius W. *Goethe im Urtheile seiner Zeitgenossen: Zeitungskritiken, Berichte, Notizen, Goethe und seine Werke betreffend, aus den Jahren 1772–1812.* 3 vols. Berlin: Friedrich Luckhardt, 1885.

Calvert, George H. *Goethe: His Life and Works.* Boston: Lee and Shepard, 1886.

Carlyle, Thomas. "Death of Goethe" and "Goethe's Works." Cited here from Carlyle's *Critical and Miscellaneous Essays* (1872). 7 vols. London: Chapman and Hall.

Eichendorff, Joseph von. *Der deutsche Roman des 18. Jahrhunderts in seinem Verhältnis zum Christentum.* Leipzig: Brockhaus, 1851. Quoted from *Werke.* Vol. 6:468–71. Frankfurt: Deutscher Klassiker Verlag, 1993.

Engel, Eduard. *Goethe: Der Mann und das Werk.* 2 vols. Berlin: Concordia Deutsche Verlagsanstalt, 1909. Quoted here from the 11th ed., 1921. Hamburg: Westermann.

François-Poncet, André. *Les Affinités Électives.* Paris: F. Alcan, 1910. Quoted here from the 1951 German translation: *Goethes Wahlverwandtschaften: Versuch eines kritischen Kommentars.* Mainz: Florian Kupferberg Verlag.

Gervinus, G[eorg] G[ottfried]. *Geschichte der deutschen Dichtung V: Neuere Geschichte der poetischen National-Literatur der Deutschen. Zweiter Theil: Von Göthes Jugend bis zur Zeit der Befreiungskriege.* Leipzig: Engelmann, 1842.

Grillparzer, Franz. Diary entry (1841) #3538. Cited here from *Sämtliche Werke.* Vol. 10. Vienna: Kunstverlag Anton Schroll & Co., 1909. 319–20.

Grimm, Herman. *Goethe Vorlesungen.* Berlin: Hertz, 1877. Translation from the 1971 reprint of the 1880 English translation: *The Life and Times of Goethe.* Trans. Sarah Holland Adams. Freeport, NY: Books for Libraries Press.

Gundolf, Friedrich. *Goethe.* Berlin: Bondi, 1916. Quoted here from the 4th ed., 1918.

Haeckel, Ernst. *Natürliche Schöpfungsgeschichte.* Berlin: Georg Reimer, 1868.

Hárnik, J. "Psychoanalytisches aus und über Goethes *Wahlverwandtschaften.*" *Imago Zeitschrift für Anwendung der Psychoanalyse auf die Geisteswissenschaften* 1 (1912): 507–18.

Hebbel, Friedrich. "Vorwort" zur *Maria Magdalene* (1844). Hamburg. Quoted here from *Friedrich Hebbel: Werke.* Vol. 1. Munich: Carl Hanser Verlag, 1963. 307–38. Also partially reprinted in Mandelkow, *Goethe im Urteil* 2:270–72. Translation by T. M. Campbell in *Hebbel-Ibsen and the Analytic Exposition.* Heidelberg: Winter, 1922.

Heinemann, Karl. *Goethe.* Vol. 2. Leipzig: Seemann, 1895.

Hettner, Hermann. *Die romantische Schule in ihrem inneren Zusammenhange mit Goethe und Schiller.* Braunschweig: Bieweg, 1850. Quoted here from *Schriften zur Literatur.* Berlin: Aufbau Verlag, 1959.

Hohendahl, Peter Uwe. "Literary Criticism in the Epoch of Liberalism, 1820–1870." *A History of German Literary Criticism, 1730–1980*. Ed. Peter Uwe Hohendahl. Lincoln: U of Nebraska P, 1988.

Holub, Robert C. "Young Germany." *A Concise History of German Literature to 1900*. Ed. Kim Vivian. Columbia, SC: Camden House, 1992. 224–39.

Leppmann, Wolfgang. *The German Image of Goethe*. Oxford: Clarendon Press, 1961.

Lewes, George Henry. *The Life of Goethe*. Quoted from the 2nd ed. London: Smith, Elder and Co, 1864.

Lösch. "Ueber Göthe's Ottilie." *Album des literarischen Vereins in Nürnberg für 1852*. 168–84.

Luther, Arthur. "*Die Wahlverwandtschaften*." *Sechs Vorträge*. Leipzig: Oskar Hellmann, 1905.

M., F. K. [Friedrich Karl Meyer]. "Göthe, die *Wahlverwandtschaften* und Wilhelmine Herzlieb." *Preußische Jahrbücher* 25 (1869): 623–36.

Mandelkow, Karl Robert. *Goethe in Deutschland I: Rezeptionsgeschichte eines Klassikers (1733–1918)*. Munich: C. H. Beck, 1980.

———. *Goethe im Urteil seiner Kritiker: Dokumente zur Wirkungsgeschichte Goethes in Deutschland*. 4 vols. Munich: C. H. Beck, 1975–1984.

Meyer, Richard M. *Goethe*. Vol. 2. Berlin: Hofmann & Co, 1895.

Nietzsche, Friedrich. *Zur Genealogie der Moral. Eine Streitschrift*. Cited here from *Studienausgabe*. 4 vols. Frankfurt: Fischer, 1968. English trans. by Francis Golffing, New York: Doubleday, 1956.

Reiss, Hans. *Goethe's Novels*. New York: St. Martin's Press, 1969.

Rosenkranz, Karl. *Göthe und seine Werke*. Königsberg: Bornträger, 1847.

Rötscher, Heinrich Theodor. "Die 'Wahlverwandtschaften' von Goethe in ihrer weltgeschichtlichen Bedeutung, ihrem sittlichen und künstlerischen Werthe nach entwickelt." *Abhandlungen zur Philosophie der Kunst* 2. Abtheilung. Berlin: Duncker und Humblot, 1838.

Scherer, Wilhelm. *Geschichte der deutschen Litteratur*. Berlin: Weidmann, 1883. Translation from the 1890 *A History of German Literature*. Trans. F. C. Conybeare. Ed. F. Max Müller. Vol. 2. New York: Charles Scribner's Sons.

Schmidt, Julian. *Geschichte der Deutschen Literatur seit Lessing's Tod*. Vol. 2. Quoted here from the expanded 4th ed. Leipzig: Friedrich Ludwig Herbig, 1858.

————. *Geschichte der Deutschen Litteratur von Leibniz bis auf unsere Zeit.* Vol. 4: 1797–1814. Berlin: Wilhelm Herz, 1890.

Snider, Denton J. *Goethe's Life-Poem: As Set Forth in His Life and Works.* St. Louis: Sigma Publishing Co, 1915.

Sommerfeld, Martin. "Goethes *Wahlverwandtschaften* im 19. Jahrhundert." Jahrbuch d. fr. dt. Hochstifts. (1926): 203–50.

Stahr, Adolf. "Minna Herzlieb. Goethe's 'Ottilie' in den 'Wahlverwandtschaften.'" *Westermann's Monatshefte. Ein Familienbuch für das gesammte geistige Leben der Gegenwart* 27 (March 1870): 664–76.

Thomas, Calvin. *Goethe.* New York: Holt and Company, 1917.

Vilmar, A[ugust] F[riedrich] C[hristian]. *Vorlesungen über die Geschichte der deutschen National-Literatur.* Marburg: Elwert'schen Universitäts-Buchhandlung, 1845.

Walzel, Oskar F. "Goethes 'Wahlverwandtschaften' im Rahmen ihrer Zeit." *Goethe Jahrbuch* 27 (1906): 166–206.

Weiße, Christian Hermann. "Ueber Göthe's *Wahlverwandtschaften* und ihre neuesten Beurtheilungen." *Blätter für literarische Unterhaltung* (1841). Quoted here from Weiße's *Kleine Schriften zur Aesthetik und ästhetischen Kritik* (1867). Ed. by Rudolf Seydel. Leipzig: Breitkopf und Härtel.

Witkowski, Georg. *Goethe.* Leipzig: Seemann und Gesellschaft für graphische Industrie. Quoted here from 3rd, expanded ed., 1923. Leipzig: Alfred Kröner.

Wolff, Eugen. *Goethes Leben und Werke mit besonderer Rücksicht auf Goethes Bedeutung für die Gegenwart.* Kiel and Leipzig: Lipsius & Tischer, 1895.

3: Walter Benjamin and New Critical Approaches

WALTER BENJAMIN WAS BY FAR the most influential critic of Goethe's *Die Wahlverwandtschaften* in the twentieth century. His essay, "Goethes *Wahlverwandtschaften*," written in 1921 and first published by Hugo von Hofmannsthal in the *Neue Deutsche Beiträge* (1924/25), has influenced several generations of scholars. Although it has perhaps most exerted its influence over the past twenty-five years during the renaissance of interest in Benjamin, the influence of his essay certainly goes back at least fifty years, if not to the initial date of its publication. Early citations are found in Reitz, Lockemann, Stahl, Wiese, and Brinkmann, among others. Republished in 1955, it is at least mentioned by most articles and books on *Die Wahlverwandtschaften* during the 1960s and 1970s. Beginning with the early 1980s, however, several commentators began turning to Benjamin's essay not simply to discuss particular details, but also to engage directly with his theoretical approach. The most prominent book of this type was Bolz's 1981 edited volume on *Die Wahlverwandtschaften*. Ryan notes in her review of the volume that Benjamin's essay "becomes itself a text for analysis, almost a substitute for the novel itself, in a number of the essays, thus giving rise to a virtually unquestioning canonization of Benjamin" (251).

Benjamin's essay led to the radical reassessment of several canonical readings of the novel. He challenged the centrality of the theme of marriage, the morality of Ottilie's sacrifice, the viability of studying Goethe's authorial intentions, and the critical legitimacy of reading any aspect of Goethe's life into the work, or vice versa. He further gave new prominence to the novella as the key to understanding the whole novel. Most importantly, however, he established a completely new view of the tone. He rejected reading it as a classical or tragic work, but turned instead to the role of the mythic. Benjamin therefore does not treat the novel as a didactic and moral piece of literature, but emphasizes the novel's darker side. Nowhere in the novel, he claims, does the landscape appear in sunlight (132).[1] His brooding interpretation of the novel is even reflected in his characterization of Goethe. For Benjamin, as for many of Goethe's commentators, Goethe is an Olympian, but he means something completely different than the standard expression of apotheosis. For Benjamin "Olympian" means "die dunkle, in sich selbst versunkene, mythische Natur, die in sprachloser Starre dem Goetheschen Künstlertum innewohnt" [147; the dark, deeply self-absorbed, mythic nature that, in speechless rigidity, indwells Goethean artistry: 314].

Benjamin's essay operates on several levels. On one level, it is a critical (indeed at times a savage) review of the previous scholarship. Indeed, he mentions almost every important critic who had ever written on the novel, though saving his worst barbs for Gundolf. On another level, Benjamin offers a modern and to a large degree alternative interpretation of the novel that revisits many of the standard interpretations. And finally, on yet another level, the essay serves as a manifesto of a new method of criticism. On the one hand, this criticism treats an aesthetic object as having an independent existence apart from the author and his life story. On the other hand, it relativizes the object, seeing it as subject to constant reinterpretation by different critics of different ages. In more general terms, Benjamin's method of criticism rejects the largely descriptive commentaries that had characterized the criticism of his day and tries instead to establish a more philosophical approach.

Benjamin's *Wahlverwandtschaften* essay was his first major work since his dissertation on the German Romantics, and many scholars have noted the influence of Romantic literary theory upon it. First, he was following Schlegel in both treating an individual novel by Goethe and in attempting to make the criticism into a work of art itself (McCole 117–18, Wolin 53, Rosen 133, Jennings 133–34, Witte 39). His essay was therefore an attempt to combine criticism, philosophy of criticism, and art. Second, "his methodological guide" was the "'idea of illuminating a work entirely from within'" (McCole 117). He therefore closely reads and analyzes the text and does not turn to either historical or biographical details in his interpretation of it. Indeed, in those instances in which he quotes Goethe on *Die Wahlverwandtschaften*, he generally does so to demonstrate Goethe's unawareness or unconsciousness of key aspects of the novel. For Benjamin, as for the earlier Romantic critics, a work of art stood on its own and could be interpreted without recourse to outside sources.

Benjamin's essay is in large part a direct attack on Gundolf's methodology in his treatment of both Goethe's life and *Die Wahl-verwandtschaften*. In a fragment written about 1917, Benjamin gives a good sense of the criticism that will emerge in his *Wahlver-wandtschaften* essay a few years later. He recognizes that Gundolf is attempting to go beyond a positivistic methodology and found a new critical approach, but he views Gundolf as having utterly failed in his project:

> aber wie kalt ist Gundolf wo es gilt Goethes Werk und Dasein symbolisch für bestimmtes, und doch wohl für zukünftiges Leben und *Leiden* zu sehen. Da begnügt er sich ein Fädchen zwischen Goethe und irgendwelcher moderner Literatur zu spinnen weil ihm der Sinn des Goethischen für die bestimmtesten und tiefsten Aufgaben des gegenwärtigen Lebens verschlossen ist. Kein Wunder: diesen Aufgaben hat er selbst sich verschlossen. (Und in dieser Hinsicht, kann man sagen, fühlt noch der letzte Kanzlist der Literaturgeschichtsschreibung richtiger, wenn er sein kleines Urteil über Wert und Unwert Vergänglichkeit und Unsterblichkeit der Dichter und Werke registriert. Wiewohl Gundolfs Streben offenbar aus dem Gegensatz zu der Armseligkeit solchen Verfahrens entstanden ist, hat seine Schwäche ihm nicht erlaubt es in Wirklichkeit durch die Tat zu zernichten.) (827–28)

> [But how cold Gundolf is when confronted by the need to interpret Goethe's life and works as symbols of specific yet also future life and *suffering*. When that happens he falls back on the device of spinning a thread between Goethe and one or another aspect of modern literature, because the meaning of Goethe's life for the most specific and profound tasks of modern life is a closed book to him. It is no wonder: these are tasks to which he has closed his own mind. (In this respect we may say that the most insignificant scrivener of literary history exhibits a superior sensibility when he registers his own little judgments about the value or lack of value, or immortality and its opposite, or poets and their works. Even though Gundolf's own writings arose from his reaction against the spiritual poverty of such a procedure, his own weaknesses have prevented him from destroying it through his own actions.) (99)]

In this fragment, Benjamin describes Gundolf's project as "die Verfälschung des Lebens des historischen Menschen Goethe zu dem eines mythischen Heros" [827; the falsification of a historical individual, namely Goethe, by transforming him into a mythical hero: 98]. In creating this image, Benjamin argues that Gundolf does much more damage than a traditional biographer. Gundolf offers the reader only an "optical illusion" that creates a demigod of Gundolf's own creation:

> In der Tat weiß Gundolf schließlich nichts bündiges über Goethe zu sagen, einzelne Einsichten verflüchtigen sich zu Redensarten wo sie auf das Ganze bezogen werden sollen und überall haben sich statt der einfachsten Begriffe die horribelsten Worte eingestellt. Das ganze ist eine Blasphemie auf den Begriff der Idee, der er keinen Gegenstand gibt und auf den Gegenstand, den er zum Popanz macht weil er ihn von der Idee aus unmittelbar darzustellen sucht. (In diesem Nichts findet er den Raum für seine sämtlichen Velleitäten, seinen willkürlichen und leeren Sprachwust.) (827)

> [In reality, Gundolf has nothing convincing to say about Goethe; individual insights disintegrate into empty phrases when he tries to expand them into larger judgments, and at every point simple concepts have been replaced by the most rebarbative expressions. The whole thing is a blasphemous travesty of the idea, to which he gives no object, and of the object, whom he turns into a puppet because he attempts to portray him directly in terms of his idea. (In this void he finds space for all his whims and fancies, his arbitrary and inane linguistic hodge-podge). (98)]

I have quoted from this fragment in detail because it sheds light upon Benjamin's project within his *Wahlverwandtschaften* essay. In this 1917 fragment, Benjamin already outlines his main objections to Gundolf's approach. It is hollow because it is based upon an empty notion of criticism that Gundolf himself as created. Because Gundolf's approach is unfounded, his results are highly questionable. In particular, Benjamin finds fault with Gundolf's efforts to elevate Goethe into a kind of god. As a whole, the fragment points to two aspects of criticism: the first is Gundolf's methodology; the second is his created image of Goethe. Benjamin takes up both points throughout his essay on *Die Wahlverwandtschaften*.

The very first lines of Benjamin's *Wahlverwandtschaften* essay announce the goal of the whole project, a project which initially seems to share the same goal as Gundolf's. Benjamin, like Gundolf, desires to go beyond the positivistic study of Goethe and his works that had characterized the end of the nineteenth century and the beginning of the twentieth. Like Gundolf, he also wishes to go beyond the philological school and discover the intellectual core of the text. However, it becomes almost immediately clear that Benjamin's project is quite different than Gundolf's. Benjamin hopes to succeed where Gundolf has failed: in establishing a new critical approach that is philosophical in nature, and which attempts to reach the goal of Romantic criticism, namely creating a work of art.

The entire essay is divided into three parts: the first part explains Benjamin's methodology and then discusses the mythic elements within the novel; the second takes to task Goethe's biographers, especially Gundolf, and then examines the role of the novella within the novel; and the third explores the meaning of semblance and beauty as they are portrayed within the novel and then analyzes the themes of hope and reconciliation. The three parts, moreover, are constructed according to the dialectical model of thesis, antithesis, and synthesis. Part I presents the thesis of the mythic within the novel and examines the negative power of guilt. This part is characterized by images of darkness, death, and blindness. Part II examines the antithesis of guilt: redemption. It further examines this antithesis within a structural argument about the novella as the antithesis of the main novel. This section is characterized by its discussion of life and light. Part III acts as a synthesis in that it investigates the concept of hope at the conclusion of the main novel. Unlike a Hegelian dialectic, however, Benjamin's does not end with a true synthesis or reconciliation of opposites. The last section concludes with only the appearance of a reconciliation. Thus, whereas Part II examines the theme of redemption for the characters in the novella, Part III postulates the semblance of redemption for the characters in the novel — a semblance which is created by hope.

Writing about Benjamin's essay poses numerous difficulties. First, it is a difficult text that is considered to be his most esoteric (Smith 105). Rosen notes that its esotericism is characteristic of the age (152–53) — an age that produced Joyce's *Ulysses* (1922), Eliot's

The Waste Land (1922), Rilke's *Die Sonette an Orpheus* (Sonnets to Orpheus, 1923), and Yeats's *A Vision* (1926). Second, and most importantly, Benjamin's very methodology protests against explicit arguments. His essay is intentionally esoteric due to his theory of beauty as it is developed in Part III. Benjamin argues that true beauty within any work of art has something expressionless about it. It is therefore impossible for the critic to write directly and explicitly about it. Any means of criticism that attempts to get to the core of the work's beauty, he will argue in Part III, only succeeds in destroying what is beautiful about the work in the process. The job of the critic, therefore, is not to uncover the core or the "secret" of the work, but to enable the reader to sense the mystery of the inexpressible within it. The critic, according to Benjamin, also has the task of demonstrating the reasons why other modes of criticism, especially those that attempt to get to a canonical core or idea of a text, do not work. When it comes to analyzing Benjamin's discussion of the novel, it is much easier to discuss the latter function of the critic than the former. Benjamin is much more explicit in his criticisms of earlier critics than he is in articulating his own project. It is, after all, a difficult task to talk about the inexpressible within a critical work. Third, I recognize that as Benjamin considers his own essay a work of art, it may be indeed a violation of his method to try to give an explication of the essay. Yet, as the purpose of this book is to examine not Benjamin himself, but his interpretation of the novel and the influences that his interpretation has had, it is important to try to draw an admittedly rough image of the whole, as it is the various aspects of this rough image that have been discussed throughout the years.

Thesis

The first part of Benjamin's essay draws a distinct line between commentary and critique: commentary writes about what is most evident within a text, its material content, while critique attempts to go below the surface to discuss the truth content. Benjamin immediately begins his essay by outlining his goal — that of writing a critique as opposed to a commentary: "Die Kritik sucht den Wahrheitsgehalt eines Kunstwerks, der Kommentar seinen Sachgehalt" [125; Critique seeks the truth content of a work of art; commentary, its material content: 297]. Benjamin is somewhat cryptic as to the exact meaning of and the differences between the truth and material contents. He begins the explanation of the two contents by outlining their relationship to each other, which is complex and changes over time. When a work of literature is written, the material content and the truth content are closely linked together, only to drift apart over time, "weil der letzte [Wahrheits-gehalt] immer gleich verborgen sich hält, wenn der erste [Sachge-halt] hervordringt" [125; because the truth content always remains to the same extent hidden as the material content comes to the fore: 297]. The material content is associated with the text at the time of its composition. It is the meaning endowed by the author, seen by his or her contemporaries, and influenced by the historical time period. The truth content of the work, however, is one independent of the historical and authorial aspects of its composition. This meaning can be discovered solely within the text and without recourse to any background meaning. The work therefore has a dual existence: both within time and out of time. Rosen similarly argues that the work has a double transcendence:

> on the one hand the work gradually reveals a meaning accessible without a knowledge of the time in which it arose, and on the other it preserves for posterity some aspect of that time. . . . Commentary and criticism are Benjamin's names for the two ways of approaching this double nature of literature. Commentary deals with the sense of the past life evoked by the work; criticism with the way the work detaches itself from that life. Commentary is philological in its method: criticism is philosophical. They are interdependent; without commentary, criticism is self-indulgent reverie; without criticism, commentary is frivolous information. (137)[2]

Rosen further argues that the esoteric quality of Benjamin's writing stems from the fact that he tries "to give full weight to both sides of the dual nature of literature" (154). He therefore tries not to do away with the analysis of material contents, but to incorporate the material into his more philosophical treatment of the whole.

In one of the more famous passages of the essay, Benjamin compares the commentator (or one who investigates the material content) to a chemist, the critic (or one who investigates the truth content) to an alchemist:

Will man, um eines Gleichnisses willen, das wachsende Werk als den flammenden Scheiterhaufen ansehn, so steht davor der Kommentator wie der Chemiker, der Kritiker gleich dem Alchimisten. Wo jenem Holz und Asche allein die Gegenstände seiner Analyse bleiben, bewahrt für diesen nur die Flamme selbst ein Rätsel: das des Lebendigen. So fragt der Kritiker nach der Wahrheit, deren lebendige Flamme fortbrennt über den schweren Scheitern des Gewesenen und der leichten Asche des Erlebten. (126)

[If, to use a simile, one views the growing work as a burning funeral pyre, then the commentator stands before it like a chemist, the critic like an alchemist. Whereas, for the former, wood and ash remain the sole objects of his analysis, for the latter only the flame itself preserves an enigma: that of what is alive. Thus, the critic inquires into the truth, whose living flame continues to burn over the heavy logs of what is past and the light ashes of what has been experienced. (298)]

A commentator therefore looks at that which is unchangeable within a text: the historical background, the artist's technique, its philological content. He is therefore like the hard scientist, a chemist, who studies the demonstrable aspects of the text's composition. A critic, in contrast, has the task of constantly reexamining the text. If it is still "alive," or still philosophically meaningful to the reader years after the author wrote it, then it is up to the critic to discover why — what aspect of the work reflects a truth that is relevant. The truth content therefore is the philosophical meaning behind the surface text that the critic tries to discover in his/her analysis. By comparing the critic to an alchemist, Benjamin emphasizes that the results of the study are not openly verifiable, as are the commentator's, but contain a mystical strain.

Benjamin's approach places a new emphasis upon the critic, while simultaneously downplaying the role of the author and his/her contemporary commentators. He argues that the critic, who writes about a text years after its composition, is in a much better position to uncover the truth content than either the author or his/her contemporaries. Because of the close intertwining of the truth and material contents at the time of the work's composition, contemporaries may sense only the existence but not the meaning of the truth. The truth that they are able to discover is but a "bewegende Wahrheit" [moving truth], while the critic, who analyzes the work once the truth and material contents have separated, may study the "ruhende Wahrheit" [resting truth].

Benjamin's critique is a radical departure from the criticism of the time. As suggested in chapters 1 and 2, the first hundred years of the novel's interpretation is characterized by three main trends: accepting Goethe's own words (or those of his approved critics), reading the novel in light of Goethe's life, and the more recent one of reading the novel as the product of an historical era. Benjamin soundly rejects these approaches. He rejects the latter two approaches because they do not speak to the truth content (or for that matter to the material content either) and the first because the author himself may not be aware of the real content, or he may be indeed intentionally hiding that content from the reader. Therefore, rather than helping the critic interpret the novel, Goethe's words may in fact hinder him or her. In addition, that Goethe promoted authorized interpretations only served to stifle further analysis of the novel. As his reputation grew in the nineteenth and early twentieth centuries, critics became less likely to follow their instincts and depart from the accepted, positive interpretations. Benjamin also points out that Goethe's purpose in commenting upon the novel was not so much to aid interpretation, but to defend his work from critical attacks. Most importantly, Benjamin notes that Goethe intentionally tried to prevent his readers from discovering the novel's real content — a content of which Goethe himself was not fully conscious. In other words, Benjamin argues that it is largely useless to try to determine Goethe's authorial intent, because the true content of the novel may have nothing to do with it:

> Das Verständnis der *Wahlverwandtschaften* aus des Dichters eigenen Worten darüber erschließen zu wollen, ist vergebene Mühe. Gerade sie sind ja dazu bestimmt, der Kritik den Zugang zu verlegen. Dafür aber ist der letzte Grund nicht die Neigung Torheit abzuwehren. Vielmehr liegt er eben in dem Streben, alles jenes unvermerkt zu lassen, was des Dichters eigene Erklärung verleugnet. (145)

> [To wish to gain an understanding of *Elective Affinities* from the author's own words on the subject is wasted effort. For it is precisely their aim to forbid access to critique. The ultimate reason

for this is not the inclination to ward off foolishness but the effort
to keep unperceived everything that denies the author's own explanation. (313)]

Benjamin goes on to say that neither Goethe nor anyone of his
time period could really know or understand the significance of the
mythic, which for Benjamin, as discussed below, formed the core
of his investigation in the first, or "thesis" part of his essay. Benjamin does not mean to say that Goethe is totally blind to the mythic
forces that he created within his novel. The fact that Goethe destroyed all of his drafts of the novel indicates that he was aware of
some of its mythic contents:

> Deutlicher als alles spricht aber die Vernichtung der Entwürfe.
> Denn es möchte schwerlich Zufall sein, daß von diesen nicht
> einmal ein Bruchstück aufbehalten blieb. Vielmehr hat der Dich-
> ter offenbar ganz vorsätzlich alles dasjenige zerstört, was die
> durchaus konstruktive Technik des Werkes gezeigt hätte. — Ist
> das Dasein der Sachgehalte dergestalt versteckt, so verbirgt ihr
> Wesen sich selbst. Alle mythische Bedeutung sucht Geheimnis.
> (146)

> [The destruction of the drafts, however, speaks more clearly than
> anything else. For it could hardly be a coincidence that not even
> a fragment of these was preserved. Rather, the author had evi-
> dently quite deliberately destroyed everything that would have
> revealed the purely constructive technique of the work. — If the
> existence of the material contents is in this way concealed, then
> the essence of those contents conceals itself. All mythic meaning
> strives for secrecy. (313–14)]

Benjamin argues that Goethe's consciousness of the mythic content was primarily on the level of its material and not its truth
content. On that level, he sought to destroy all evidence of the
technique behind the structure of the novel as the very structure
might give away some of the "secrets" of the mythic, which according to Benjamin always seeks to remain hidden. In part, Benjamin argues that Goethe hides the material content precisely
because he himself does not fully grasp the truth content: "So
konnte Goethe sich durch die Technik der Betonung der mythischen Mächte in seinem Werke versichern. Welche letzte Bedeutung sie haben, mußte ihm wie dem Zeitgeist entgehen" [146;
Thus, through technique, Goethe could assure himself of stressing

the mythic powers in his work. Their ultimate existence had to escape him, as it did the *Zeitgeist:* 313].

After setting the stage for his own critique, Benjamin turns to the novel itself. He begins by contextualizing Goethe's treatment of marriage within Enlightenment thought. He juxtaposes Kant's and Mozart's views on marriage as the two most extreme views of the age, and then poses the question whether Goethe's novel is closer to Kant's extremely cold and rational definition of marriage in the *Die Metaphysik der Sitten* (The Metaphysics of Morals, 1797)[3] or to Mozart's exploration of conjugal love in *Die Zauberflöte* (The Magic Flute, 1791). The most famous, and most quoted, argument of Benjamin's essay arises from this discussion. In contrast to almost every commentary (with the notable exception of Gundolf's), Benjamin argues that marriage is not the main theme of the novel:

> Der Gegenstand der Wahlverwandtschaften ist nicht die Ehe. Nirgends wären ihre sittlichen Gewalten darin zu suchen. Von Anfang an sind sie im Verschwinden, wie der Strand unter Wassern zur Flutzeit. Kein sittliches Problem ist hier die Ehe und auch kein soziales. Sie ist keine bürgerliche Lebensform. In ihrer Auflösung wird alles Humane zur Erscheinung und das Mythische verbleibt allein als Wesen. (131)

> [The subject of *Elective Affinities* is not marriage. Nowhere in this work are its ethical powers to be found. From the outset, they are in the process of disappearing, like the beach under water at floodtide. Marriage here is not an ethical problem, yet neither is it a social problem. It is not a form of bourgeois conduct. In its dissolution, everything human turns into appearance, and the mythic alone remains as essence. (302)]

This passage is so often quoted because it appears to be contradicted by the events in the novel. Benjamin, however, carefully explains what he means. The novel is not about marriage; it is instead about the decay of the institution. The novel therefore does not investigate the social power of marriage, as Hebbel argued in his preface to *Maria Magdalene* (309; cf. Benjamin 189–90), but the powers that become unleashed once this institution is in decline. Thus, for Benjamin, it is clear that Mittler in no way can be the mouthpiece, as many commentators had argued, for Goethe's own views. Where Mittler tries to establish and enforce the foundation of marriage, Goethe wanted to show those forces that arise from its decay (130). In particular, Benjamin highlights the powers of fate that emerge with the disintegration of marriage (159).

That Benjamin focuses on the decay of marriage and the forces behind it is closely connected to his idea of the mythic within the novel. Mythic forces exert their power over the characters precisely because the institution of marriage is disintegrating. Benjamin appears to link the declining institution of marriage to the greater decline of religion during the Enlightenment. He notes that the characters are to a large degree free of tradition and religious feeling. Yet, Benjamin argues that it is precisely religious belief that keeps mythic forces in check. The fact that the enlightened characters are almost free of superstition gives mythic forces greater power over their lives. He cites the characters' treatment of the cemetery as a particularly good example to illustrate this point:

> Keine bündigere Lösung vom Herkommen ist denkbar, als die von den Gräbern der Ahnen vollzogene, die im Sinne nicht nur des Mythos sondern der Religion den Boden unter den Füßen der Lebenden gründen. Wohin führt ihre Freiheit die Handelnden? Weit entfernt, neue Einsichten zu erschließen, macht sie sie blind gegen dasjenige, was Wirkliches dem Gefürchteten einwohnt. Und dies daher, weil sie ihnen ungemäß ist. Nur die strenge Bindung an ein Ritual, die Aberglaube einzig heißen darf, wo sie ihrem Zusammenhange entrissen rudimentär überdauert, kann jenen Menschen Halt gegen die Natur versprechen, in der sie leben. Geladen, wie nur mythische Natur es ist, mit übermenschlichen Kräften, tritt sie drohend ins Spiel. Wessen Macht, wenn nicht ihre, ruft den Geistlichen hinab, welcher auf dem Totenacker seinen Klee baute? (132)

[One cannot imagine a more conclusive liberation from tradition than that liberation from the graves of the ancestors, which, in the sense not only of myth but of religion, provide a foundation for the ground under the feet of the living. Where does their freedom lead those who act thus? Far from opening up new perspectives for them, it blinds them to the reality that inhabits what they fear. And this because these perspectives are unsuited to them. Nothing but strict attachment to ritual — which may be called superstition only when, torn from its context, it survives in rudimentary fashion — can promise these human beings a stay against the nature in which they live. Charged, as only mythic nature is, with superhuman powers, it comes menacingly into play. Whose might, if not that of mythic nature, calls down the minister who cultivates his clover on the land of the dead? (302–3)]

Benjamin implies that religion in the past succeeded in controlling the darker forces of mythic nature. It is as if the decline of Christianity unleashes the powers of pagan nature over the characters. They believe themselves to be free and in control over nature. Yet these very beliefs are the source of their ultimate misfortune. Their belief in the control of nature backfires. For example, their newly rejoined lake leads to several accidents and becomes a backdrop of a tragic scene. Once human beings lose their religious sense, the world around them becomes ominous: seemingly dead objects acquire power. Here Benjamin agrees with Gundolf on the significance of the details within the novel. Benjamin, however, emphasizes how the objects take on a mythic importance. He cites the example of the house as a prime example of this phenomenon: "So rückt hier im Maße wie das Haus vollendet wird das Schicksal nah. Grundsteinlegung, Richtfest und Bewohnung bezeichnen ebensoviele Stufen des Unterganges" [139; Thus, to the extent that the house approaches completion, fate closes in. The laying of the foundation stone, the celebration of the raising of the roof beams, and moving in mark just so many stages of decline: 308]. Benjamin, who was the first to emphasize the numerous symbols of death in the novel, further links these symbols to the theme of moral decay (135–36).

Benjamin's interpretation of these mythic forces is further connected to his scorn for an ethical view of the novel. He characterizes Solger's and Bielschowsky's attempts to establish an ethical teaching from the novel as foolish for several reasons. First, fictional characters cannot be subject to ethical judgment — such a judgment can only be executed on human beings. Rather than judging characters according to ethical standards, Benjamin argues that a critic ought to try to understand morally what happens in the novel as a whole. Second, the characters, due to their loss of religion and close connection to nature, have lost the feeling for what is moral. Therefore, just as the novel is not about marriage but its decline, so too is it not a didactic, moral tale, but about the disintegration of ethics. Benjamin cites Goethe's own words to Riemer (FA 2, 6:516–17; 6/10 December 1809; see chapter 1) about the conflict in the novel and its ultimate moral ending as an instance in which the author himself does not understand the full scope of his work. Benjamin proclaims that no struggle between duty and passion takes place on any level within the novel. If the ethical appears, it appears only to show its defeat (144). Benjamin notes that Goethe's harshest critics, de Valenti and Baumgartner, also noticed the same propensity (142). They too argued that ethical forces were defeated by pagan forces. Benjamin, however, avoids a value judgment on this aspect of the novel. That the characters have lost a sense of ethics does not warrant moral condemnation. He explains:

> Nicht ein Urteil über ihr Handeln ist hier gemeint, sondern eines über ihre Sprache. Denn fühlend doch taub, sehend doch stumm gehen sie ihren Weg. Taub gegen Gott und stumm gegen die Welt. Rechenschaft mißlingt ihnen nicht durch ihr Handeln sondern durch ihr Sein. Sie verstummen. (134)

> [This is meant as a judgment not on their actions but rather on their language. Feeling, but deaf, seeing, but mute, they go their way. Deaf to God and mute before the world. Rendering account eludes them, not because of their actions but because of their being. They fall silent. (304–5)]

Benjamin will return to the importance of silence and its relation to morality in the third part of the essay when he addresses Ottilie. Here, the important fact is that, like Gundolf, he rejects the thesis that the novel is either moral or immoral. He rejects the notion that the novel has a didactic function, that it is in any way a "fabula docet" (145).

While Benjamin agrees with Gundolf that the novel is not a moral tale, he disagrees vehemently on the function of fate. Benjamin takes strong issue with Gundolf's comparison of fate to the development of plants (Gundolf 553–54). The two things are by no means similar in Benjamin's philosophy because fate does not affect the life of innocent plants. Fate can only affect human lives. Benjamin criticizes Gundolf's conception of fate because it does not emphasize the connection between fate and guilt. Benjamin's understanding of this relationship resembles that of natural sin: guilt is passed on from one generation to the next. In this context, he agrees with Bielschowsky's characterization of the baby as the child of deception, who must die because of the guilt of his parents (Bielschowsky 2:276). Benjamin explains:

> Soviel ist an dieser Vermutung Bielschowskys unumstößlich: daß er ganz der Schicksalsordnung entspricht, wenn das Kind, das neugeboren in sie eintritt, nicht die alte Zerrissenheit entsühnt, sondern deren Schuld ererbend vergehen muß. Nicht von sittlicher ist hier die Rede — wie könnte das Kind sie erwerben — sondern von natürlicher, in die Menschen nicht durch Entschluß und Handlung, sondern durch Säumen und Feiern geraten. Wenn sie, nicht des Menschlichen achtend, der Naturmacht verfallen, dann zieht das natürliche Leben, das im Menschen sich die Unschuld nicht länger bewahrt als es an ein höheres sich bindet, dieses hinab. Mit dem Schwinden des übernatürlichen Lebens im Menschen wird sein natürliches Schuld, ohne daß es im Handeln gegen die Sittlichkeit fehle. (138–39)

[This much is incontrovertible in Bielschowsky's conjectures: it corresponds wholly to the order of fate that the child, who enters it as a newborn, does not expiate the ancient rift but, in inheriting its guilt, must pass away. It is a question here not of ethical guilt (how could the child acquire it?) but rather of the natural kind, which befalls human beings not by decision and action but by negligence and celebration. When they turn their attention away from the human and succumb to the power of nature, then natural life, which in man preserves its innocence only so long as natural life binds itself to something higher, drags the human down. With the disappearance of supernatural life in man, his natural life turns into guilt, even without his committing an act contrary to ethics. (308)]

Unlike the Christian notion of sin, however, guilt does not arise from the transgression of an ethical command, but arises when natural forces become the predominant ones in the lives of human beings. Human beings do not even have to break an ethical command to feel guilty because their existence in the nonreligious world in which they live creates guilt. Benjamin's conception of guilt is thus connected to religion only to the extent that this natural guilt arises when religion has ceased to play an important role.

Benjamin's further departs from traditional scholarship in his treatment of Ottilie. Many of the novel's defenders argue, as do Abeken and Solger whom he cites, that the novel is moral because it is fitting for Ottilie to die: she has loved a married man and destroyed a marriage. These critics further argue, however, that the reader is able to forgive her because she is unconscious of her passion until it is too late. Then, when she realizes what she has done, she commits suicide to escape her sinful existence. While Benjamin, too, concludes that Ottilie is a martyr, he sees her as a very different kind of martyr than either Solger or Abeken. He argues that she does not sacrifice herself nor is she a victim of fateful forces. Instead, he views her as a sacrifice in the more pagan sense. She is sacrificed as an innocent victim to expiate the more guilty ones: "Die Sühne nämlich ist im Sinne der mythischen Welt, die der Dichter beschwört, seit jeher der Tod der Unschuldigen. Daher stirbt Ottilie, wundertätige Gebeine hinterlassend, trotz ihres Freitods als Märtyrerin" [140; For atonement, in the sense of the mythic world that the author conjures, has always meant the death of the innocent. That is why, despite her suicide, Ottilie dies as a martyr, leaving behind her miraculous remains: 309]. In contrast to Abeken and Solger, Benjamin emphasizes Ottilie's passive role. She does not act to sacrifice herself, but becomes the passive offering of the forces around her.

Antithesis

The second and shortest part of Benjamin's essay follows the general structure of his first part. He begins by outlining methodological concerns before then addressing specific interpretive aspects of the novel. However, where the theoretical discussion of Part I serves to outline Benjamin's own methodology, the theoretical portion of Part II is a critique of the biographical method in general and Gundolf's biography in particular. In his treatment of the novel, Part II serves as the antithesis to his investigation of Part I. In Part II he examines the themes, characterization and tone of the novella as being the antithesis to the mythic portrayal of the novel that he provided in Part I. Where Part I is characterized by discussion of blindness, darkness, and death, Part II focuses on light, life, and redemption.

Benjamin begins Part II with a scathing attack on using biographical data as a means of interpreting literary works of art. Such techniques are flawed at the onset, he argues, since they operate under the false assumption that a work cannot be understood except within the context of an author's life. They therefore afford privilege to the artist's life over the work of art, whereas the exact opposite ought to be the case. Benjamin implies that those who write biographies do so because they are incapable of grasping the deeper meaning of texts. He is likewise critical of their products, which he sees as an attempt to make works of art accessible to lazy understanding. He therefore characterizes the biographical approach as arising out a deficiency of understanding. Benjamin, like Gundolf, has a hierarchical understanding of criticism: not everyone is capable of understanding the texts. And because the study of texts is often difficult, they remain to many people forever inaccessible. Biographers are categorized within this class. Because they do not understand the art, they substitute the more simplistic study of an author's life for a philosophical exposition.

Benjamin argues that a critic should never follow a biographical approach or even give it credence. If one is to gain an understanding of the work's contents and essence, Benjamin argues, it can only be done by studying the works themselves and not the author's life. Benjamin's critic will keep in mind:

> daß der einzige rationale Zusammenhang zwischen Schaffendem und Werk in dem Zeugnis besteht, das dieses von jenem ablegt. Vom Wesen eines Menschen gibt es nicht allein Wissen nur durch seine Äußerungen, zu denen in diesem Sinn auch die Werke gehören — nein, es bestimmt sich allererst durch jene. (155–56)

> [the sole rational connection between creative artist and work of art consists in the testimony that the latter gives about the former. Not only does one gain knowledge of the essence of a human being through his outward manifestations (and in this sense the works, too, are a part of his essence); no, such knowledge is determined first and foremost by the works. (321)]

For the critic, the work must form the center of his or her analysis, not only because this is the only way in which to gain any knowledge about the meaning of the text, but also because it is the only real way that we gain any knowledge about the author. The author's existence is most palpable within his works. To understand something about the work is to understand something about the artist. Moreover, the search for biographical details as a means to explicate the text denigrates the author's power of imagination. This approach assumes that the experience is more telling than what the author created from it. In addition, Benjamin even argues that the artist, to an extent, creates his or her own experiences. Life is not something that the artist passively experiences, but it can be something that the artist actively shapes in order to enable the creation of a work of art. In this respect, the work of art, not the experience itself, ought to become the central concern.

From his general condemnation of the biographical method, Benjamin then begins his specific attack of Gundolf's biography. Conflating Bielschowsky's approach to biography with Gundolf's, he quotes Bielschowsky (1:6) on Goethe's life being itself a work of art and implies that Gundolf followed the principle in his biography: "Das gedankenloseste Dogma des Goethekults, das blasseste Bekenntnis der Adepten: daß unter allen Goetheschen Werken das größte sein Leben sei — Gundolfs *Goethe* hat es aufgenommen. Goethes Leben wird demnach nicht von dem der Werke streng geschieden" [160; The most thoughtless dogma of the Goethe cult, the most jejune confession of the adepts, asserts that among all the works of Goethe, the greatest is his life; Gundolf's *Goethe* took this up. Accordingly, Goethe's life is not rigorously distinguished from that of the works: 324]. This conflation of Bielschowsky's and Gundolf's approaches is to a certain extent unfair (although Witte for one argues that the criticism is justifiable, 39), because Gundolf himself was critical of Bielschowsky and his school and claims to set his work in direct opposition: whereas Bielschowsky privileged the life above the works, Gundolf claims to do the reverse (2). Benjamin argues, however, that Gundolf indeed conflates Goethe's life with his works, because this is the only way in which he is able to create the mythic, heroic image of Goethe. And because this image is based upon an assumption that Benjamin believes to be false (the convergence of life and works), he finds it to be a completely hollow and meaningless one.

Benjamin is critical of Gundolf's hero-worship for several different reasons. In creating a mythic image of Goethe, Gundolf propounds a false aesthetic philosophy. Goethe is not a god, nor is he especially singled out by God to create art. Such a view of creation is based upon external elements and looks for the mythic outside of the artist. Benjamin argues, however, that real literary productions arise from within the artist: "Nicht von Gott steigt solche Dichtung nieder, sondern aus dem Unergründlichen der Seele empor; sie hat am tiefsten Selbst des Menschen Anteil" [159;

Such poetry does not descend from God but ascends from what in the soul is unfathomable; it has a share in man's deepest self: 323]. Second, Gundolf's emphasis upon Goethe as a god-like creator wrongly displaces the proper emphasis from the works to Goethe himself— from the created product to the creator. Third, Gundolf's elevation of Goethe hides the faulty methodology of the entire work. While Benjamin acknowledges Gundolf's intention to counter simplistic biographies (161), he argues that in the end, Gundolf's work is much worse than those of earlier biographers. They only make claim to uncovering aspects of the material content (and Benjamin even questions the validity of this claim). Gundolf, in contrast, through his melding of Goethe's life and works, claims to have uncovered both the material and the truth contents and to find both clearly discernible. Gundolf is able to make this claim because he already treats Goethe as a hero, as a mythic being like Hercules whose deeds in a sense do represent the sum of his life.

Of course, Benjamin, in Part I, claimed that the only way in which one can gain access into an artist's true essence was through his works. But he accuses Gundolf of examining Goethe's works not as a means of understanding their truth content or of discovering part of Goethe's true essence, but primarily as a means of deifying his life. Because Benjamin believes that the truth content is often unknown even to the artist himself, biographical details do not serve the critic. In the end, he argues that biography serves neither commentary (the discussion of material content) nor criticism (the discussion of the truth content). He illustrates this point by comparing Baumgartner's biography to Gundolf's. While both fail in their endeavors, they fail for different reasons:

Wo die letztere [Baumgartners] geradenwegs die Ergründung des Wahrheitsgehalts unternimmt, ohne den Ort seines Vergrabenseins auch nur zu ahnen, und daher die kritischen Ausfälle ohne Maß häufen muß, versenkt sich Gundolf in die Welt der Sachgehalte des Goetheschen Lebens, in denen er doch nur vorgeblich dessen Wahrheitsgehalt darstellen kann. Denn menschliches Leben läßt sich nicht nach Analogie eines Kunstwerks betrachten. (161)

[Whereas the latter [Baumgartner's] undertakes to fathom the truth content directly (without, however, having the slightest

inkling of the place where it is buried) and hence must pile one
critical failure upon another to an inordinate extent, Gundolf
plunges into the world of the material contents of Goethe's life,
in which, to be sure, he can only allegedly present their truth
content. For human life cannot be considered on the analogy of a
work of art. (325)]

According to this passage, Baumgartner, unlike Gundolf, attempts
to get to the heart of the meaning of Goethe's works. He is, however, completely wrong about where to look for it and manages
only to base one critical mistake upon the other. Gundolf, on the
other hand, spends his time occupied with the material content —
with Goethe's life — and attempts to make statements about the
truth content based upon that. Benjamin argues that human life
cannot be analyzed in the same way as a work of art. He thus challenges the premise of Gundolf's endeavor and along with it, the
results: "So erscheint mit der erlogenen Monumentalität des Goetheschen Bildes die gefälschte Legalität seiner Erkenntnis" [164;
Thus, along with the fake monumentality of the Goethean image
appears the counterfeit legitimacy of the knowledge of that image:
327]. Benjamin even accuses Gundolf of intentionally obscuring
his faulty methodology through the use of esoteric terminology.
Indeed, Benjamin is the most savage in his criticisms of Gundolf
when he addresses his writing style. After quoting a passage from
Gundolf on the definition of marriage, Benjamin notes: "Eine
Darlegung, die der blutrünstige Mystizismus des Ausdrucks allein
von der Denkart einer Knallbonboneinlage unterscheidet" [163; A
formulation that is distinguished from the mentality of a fortune-
cookie motto only by the bloodthirsty mysticism of the wording:
326].

It is ironic that Benjamin accuses Gundolf of esotericism and
mysticism. If reader accessibility is a criterion, then Benjamin
clearly fails, for his text is much more difficult to comprehend than
Gundolf's. However, Benjamin's complaint is not that Gundolf
uses esoteric terminology, but that he uses it to cover a false methodology. In contrast, Benjamin would argue that his own esotericism is not meant to "hide" a faulty methodology, but to
illuminate a viable one. His esotericism is meant as a model for the
only type of criticism that can attempt a critique without destroying the beauty of the whole. As I will discuss below, the third part

of the essay explains Benjamin's esotericism within the context of a philosophy of beauty. Benjamin is so harshly critical of Gundolf in this section because he wants to prove how inadequate Gundolf's method is in bringing to light the meaning of *Die Wahlverwandt-schaften*. In particular, Benjamin points to the fact that Gundolf did not take the novella into account as a symptom of what is wrong with his method. By focusing upon Goethe's life instead of upon textual details, Benjamin argues that Gundolf misses one of the most important keys to reading the novel as a whole.

Benjamin's analysis of the novella is pathbreaking for several reasons. First, it is the first extended treatment of the novella found within the pages of *Die Wahlverwandtschaften*. Second, and most importantly, through his discussion of the novella, he demonstrates one of his main principles of analysis: using elements of the text to interpret the text as a whole. He therefore does not turn to bio-graphical facts or even to the background historical details, but to textual clues within the work to interpret it. He reads the novella as the antithesis of the novel. In Part I, Benjamin examined the thesis of the novel's dark and brooding treatment of the mythic. In Part II, he treats the novella as the antithesis, an antithesis, moreover, that "sheds light" on the whole. Benjamin interprets the ending of the novella as a happy one that illuminates why the characters in the novel suffer such a different fate. By juxtaposing the thesis of the novel against the antithesis of the novella, he is able to demon-strate several of his earlier statements about the role of myth within the novel. He thus is able to take a discussion about the structure of novellas generally and show how this structure has an interpre-tive function for *Die Wahlverwandtschaften*.

Before discussing the novella, Benjamin outlines how the entire novel has the qualities of a novella. Like many prior commentators, he remarks on how the tone of the writing keeps the reader at a certain distance. The characters are not portrayed as real people, but are more like types. The sympathy of the reader is therefore never fully aroused. For Benjamin, this aspect of the novel is sig-nificant in that it makes the whole "novella-like": "Denn wenn der Roman wie ein Maelstrom den Leser unwiderstehlich in sein Inne-res zieht, drängt die Novelle auf den Abstand hin, drängt aus ih-rem Zauberkreise jedweden Lebenden hinaus. Darin sind *Die Wahlverwandtschaften* trotz ihrer Breite novellistisch geblieben"

[168; For if the novel, like a maelstrom, draws the reader irresistibly into its interior, the novella strives toward distance, pushing every living creature out of its magic circle. In this way, despite its breadth *Elective Affinities* has remained novella-like: 330]. The fact that *Die Wahlverwandtschaften* is novella-like serves to link it closely to the novella within its pages and demands the juxtaposition of the two.

The comparison between the novel and the novella is a complex one in which Benjamin attempts to sketch contrasting relationships to freedom, sacrifice, and fate. Central to his discussion is the observation that the novel and novella present diametrically opposed relationships of the lovers to the people around them. The love of Ottilie and Eduard is characterized by its hidden nature and Eduard's attempts to seclude Ottilie away from the outside community. Eduard even demands that Ottilie separate herself from even the memory of her father when he requests that she relinquish the locket containing his picture. Ottilie complies with his request and abandons her connection to the others to give herself wholly to Eduard. The lovers in the novella, in contrast, are always surrounded by others. Even once they realize their love for each other, they do not hide their love, but feel the necessity of obtaining approval of the outside community: they desire a paternal blessing of their union. Because they face the crisis of their love in front of the community, love triumphs in their openness. The seclusion that characterizes Eduard and Ottilie's love, in contrast, only leads to their ruin.

Benjamin argues that the characters' relationship to the human community is directly related to their level of freedom. The characters in the novel are much more free from human ties, but as a consequence, they are much more subject to the powers of fate. Thus, whereas in Part I Benjamin argues that the decline in religious sentiment led to the increase in the power of the mythic over the characters, so here does the diminished power of traditional familial and communal ties open the characters more to the vicissitudes of external, mythic forces. The only way in which the characters in the novel can regain their lost sense of community is through sacrifice. Because the characters in the novella have never separated themselves from the community, no sacrifice is necessary on their part. Benjamin emphasizes that in no way ought the reader to interpret either the neighbor girl's or boy's actions as in any way connected to sacrifice. In fact, he argues that the girl's jump into the water is the rejection of sacrifice:

> Ihren Frieden erkaufen die Liebenden in der Novelle nicht durch das Opfer. Daß der Todessprung des Mädchens jene Meinung nicht hat, ist aufs zarteste und genaueste vom Dichter bedeutet. Denn nur dies ist die geheime Intention, aus der sie den Kranz dem Knaben zuwirft: es auzusprechen, daß sie nicht "in Schönheit sterben," im Tode nicht wie Geopferte bekränzt sein will. (170)

> [The lovers in the novella do not obtain their freedom through sacrifice. That the girl's fatal leap does not have that meaning is indicated by the author in the most delicate and precise manner. For this alone is her secret intention when she throws the garland wreath to the boy: to assert that she does not want to "die in beauty," be wreathed in death like a sacrifice. (332)]

That the girl does not sacrifice herself is an indication for Benjamin that she is not attempting to gain freedom — an attempt which brings about the powers of fate over the lovers in the novel. While Benjamin's argument is quite difficult to follow, he appears to argue that neither the girl nor the boy initially acts to overturn parental wishes or societal norms. Then when they find themselves together in the cottage, they consider and reject the possibility of running away from their families. Their decision to become a couple is not done in the spirit of trying to gain freedom over the laws of convention, but they attempt to gain the desired object within the confines of the community. That neither the girl nor the boy in the novella actively set out to gain freedom ultimately leads to a happy ending:

> Weil diese Menschen nicht um einer falsch erfaßten Freiheit willen alles wagen, fällt unter ihnen kein Opfer, sondern in ihnen die Entscheidung. In der Tat ist Freiheit so deutlich aus des Jünglings rettendem Entschluß entfernt wie Schicksal. Das chimärische Freiheitsstreben ist es, das über die Gestalten des Romans das Schicksal heraufbeschwört. Die Liebenden in der Novelle stehen jenseits von beiden und ihre mutige Entschließung genügt, ein Schicksal zu zerreißen, das sich über ihnen ballen, und eine Freiheit zu durchschauen, die sie in das Nichts der Wahl herabziehn wollte. Dies ist in den Sekunden der Entscheidung

der Sinn ihres Handelns. Beide tauchen hinab in den lebendigen Strom, dessen segensreiche Gewalt nicht minder groß in diesem Geschehen erscheint, als die todbringende Macht der stehenden Gewässer im andern. (170–71)

[Because these human beings do not risk everything for the sake of a falsely conceived freedom, no sacrifice falls among them; rather, the decision befalls within them. In fact, freedom is as clearly removed from the youth's saving decision as is fate. It is the chimerical striving for freedom that draws down fate upon the characters in the novel. The lovers in the novella stand beyond both freedom and fate, and their courageous decision suffices to tear to bits a fate that would gather to a head over them and to see through a freedom that would pull them down into the nothingness of choice. In the brief instants of their decision, this is the meaning of their action. Both dive down into the living current, whose beneficent power appears no less great in this even than the death-dealing power of the still waters in the other. (332)]

The characters are free from fate precisely because they are not free from conventional ties. The characters in the novel, in contrast, are free from conventional ties, but as a consequence are not free from the powers of fate. Benjamin further argues that symbolic importance of the wedding clothes further suggests how free the characters in the novella are from the powers of fate. He argues that as Ottilie's shroud is also viewed as a bridal gown (Nanny characterizes it as such), so too, by analogy, can we view the wedding clothes as burial clothes in the novella. These shrouds in the novella symbolize, according to Benjamin, an immunity from death. The characters are free from death in the same way as they are free from fate. They have avoided the striving toward freedom that leads to death, and in avoiding this path, they become free from it.

While Benjamin does not cite passages from the novella to illustrate his point, I believe his meaning becomes more clear if one turns to the following passage in *Die Wahlverwandtschaften:*

Sich vom Wasser zur Erde, vom Tode zum Leben, aus dem Familienkreise in eine Wildnis, aus der Verzweiflung zum Entzükken, aus der Gleichgültigkeit zur Neigung, zur Leidenschaft gefunden zu haben, alles in einem Augenblick — der Kopf wäre nicht hinreichend, das zu fassen, er würde zerspringen oder sich verwirren. Hiebei muß das Herz das beste tun, wenn eine solche Überraschung ertragen werden soll. (*FA* 1, 8:478)

[To go from water to land, death to life, from the family to wilderness, despair to delight, indifference to affection and passion, and all this in one moment — the mind could scarcely contain it all; it would burst or go mad. Only the heart can bear such a shattering sequence of events. (11:229)]

The language in the novella implies that in a certain way, the characters died and were resurrected. They have found new life after their seeming death in the water. Read in this way, one can see how Benjamin would view them as being now free from death. As resurrected beings, they have no fear of death. They have already submitted to it and conquered. Their "burial" clothes subsequently also symbolize the clothes of their new, resurrected life. Benjamin stresses their changed existence after this event. They are not even initially recognized by their families. Their burial shrouds, so to speak, momentarily conceal their new existence from their families. Benjamin, furthermore, warrants a reading of these characters as resurrected beings when he argues that the mythic themes in the novel correspond to themes of redemption in the novella (171). In other words, whereas the novel emphasizes death and the powers of fate, the novella illustrates the redemption of the characters. For Ottilie, the water symbolizes her lack of freedom and the powers of fate that lead to her death. For the characters in the novella, the water symbolizes their new life as one free from fate. Accordingly, Benjamin argues that the final feeling at the end of the novella is bliss [Seligkeit] (171).

Synthesis

Whereas in Part I Benjamin examined the differences between commentary and critique and in Part II exhibited what was wrong with earlier interpretative attempts, in Part III he endeavors to display critique in action. Here, he simultaneously offers his critique of the novel and explains the nature of critical inquiry. Unlike the second section, which began with a discussion of theory before turning to the novel, this one more closely intertwines the two. It therefore offers through its structure an example of the synthesis between theory and practice. On the one hand, Benjamin thus outlines his philosophy of beauty and the critic's role in writing about it. On the other hand, he outlines the significance of beauty and the semblance of beauty within the novel. He concludes the entire essay with a discussion of hope. This discussion further serves to distance his criticism of *Die Wahlverwandtschaften* from Gundolf's. Both Benjamin and Gundolf model part of their analysis upon Goethe's poem, "Urworte, Orphische" (Primal Words, Orphic, 1817/18). As Benjamin notes, Gundolf includes a discussion of the stanzas dealing with the daemonic, chance, the erotic, and necessity, but not that of hope (157–58). Yet, for Benjamin, the concept of hope is one of the keys to understanding the conclusion of the novel.

At the center of Benjamin's discussion in Part III is the notion of beauty as a veiled object. He maintains that beauty operates on several different levels within a work of art. That which is externally visible in a work of art is its "Schein" [semblance]. While beauty is not possible without its semblance, it is also not what is most essential about it. Semblance does not comprise beauty's existence because the existence of beauty does not reside in the visible realm, nor does it reside in the realm of what can be explained with words. The essence of beauty in Benjamin's schema is "das Ausdruckslose" [the expressionless]. Although its essence is closely related to its appearance or semblance, the two are nevertheless different:

> Zum Schein nämlich steht das Ausdruckslose, wiewohl im Gegensatz, doch in derart notwendigem Verhältnis, daß eben das Schöne, ob auch selber nicht Schein, aufhört ein wesentlich Schönes zu sein, wenn der Schein von ihm schwindet. Denn dieser gehört ihm zu als die Hülle und als das Wesensgesetz der Schönheit zeigt sich somit, daß sie als solche nur im Verhüllten erscheint. Nicht also ist, wie banale Philosopheme lehren, die Schönheit selbst Schein. . . . Nicht Schein, nicht Hülle für ein anderes ist die Schönheit. Sie selbst ist nicht Erscheinung, sondern durchaus Wesen, ein solches freilich, welches wesenhaft sich selbst gleich nur unter der Verhüllung bleibt. Mag daher Schein sonst überall Trug sein — der schöne Schein ist die Hülle vor dem notwendig Verhülltesten. Denn weder die Hülle noch der verhüllte Gegenstand ist das Schöne, sondern dies ist der Gegenstand in seiner Hülle. Enthüllt aber würde er unendlich unscheinbar sich erweisen. Hier gründet die uralte Anschauung, daß

in der Enthüllung das Verhüllte sich verwandelt, daß es "sich selbst gleich" nur unter der Verhüllung bleiben wird. (194–95)

[Although the expressionless contrasts with the semblance, it stands in such a fashion of necessary relationship to the semblance that precisely the beautiful, even if it is itself not semblance, ceases to be essentially beautiful when the semblance disappears from it. For semblance belongs to the essentially beautiful as the veil and as the essential law of beauty, shows itself thus, that beauty appears as such only in what is veiled. Beauty, therefore, is not itself semblance, as banal philosophemes assert. . . . Beauty is not a semblance, not a veil covering something else. It itself is not appearance but purely essence — one which, of course, remains essentially identical to itself only when veiled. Therefore, even if everywhere else semblance is deception, the beautiful semblance is the veil thrown over that which is necessarily most veiled. For the beautiful is neither the veil nor the veiled object but rather the object in its veil. Unveiled, however, it would prove to be infinitely inconspicuous. Here is the basis of the age-old view that that which is veiled is transformed in the unveiling, that it will remain "like unto itself" only underneath the veiling. (350–51)]

The essence of beauty is related to Plato's ideal forms, and indeed Benjamin even quotes from Plato's *Phaedrus* on ideal beauty and our memory of it. Whenever one sees a particular object, the visible aspect of this object is its semblance. The semblance is not true beauty, which only exists in the ideal world, but simply reminds one of that ideal beauty. We can recognize it as belonging to the beautiful only because we have a prior notion, a notion that cannot be made visible nor completely articulated, within our minds. Benjamin emphasizes that the true essence of beauty is never visible, but remains necessarily veiled in mystery. Therefore, while the veil, or the semblance, is not itself the beautiful, it is a necessary, albeit purely exterior covering that enables us to sense the beautiful and recognize that it exists. Unlike Plato, Benjamin argues that the beautiful will be destroyed if we probe its essence. Beauty for him has a sacredness that the critic ought not to violate. One cannot "uncover" the essence of beauty without destroying that essence because part of the beautiful's essence is the mystery that surrounds it.[4]

Benjamin accuses the earlier critics of *Die Wahlverwandtschaften* of precisely this kind of "uncovering." Their type of criticism, accordingly, makes the work of art more banal: it destroys the work's essence by trivializing it. Benjamin accuses these critics of expressing the relationship between truth and beauty in the shallow formula, "beauty is truth become visible." He cites as an example of this type of criticism Solger's positive assessment of Ottilie as a moral being (194): such an assessment of the work reduces it to a mere moral formula and does not appreciate the greater artistry within it. One of Benjamin's main theoretical objections to such canonical readings as Solger's is that they purport to find a unified, coherent meaning within the text. Benjamin's concept of the expressionless, however, denies and indeed undermines the existence of a work's totality. There can never be a unified, coherent interpretation of a work of art because the expressionless keeps the semblance of beauty and the essence of beauty from joining. Stated in another way, as the relationship between the material content (semblance) and the truth content (essence) constantly changes over time, static, canonical interpretations are impossible. The critic always must reassess the meaning of the work.

Benjamin's critic, therefore, goes about his or her task with a completely different goal than the traditional one of unlocking the core, or the secret, of the work's essence. The critic is not to search for beauty as a kind of Platonic ideal or to search for a single idea within the text, but is to create a critique that highlights the mystery behind the beautiful: the secret behind the veil which can never be lifted. "Critique," as Smith writes of Benjamin's approach, "must make the intuition of beauty possible while defending its integrity" (109). Benjamin explains the relationship of the critic to the essence of the beautiful:

> Also wird allem Schönen gegenüber die Idee der Enthüllung zu der der Unenthüllbarkeit. Sie ist die Idee der Kunstkritik. Die Kunstkritik hat nicht die Hülle zu heben, vielmehr durch deren genaueste Erkenntnis als Hülle erst zur wahren Anschauung des Schönen sich zu erheben. Zu der Anschauung, die der sogenannten Einfühlung niemals und nur unvollkommen einer reineren Betrachtung des Naiven sich eröffnen wird: zur Anschauung des Schönen als Geheimnis. Niemals noch wurde ein wahres Kunstwerk erfaßt, denn wo es unausweichlich als Geheimnis sich darstellte. Nicht anders nämlich ist jener Gegenstand zu bezeichnen, dem im letzten die Hülle wesentlich ist. Weil nur das Schöne und außer ihm nichts verhüllend und verhüllt wesentlich zu

sein vermag, liegt im Geheimnis der göttliche Seinsgrund der Schönheit. So ist denn der Schein in ihr eben dies: nicht die überflüssige Verhüllung der Dinge an sich, sondern die notwendige von Dingen für uns. (195)

[Thus, in the face of everything beautiful, the idea of unveiling becomes that of the impossibility of unveiling. It is the idea of art criticism. The task of art criticism is not to lift the veil but rather, through the most precise knowledge of it as a veil, to raise itself for the first time to the true view of the beautiful. To the view that will never open itself to so-called empathy and will only imperfectly open itself to a purer contemplation of the naive: to the view of the beautiful as that which is secret. Never yet has a true work of art been grasped other than where it ineluctably represented itself as a secret. For that object, to which in the last instance the veil is essential, is not to be characterized otherwise. Since only the beautiful and outside it nothing — veiling or being veiled — can be essential, the divine ground of the being of beauty lies in the secret. So then the semblance in it is just this: not the superfluous veiling of things in themselves but rather the necessary veiling of things for us. (351)]

The relationship between the critic and the work of art resembles that between a sacred text and a devotee. One is never to question the essence of a sacred text but must examine the mystery and the seeming beauty that surrounds it. To question the essence would be to doubt its existence as sacred, which in turn would destroy the sacredness of the text. The critic of a work of art similarly cannot set out to explain the source of beauty in the text because to do so would destroy the beauty. The philosophical quest of the critic is to show that the highest philosophical problem is the formulation of the work's truth content. The critic, however, stops before giving the actual formulation "wie aus Ehrfurcht vor dem Werk, gleich sehr jedoch aus Achtung vor der Wahrheit" [173; as if in awe of the work, but equally from respect for the truth: 334]. As Smith explains: "The secret of a work's beauty cannot be discovered by lifting its veil, by destroying its husk, that is by penetrating a surface or appearance. All such approaches alter — and hence Benjamin would say 'destroy' — the work in the process. The interpreter's strategy must be instead to comprehend and then articulate the grounds *why* such an approach cannot succeed" (109). Although the critic approaches the text with a reverential attitude, it is not with the goal of creating a canonical reading, but indeed its opposite. Canonical readings arise when critics claim that one particular truth exists within the text. For Benjamin, each critic and each age approaches the text anew and discovers new things about it. Criticism never ossifies, but remains alive like the metaphor of the flame in Part I.

When Benjamin turns his theory of semblance and beauty upon interpreting the novel, he focuses primarily upon Ottilie and her semblance-like qualities. In one of his most famous departures from earlier interpretations of the novel, he rejects the notion that Ottilie acts in a moral way or that she is an innocent being. Benjamin notes that Goethe symbolizes Ottilie's chastity in two great scenes: one in which she portrays the Virgin Mary in the living picture and one in which she holds the dead child in her arms. In both instances, Ottilie plays the part of a virgin mother. Ottilie's portrayal as the Virgin Mary, Benjamin argues, is indeed artificial because Ottilie in no way represents the ethical purity of the Mother of God. Instead it is her role as the virgin mother of the dead child that "enthüllt das wahre Wesen" [unveils the true essence] of her chastity. Her chastity is not related to innocence, but to the "Schein einer Unschuld des natürlichen Lebens" [semblance of an innocence of natural life]. It is a chastity that is closely related to guilt. Her chastity is only a semblance of innocence because it is not really linked to innocence but to sexuality. Benjamin interprets Ottilie's chastity within the context of Christian notions of it. He judges the Christian attempt, like Ottilie's, to drive away the forces of sexuality through the life of virginity to be misguided because it does not lead to a life of innocence, but instead inspires physical desire. While Benjamin believes that there exists a life of natural innocence, it is not be found in any way within the body, but in the spirit:

> [Eine natürliche Unschuld des Lebens] aber ist nicht an die Sexualität — und sei es verneinend — sondern einzig an ihren Gegenpol den — gleichermaßen natürlichen — Geist gebunden. Wie das sexuelle Leben des Menschen der Ausdruck einer natürlichen Schuld werden kann, so sein geistiges, bezogen auf die Einheit seiner gleichviel wie beschaffenen Individualität, der Ausdruck einer natürlichen Unschuld. (174)

[The natural innocence of life, however, is tied not to sexuality —
not even in the mode of denial — but rather solely to its anti-
pode, the spirit (which is equally natural). Just as the sexual life of
man can become the expression of natural guilt, his spiritual life,
based on the variously constituted unity of his individuality, can
become the expression of natural innocence. (335)]

Benjamin explains that virginity always remains an ambiguous
symbol. While it symbolizes purity, its very purity in turn becomes
the object of sexual desire and indeed incites sexual desire:

Und eben diese Zweideutigkeit kehrt höchst bezeichnender Weise in dem christlichen Symbol der Unschuld, in der Lilie, wieder.
Die strengen Linien des Gewächses, das Weiß des Blütenkelches
verbinden sich mit den betäubend süßen, kaum mehr vegetabilen
Düften. Diese gefährliche Magie der Unschuld hat der Dichter
der Ottilie mitgegeben und sie ist aufs engste dem Opfer ver-
wandt, das ihr Tod zelebriert. Denn eben indem sie dergestalt
unschuldig erscheint, verläßt sie nicht den Bannkreis seines Voll-
zugs. Nicht Reinheit sondern deren Schein verbreitet sich mit
solcher Unschuld über ihre Gestalt. (175)

[And precisely this ambiguity returns in an extremely characteristic manner in the Christian symbol of innocence, the lily. The se-
vere lines of the plant, the whiteness of the calyx, are joined to
numbingly sweet scents that are scarcely still vegetal. The author
has also given Ottilie this dangerous magic of innocence, which is
most intimately related to the sacrifice celebrated by her death.
For the very fact that she appears innocent in this manner prevents her from escaping the spell of that consummation. Not purity but its semblance spreads itself out with such innocence over
her form. (335–36)]

Real innocence requires spiritual or intellectual engagement, but
Ottilie's is rooted in the physical. Her seeming purity is based upon
her physical virginity and her "sacrifice" upon her ability to overcome the bodily desire for food. Because her innocence is based on
physical aspects, according to Benjamin's definition, her innocence
is not real, but only has the semblance of innocence. Benjamin will
base his interpretation of the novel's conclusion (discussed below)
as stemming from this semblance. Thus, because the characters in
the novella are truly innocent, they are able happily to reconcile.
Ottilie's seeming innocence, however, only leads to the hope of a
semblance of redemption at the end.

Because Benjamin questions Ottilie's innocence, he argues against interpretations, such as Gundolf's and François-Poncet's, that stress her sacredness. He argues that her chastity is not at all sacred, but to the contrary is linked to her moral ambiguity. He suggests that Ottilie's silence is the most telling aspect of her lack of true innocence. If true innocence is grounded in the spiritual life, then Ottilie's silence for him is an indictment against her spirituality. Morality requires decision making. Passive existence can never be called moral. Ottilie is not holy or sacred, but exists in an ambiguous moral plane of unreflective existence. Benjamin compares her several times to a plant to emphasize that just as one cannot speak of the moral life of a plant, so too one cannot speak of the silent Ottilie's morality. That she is even silent about her own death demonstrates for Benjamin that her death is not the result of a moral decision:

> Denn wenn irgendwo, so zeigt sich im Entschluß die moralische Welt vom Sprachgeist erhellt. Kein sittlicher Entschluß kann ohne sprachliche Gestalt, und streng genommen ohne darin Gegenstand der Mitteilung geworden zu sein, ins Leben treten. Daher wird, in dem vollkommenen Schweigen der Ottilie, die Moralität des Todeswillens, welcher sie beseelt, fragwürdig. Ihm liegt in Wahrheit kein Entschluß zugrunde sondern ein Trieb. Daher ist nicht, wie sie es zweideutig auszusprechen scheint, ihr Sterben heilig. (176)

> [For if the moral world shows itself anywhere illuminated by the spirit of language, it is in the decision. No moral decision can enter into life without verbal form and, strictly speaking, without thus becoming an object of communication. That is why in Ottilie's complete silence, the morality of the will to die that animates her becomes questionable. In truth, what underlies it is not a decision but a drive. Therefore, her dying is not — as she seems ambiguously to express it — sacred. (336)]

Benjamin argues that one cannot be moral if one does not actively decide upon a path. Similarly, a character cannot be considered tragic unless that character has actively pursued a course of action. Ottilie is neither a moral nor a tragic figure because she is passive and unreflective. He discounts the nobility of Ottilie's sacrifice through starvation by reminding the reader that Ottilie deprived herself of food at the boarding school when it clearly served no moral purpose. Thus, while Ottilie remains a victim in that she is sacrificed at the end of the novel as a means of expiating the guilt of all of the characters, she does not sacrifice *herself.* She remains for Benjamin a passive character.

Although Benjamin denies that Ottilie's existence is sacred, he does not therefore label Ottilie as immoral in the traditional sense. Unlike the religious critics who characterize Ottilie as immoral due to her role in breaking up Charlotte and Eduard's marriage, Benjamin calls Ottilie's existence an unhallowed one because of her passivity:

> Nicht so sehr darum ist das Dasein der Ottilie, das Gundolf heilig nennt, ein ungeheiligtes, weil sie sich gegen eine Ehe, die zerfällt, vergangen hätte, als weil sie, im Scheinen und im Werden schicksalhafter Gewalt bis zum Tod unterworfen, entscheidungslos ihr Leben dahinlebt. (176)

> [Ottilie's existence, which Gundolf calls sacred, is an unhallowed one, not so much because she trespassed against a marriage in dissolution as because in her seeming and her becoming, subjected until her death to a fateful power, she vegetates without decision. (337)]

Benjamin even praises Julian Schmidt's assessment of Ottilie in that he too emphasizes the strangeness behind her silence. Benjamin thus agrees with "dem hausbacknen Verstand" [the pedestrian common sense] of Schmidt, when he states that the reader would better understand Ottilie's character if her passion had been stronger and if she had articulated her feelings (Schmidt 172).

Benjamin's discussion of Ottilie in Part III focuses on the semblance of her innocence and the semblance of her beauty. He even directly associates her with the veil, the metaphor that he uses for the semblance of beauty generally: she is the gentle, veiled beauty at the center of the novel (186). After quoting Goethe's words to Zelter about the veiled meaning within the novel (*FA* 2, 7:485; 26 August 1809), Benjamin claims that the veil was more than an image to Goethe: "es ist die Hülle, welche immer wieder ihn bewegen mußte, wo er um Einsicht in die Schönheit rang" [197; it is the veil that again and again had to affect him where he was struggling for insight into beauty: 352]. Benjamin explains that three characters best illustrate this struggle: Mignon, Helena, and Ottilie. Each of them, according to Benjamin, are closely linked with veiled images: Mignon to the clothes that she will shed only in the afterlife; Helena to the clothes that she leaves behind in Faust's arms; and Ottilie's body, which is left behind after her death and miraculously does not decay.

Ottilie's semblance becomes of central importance to Benjamin's overall interpretation of the novel in that he links it to the semblance of reconciliation at the end of the novel. In Part III, Benjamin once again juxtaposes the novella against the novel. Earlier, he explained how the characters in the novella find redemption in their decisive acts of jumping into the water. Now he explains why the conclusion of the novel as a whole is but a semblance of redemption — where one is left only with hope for the dead couple. In other words, whereas Benjamin believes that we have every reason to believe in the happy ending of the novella, the conclusion of the novel leaves one with real reason to doubt the semblance of their reconciliation at the end.

In contrasting the novel with the novella, Benjamin once again uses the religious language of redemption:

> Wahre Versöhnung gibt es in der Tat nur mit Gott. Während in ihr der Einzelne mit ihm sich versöhnt und nur dadurch mit den Menschen sich aussöhnt, ist es der scheinhaften Versöhnung eigen, jene untereinander aussöhnen und nur dadurch mit Gott versöhnen zu wollen. Von neuem trifft dies Verhältnis scheinhafter Versöhnung zur wahren auf den Gegensatz von Roman und Novelle. (184)

> [Whereas in true reconciliation the individual reconciles himself with God and only in this way conciliates other human beings, it is peculiar to semblance-like reconciliation that the individual wants others to make peace with one another and only in this way become reconciled to God. The relation of semblance-like reconciliation to true reconciliation again evokes the opposition between novel and novella. (342)]

The characters in the novella act in a way that is diametrically opposed to those in the main novel. The neighbor children actively risk everything. They jump in the water and place their own lives at risk in order to be together. Because they are willing to risk everything, their love achieves their desired reconciliation with each other. Benjamin sees such an action as a religious one. In risking their lives, each appears before God and shows his or her willingness to die and be reconciled with God. And only because each is willing to take this risk, do they wind up together.

At the center of the difference between the characters in the novel and those in the novella is their relationship to love. Benjamin maintains that true love does not reign in the relationship between Eduard and Ottilie, but rather passion. True love is not helpless, whereas the semblance of love is. The characters in the novella have true love for each other, and they therefore find a way to reunite. Ottilie and Eduard remain passive and helpless. And just like the mythic may be tamed only through religion, so too may the destructive power of passion be controlled by another force: affection (186). Thus, the lover in the novella does not even see his beloved's naked body because his sole concern is for her safety after the accident (196). Eduard and Ottilie's love, according to Benjamin, is never tempered by affection. Most importantly for Benjamin's argument, however, is that love becomes "vollkommen nur wo sie über ihre Natur erhoben durch Gottes Walten gerettet wird" [187; perfect only where elevated above its nature, it is saved through God's intervention: 344–45]. Benjamin argues that Ottilie's death is of an entirely different character than the neighbor girl's leap into the water. Where the girl hopes to be rescued and reconciled with her love, Ottilie's sacrifice is one "welches in Gottes Hand nicht das teuerste Gut, sondern die schwerste Bürde legt und seinen Ratschluß vorwegnimmt. So fehlt alles Vernichtende wahrer Versöhnung durchaus ihrem Schein, wie denn selbst, soweit möglich, von der Todesart der Ottilie alles Schmerzhafte und Gewaltsame fernbleibt" [184–85; that puts in God's hand not the most precious good but the most difficult burden, and anticipates his decree. Thus, her semblance is thoroughly lacking in all the annihilating character of true reconciliation, just as, insofar as possible, everything painful and violent remains remote from the manner of her death: 343]. Ottilie does not decide to risk her life in order to try to find happiness or to try to put into God's hands the decision of what she ought to do. Rather, she dies having already decided her fate and Eduard's: "Dem Tod muß die Schönheit verfallen, die nicht in der Liebe sich preisgibt" [198; Beauty that does not surrender itself in love must fall prey to death: 353].

That Ottilie chooses such a non-violent, peaceful way of dying is further indicative of the greater suppression of passion in the novel. In the novella, passions are allowed to explode and come to the surface; in the novel, the bourgeois code demands the suppression of anger, shame, revenge, and despair. Because the characters believe themselves to be civilized and because they are able to hold their passions in check, they believe that they have triumphed over them. Their bourgeois existence, however, cannot lead to happiness:

> Denn was hundertfach der Dichter verschweigt, geht doch einfach genug aus dem Gange des Ganzen hervor: daß nach sittlichen Gesetzen die Leidenschaft all ihr Recht und ihr Glück verliert, wo sie den Pakt mit dem bürgerlichen, dem reichlichen, dem gesicherten Leben sucht. (185)

> [For what the author shrouds in silence a hundred times can be seen quite simply enough from the course of things as a whole: that, according to ethical laws, passion loses all its rights and happiness when it seeks a pact with the bourgeois, affluent, secure life. (343)]

Benjamin already established in Part I that mythic forces gain power once the influence of religion declines. Because the characters feel bound to the ethical laws primarily out of convention, the power of the mythic cannot be overcome or suppressed solely by the ethical. Instead, the mythic realm of passion exerts its influence and demands a sacrifice. The characters in the novel therefore have the worst of both worlds. Because they attempt to adhere to the realm of convention, they give up the possibility of happiness. However, because they adhere to convention solely from bourgeois reasons, as opposed to religious ones, the mythic is able to triumph over them. Their suppressed passions therefore become symbolic of an upcoming upheaval:

> Denn hier regiert die Stille vor dem Sturm, in der Novelle aber das Gewitter und der Friede. Während Liebe die Versöhnten geleitet, bleibt als Schein der Versöhnung nur die Schönheit bei den andern zurück. (185)

> [For what reigns here is the quiet before a storm; in the novella, however, thunderstorm and peace prevail. While love guides the

reconciled, only beauty, as a semblance of reconciliation, remains behind with the others. (343)]

The novella, in a way, therefore represents an image of the world in which religious belief combined with ethical laws exerts more power over the mythic, over passion. While Goethe refrains from framing the novella in terms of religion, Benjamin argues that the end effect is the same. That the characters in the novella place their trust in God's will ensures that they will gain new life together. In the novella, Goethe shows

> das Leben der beiden gerettet in eben dem Sinne, in dem es den Frommen die Ehe bewahrt; in diesem Paare hat er die Macht wahrer Liebe dargestellt, die in religiöser Form auszusprechen er sich verwehrte. Demgegenüber steht im Roman in diesem Lebensbereich das zwiefache Scheitern. Während die einen, vereinsamt, dahinsterben, bleibt den Überlebenden die Ehe versagt. Der Schluß beläßt den Hauptmann und Charlotten wie die Schatten in der Vorhölle. Weil in keinem der Paare der Dichter die wahre Liebe konnte walten lassen, welche diese Welt hätte sprengen müssen, gab er unscheinbar aber unverkennbar in den Gestalten der Novelle ihr Wahrzeichen seinem Werke mit. (188)

> [the life of the two lovers saved in precisely the sense in which marriage preserves it for the pious ones; in this pair he depicted the power of true love, which he prohibited himself from expressing in religious form. Opposed to this, in the novel, within this domain of life, is the double failure. While the one couple, in isolation, dies away, marriage is denied to the survivors. The conclusion leaves the captain and Charlotte like shades in Limbo. Since the author could not let true love reign in either of the couples (it would have exploded this world), in the characters of the novella he supplied his work inconspicuously but unmistakably with its emblem. (345)]

The lovers in the novella have a presentiment [Ahnung] of a life of bliss (196). The characters in the novel, on the contrary, do not have such a presentiment. Goethe holds out for them merely the hope of such a life.

In order to explain the meaning of hope, Benjamin turns to Goethe's own words on the novel. While such an approach seems a clear violation of Benjamin's critical methodology, he does examine the words in a different spirit from earlier commentators. Unlike previous scholars, who take Goethe's words at face value, Benjamin seeks to find in them a secret of the novel of which Goethe himself was not aware (199). In other words, just as Goethe remains unconscious of much of the truth content of his own novel, so too is he unconscious of the greater significance of his own words for the interpretation of the whole. Benjamin quotes a large portion of Sulpiz Boisserée's report of a conversation with Goethe involving the novel (*FA* 2, 7:528; 5 October 1815):

> Unterwegs kamen wir dann auf die *Wahlverwandtschaften* zu sprechen. Er legte Gewicht darauf, wie rasch und unaufhaltsam er die Katastrophe herbeigeführt. Die Sterne waren aufgegangen; er sprach von seinem Verhältnis zur Ottilie, wie er sie lieb gehabt und wie sie ihn unglücklich gemacht. Er wurde zuletzt fast rätselhaft ahndungsvoll in seinen Reden. — Dazwischen sagte er dann wohl einen heitern Vers. So kamen wir müde, gereizt, halb ahndungsvoll, halb schläfrig im schönsten Sternenlicht . . . nach Heidelberg. (Quoted here from Benjamin, 199)

> [During the journey, we came to speak of *Elective Affinities*. He emphasized how rapidly and irresistibly he had brought on the catastrophe. The stars had risen; he spoke of his relation to Ottilie, of how he had loved her and how she had made him unhappy. At the end, his speeches became almost mysteriously full of foreboding. — In between, he would recite light-hearted verse. Thus, weary, stimulated, half full of foreboding, half-asleep, we arrived in Heidelberg in the most beautiful starlight. (354)]

Benjamin believes that the stars reminded Goethe, albeit unconsciously, of his novel: "Denn unter dem Symbol des Sterns war einst Goethe die Hoffnung erschienen, die er für die Liebenden fassen mußte" [199; For in the symbol of the star, the hope that Goethe had to conceive for the lovers had once appeared to him: 354]. Benjamin is here speaking of the scene in the novel in which Ottilie and Eduard embrace after he has returned from the wars, "Die Hoffnung fuhr wie ein Stern, der vom Himmel fällt, über ihre Häupter weg" [200; *FA* 1, 8:493; Hope shot across the sky above their heads like a falling star: 355; 11:239]. This kind of hope becomes of central importance in understanding the hope offered to the reader at the end of the novel. The hope spoken of in this passage is a completely hollow one, for the embrace which engenders it actually leads to the death of the child and ultimately to Ottilie's death as well. In a twist of interpretation, Benjamin argues that the feeling of hope does not apply to the characters' hope of their future, but to Goethe's hopes for them. Because Goethe loves Ottilie, as demonstrated by the conversation above, Benjamin argues that Goethe hopes for her final redemption. Benjamin notes that "die letzte Hoffnung niemals dem eine ist, der sie hegt, sondern jenen allein, für die sie gehegt wird" [200; the last hope is never such to him who cherishes it but is the last only to those for whom it is cherished: 355]. Benjamin thus reads Goethe's relation to Ottilie and Eduard as diametrically opposed to Dante's relationship to Francesca and Paolo in the *Inferno*. Dante assumes within himself the hopelessness of the lovers when he faints away as if a corpse (200). Goethe created a very similar couple, but his narrative stance internalizes hope instead of despair. He leaves the reader of *Die Wahlverwandtschaften* with the hope for a different fate than the couple condemned in Dante's hell:

> Jene paradoxeste, flüchtigste Hoffnung taucht zuletzt aus dem Schein der Versöhnung, wie im Maß, da die Sonne verlischt, im Dämmer der Abendstern aufgeht, der die Nacht überdauert. Dessen Schimmer gibt freilich die Venus. Und auf solchem geringsten beruht all Hoffnung, auch die reichste kommt nur aus ihm. So rechtfertigt am Ende die Hoffnung den Schein der Versöhnung und der Satz des Platon, widersinnig sei es, den Schein des Guten zu wollen, erleidet seine einzige Ausnahme. Denn der Schein der Versöhnung darf, ja er soll gewollt werden: er allein ist das Haus der äußersten Hoffnung. So entringt sie sich ihm zuletzt und nur wie eine zitternde Frage klingt jenes "wie schön" am Ende des Buches den Toten nach, die, wenn je, nicht in einer schönen Welt wir erwachen hoffen, sondern in einer seligen. (200)

> [that most paradoxical, most fleeting hope finally emerges from the semblance of reconciliation, just as, at twilight, as the sun is extinguished, rises the evening star which outlasts the night. Its glimmer, of course, is imparted by Venus. And upon the slightest such glimmer all hope rests; even the richest hope comes only from it. Thus, at the end, hope justifies the semblance of reconciliation, and Plato's tenet that it is absurd to desire the semblance of the good suffers its one exception. For one is permitted

to desire the semblance of reconciliation — indeed, it must be desired: it alone is the house of the most extreme hope. Thus, hope finally wrests itself from it; and like a trembling question, there echoes at the end of the book that "How beautiful" in the ears of the dead, who, we hope, awaken, if ever not to a beautiful world but to a blessed one. (355)]

Benjamin once again contrasts the endings of the novella and novel. At the end of the novella, he maintains that the reader feels a certainty in the redemption and reconciliation of the lovers. The end of the novel, in contrast, contains but a fleeting, albeit beautiful, hope. Benjamin has already explained that Ottilie's passive behavior has ruled out a true reconciliation with Eduard. Such a reconciliation is only possible in the active world of the novella's characters. It is therefore hope alone that creates the semblance of reconciliation at the end of the novel. Ottilie and Eduard ought to suffer the fate of Francesca and Paolo, yet the reader holds out the hope that they, like the characters in the novella, will awaken to a blessed life: "Nur um der Hoffnungslosen willen ist uns die Hoffnung gegeben" [201; Only for the sake of the hopeless ones have we been given hope: 356]. Benjamin argues that the novel's dramatic crowning is in the mystery of hope (201). And just as one cannot unveil the secrets of the beautiful without destroying it, so too cannot one uncover the mystery of hope within the novel without destroying it.

Benjamin Studies

The secondary literature on Benjamin's essay often centers on Benjamin's expressed attempt to attack Gundolf. While Benjamin certainly viciously attacks Gundolf and demonstrates time and again how different his methodology is from Gundolf's, their interpretations also have some points of correspondence. These points are of particular interest because they demonstrate a growing dissatisfaction with the direction of criticism during their day. First, neither critic takes the idea of traditional marriage to be the topic of the novel. Indeed, it was Gundolf, and not Benjamin, who first made the claim that the novel was not about marriage. Second, both men attack the biographic methods of their predecessors. Both critics treat Bielschowsky with complete scorn. Finally, both men were elitist. Although their philosophical approaches arose from diametrically opposed political views, both attempted within their scholarship to address the privileged few. Both methodologies therefore fly in the face of the trend to popularize Goethe as a figure for general German consumption. Neither work was meant to be read by a general reading public, but by a small circle of intellectuals. Gundolf makes fun of the Goethe scholars, such as Bielschowsky, who attempt to write for the general public and attempts in his own work to treat Goethe's works on a higher, theoretical plane. Similarly, not only is Walter Benjamin's essay written in an extremely esoteric style, but he was pleased to publish it in such an exclusive journal as *Neue Deutsche Beiträge* — a journal that according to Witte was read "only by conservative journalists, politicians, and dilettantes with exquisite taste" (66).

Benjamin was disappointed in the initial reaction that his essay received. He had hoped that the essay's publication would elicit a response from someone in the George school. Gundolf, however, ignored the invective against him, and indeed, Witte notes, the only document about the essay's initial reception is a letter by Hofmannsthal (65). Hofmannsthal was deeply moved by the essay and wrote in a letter:

> Ich kann nur sagen, daß er [der Aufsatz] in meinem inneren Leben Epoche gemacht hat und daß sich mein Denken, soweit nicht die eigene Arbeit alle Aufmerksamkeit erzwingt, kaum von ihm hat lösen können. Wunderbar ist mir — um von dem scheinbar "Äußeren" zu sprechen — die hohe Schönheit der Darstellung bei einem so beispiellosen Eindringen ins Geheimnis: diese Schönheit entspringt aus einem völlig sicheren und reinen Denken, wovon ich wenig Beispiele weiß. (Letter to Rang, 20 November 1923)

> [I can only say that it [the essay] has marked an epochal change in my inner life and that insofar as my own work does not claim my full attention, my thinking has hardly been able to let go of it. What I find extraordinary — to speak of apparent externals — is the exalted beauty of the presentation in the context of such penetration into secret depths; this beauty emanates from a wholly secure and pure mode of thinking, to which I know few parallels. (Quoted from Witte 65)]

Benjamin's essay, however, came to new prominence in the publication of his collected works in 1955. His ever-growing popularity, which reached its climax in the 1980s, fostered a renewed interest in Goethe's *Wahlverwandtschaften*. As will be discussed in the next chapter, many of the scholars who wrote on the novel during that time took their departure from Benjamin's essay.

Finally, one must note the irony of Benjamin scholars scrutinizing the details of Benjamin's life in analyzing his essay on *Die Wahlverwandtschaften*. For example, Bernd Witte attempts to show the close parallels between Benjamin's life and his essay (cf. Brodersen 126–27). He describes, for example, how Benjamin was himself involved in relationships that paralleled those in Goethe's novel. Benjamin dedicates his essay to Jula Cohn, a woman who "belonged to the outer circle of the school or writers and artists formed by Stefan George and was a friend of Friedrich Gundolf" (Witte 58). Cohn lived together for a time with Benjamin and his wife "until living together had proved impossible" (58–59). Benjamin's wife, too, was probably having an affair with their mutual friend, Ernst Schoen (Brodersen 126). Eventually, Benjamin's attraction for Cohn destroyed his marriage. Most notably, Witte compares Benjamin's statements on Ottilie in the essay with his description of Jula Cohn:

> In his interpretation of Goethe's novel he endows, as a critic, the literary figure of Ottilie with the features of Jula Cohn. On the other hand, as a lover, he sees the relationship to his beloved as governed by "fate," thus situating it in the critical perspective that he applies to it in his essay on *The Elective Affinities*. (59)

When trying to explain Benjamin's attempts to meld Ottilie and Cohn, Witte turns to psychology:

> Benjamin turns the beloved woman closest to him into the one farthest away, by stylizing her as Ottilie, the loving woman who removes herself into the remotest possible distance, namely death. What drives him to such an act of distancing? Looking at comparable behavior of his toward other women, Asja Lacis for example, one is inclined to think that he sought to protect himself by fending off a permanent tie, because the prospect of love's death in the rhythm of daily life was intolerable to him. But questions of individual psychology are not of primary importance here. The issue is, rather, how does the actuality of love appear possible to a great lover? Only at a distance, through renunciation of fulfillment. In this it is Dante, whose distant glimpse of the beloved Beatrice on a bridge becomes the impetus for a life's

work, who appears as the model for Benjamin the critic. Like the author of *The Divine Comedy*, he transforms the beloved woman into his text and the text into what is truly beloved. (59–60)

Nor are the biographical details the only ones that critics analyze in interpreting Benjamin's essay. Others, such as Jennings, read the larger historical events of the time (the First World War) as having a significant impact on Benjamin's text.[5] Thus, whereas Benjamin attempted to do battle against the historical and biographical reductionists of Goethe's works, his own works, in that they too have become canonical, have suffered a similar fate.

Notes

[1] This statement, of course, is not true. The sun does shine in the novel. Benjamin here appears to be speaking metaphorically, yet several critics have taken him to task for this statement. See, for example, Barnes (76).

[2] Wolin also offers a similar reading (30).

[3] Benjamin quotes Kant on marriage as "die Verbindung zweier Personen verschiedenen Geschlechts zum lebenswierigen wechselseitigen Besitz ihrer Geschlechtseigenschaften — Der Zweck Kinder zu erzeugen und zu erziehen mag immer ein Zweck der Natur sein, zu welchem sie die Neigung der Geschlechter gegen einander einpflanzte; aber daß der Mensch, der sich verehelicht, diesen Zweck sich vorsetzen müsse, wird zur Rechtmäßigkeit dieser seiner Verbindung nicht erfordert; denn sonst würde, wenn das Kinderzeugen aufhört, die Ehe sich zugleich von selbst auflösen" [127; the union of two persons of different sexes for the purpose of lifelong mutual possession of their sexual organs. The goal of begetting and rearing children may be a goal of nature for which the inclination of the sexes to one another was implanted; but it is not requisite for human beings who marry to make this their end in order for their union to be compatible with rights, for otherwise the marriage would dissolve of its own accord when procreation ceases: 299].

[4] It is interesting to contrast Benjamin's notion of veiled beauty with a famous classical conception of truth as veiled: Schiller's poem, "Das verschleierte Bild zu Sais" (The Veiled Statue at Saïs, 1795). According to the poem, lifting the veil of truth leads to destruction, but not to the destruction of truth. The act destroys the happiness of the man who lifted the veil and leads him to an early grave.

[5] Jennings argues that Benjamin makes the novella within *Die Wahlverwandtschaften* into a "metafable of his own historical situation, as the projec-

tion of the experiences of the generation that survived World War I onto a group of seemingly inappropriate characters in a work of fiction" (137).

Works Cited

[Abeken, Bernhard Rudolf]. Ueber Goethes *Wahlverwandtschaften*. (Fragmente aus einem Briefe). *Morgenblatt für gebildete Stände*. No. 19–21 (22–24 January 1810). Quoted here from Härtl 1983, 121–27.

Barnes, H. G. *Goethe's Die Wahlverwandtschaften: A Literary Interpretation*. Oxford: Clarendon Press, 1967.

Baumgartner, Alexander. *Göthe: Sein Leben und seine Werke*. 3 vols. Freiburg: Herder'sche Verlagshandlung, 1882. Quoted here from 2nd, expanded ed., 1885–86.

Benjamin, Walter. "Bemerkung über Gundolf: Goethe." Unpublished during Benjamin's lifetime (ca. 1917). Quoted here from *Walter Benjamin: Gesammelte Schriften* I, 3. Ed. Rolf Tiedemann and Hermann Schweppenhäuser. Frankfurt: Suhrkamp, 1974. English from *Walter Benjamin: Selected Writings (1913–1926)*. Vol. 1. Ed. Marcus Bullock and Michael W. Jennings. Essay trans. Stanley Corngold. Cambridge: Belknap Press, 1996.

———. "Goethes *Wahlverwandtschaften*." *Neue deutsche Beiträge* (1924/25). Quoted here from *Walter Benjamin: Gesammelte Schriften* I, i. Ed. Rolf Tiedemann and Hermann Schweppenhäuser. Frankfurt: Suhrkamp. English from *Walter Benjamin: Selected Writings (1913–1926)*. Vol. 1. Ed. Marcus Bullock and Michael W. Jennings. Essay trans. Stanley Corngold. Cambridge: Belknap Press, 1996.

Bielschowsky, Albert. *Goethe: Sein Leben und seine Werke*. 2 vols. Quoted here from the 23rd ed., 1911. Munich: C. H. Beck. English from the 1911 translation *The Life of Goethe*. Trans. William Cooper. New York: G. P. Putnam's Sons.

Brinkmann, Hennig. "Zur Sprache der *Wahlverwandtschaften*." *Festschrift für Jost Trier zum 60. Geburtstag*. Meisenheim a. G.: Anton Hain, 1954. 254–76. Also published in Brinkmann's *Studien zur Geschichte der deutschen Sprache und Literatur*. 2 vols. Düsseldorf: Pädagogischer Verlag Schwann, 1965/66. Quoted here from Rösch.

Brodersen, Momme. *Walter Benjamin: A Biography*. Trans. Malcolm R. Green and Ingrida Ligers. Ed. Martina Derviş. London: Verso, 1996.

François-Poncet, André. *Les Affinités Électives*. Paris: F. Alcan, 1910. Quoted here from the 1951 German translation: *Goethes Wahlverwandtschaften: Versuch eines kritischen Kommentars*. Mainz: Florian Kupferberg Verlag.

Gervinus, G[eorg] G[ottfried]. *Geschichte der deutschen Dichtung V: Neuere Geschichte der poetischen National-Literatur der Deutschen. Zweiter Theil: Von Göthes Jugend bis zur Zeit der Befreiungskriege*. Leipzig: Engelmann, 1842.

Gundolf, Friedrich. *Goethe*. Berlin: Bondi, 1916. Quoted here from 4th ed., 1918.

Haeckel, Ernst. *Natürliche Schöpfungsgeschichte*. Berlin: Georg Reimer, 1868.

Hárnik, J. "Psychoanalytisches aus und über Goethes *Wahlverwandtschaften*." *Imago Zeitschrift für Anwendung der Psychoanalyse auf die Geisteswissenschaften* 1 (1912): 507–18.

Härtl, Heinz. *Die Wahlverwandtschaften: Eine Dokumentation der Wirkung von Goethes Roman 1808–1832*. Weinheim: Acta humaniora, 1983.

Hebbel, Friedrich. "Vorwort" zur *Maria Magdalene* (1844). Hamburg. Quoted here from *Friedrich Hebbel: Werke*. Vol. 1. Munich: Carl Hanser Verlag, 1963. 307–38. Translation by T. M. Campbell in *Hebbel-Ibsen and the Analytic Exposition*. Heidelberg: Winter, 1922.

Hofmannsthal, Hugo von. Letter to Florens Christian Rang 11 November 1923. Cited in *Die neue Rundschau* 70 (1959): 439–40.

Jennings, Michael W. *Dialectical Images: Walter Benjamin's Theory of Literary Criticism*. Ithaca: Cornell UP, 1987.

Lockemann, Theodor. "Der Tod in Goethes *Wahlverwandtschaften*." *Jahrbuch der Goethegesellschaft* 19 (1933): 48–61.

McCole, John. *Walter Benjamin and the Antinomies of Tradition*. Ithaca: Cornell UP, 1993.

Reitz, Gertrud. *Die Gestalt des Mittlers in Goethes Dichtung*. Frankfurter Quellen und Forschungen zur germanischen und romanischen Philologie. Ed. Erhard Lommatzsch, Hans Naumann, and Franz Schultz. Frankfurt: Mortiz Diesterweg, 1932. Quoted here from the facsimile reprint, 1973. Hildesheim: Dr. H. A. Gerstenberg.

Rösch, Ewald (1975). *Goethes Roman 'Die Wahlverwandtschaften.' Wege der Forschung*. Vol. 113. Darmstadt: Wissenschaftliche Buchgesellschaft, 1975.

Rosen, Charles. "The Ruins of Walter Benjamin." *On Walter Benjamin: Critical Essays and Recollections*. Ed. Gary Smith. Cambridge: MIT Press, 1988. 129–75.

Ryan, Judith. Review of *Goethes Wahlverwandtschaften: Kritische Modelle und Diskursanalysen zum Mythos Literatur*. Ed. Norbert W. Bolz. *Goethe Yearbook* 2 (1984): 250–53.

Schmidt, Julian. *Geschichte der Deutschen Literatur seit Lessing's Tod*. Vol. 2. Quoted here from 4th, expanded ed. Leipzig: Friedrich Ludwig Herbig, 1858.

Smith, Gary. "A Genealogy of 'Aura': Walter Benjamin's Idea of Beauty." *Artifacts, Representations and Social Practice*. Ed. C. C. Gould and R. S. Cohen. Netherlands: Kluwer Academic Publishers, 1994. 105–19.

Solger, Karl Wilhelm. "Über die *Wahlverwandtschaften*." First published in *Solger's nachgelassene Schriften und Briefwechsel*. Ed. Ludwig Tieck and Friedrich von Raumer. Vol. 1. Leipzig 1826: 175–85.

Stahl, E. L. "*Die Wahlverwandtschaften*." *Publications of the English Goethe Society* 15 (1946): 71–95.

Wiese, Benno von. "Goethes *Wahlverwandtschaften*." Vol. 6. Hamburg: Christian Wegner Verlag, 1951. Cited here from Wiese's *Der Mensch in der Dichtung: Studien zur deutschen und europäischen Literatur*. Düsseldorf: August Bagel Verlag, 1958.

Witte, Bernd. *Walter Benjamin: An Intellectual Biography*. Revised and enlarged English translation of *Walter Benjamin*. Reinbek bei Hamburg: Rowohlt Taschenbuch Verlag, 1985. Trans. James Rolleston. Detroit: Wayne State UP, 1991.

Wolin, Richard. *Walter Benjamin: An Aesthetics of Redemption*. New York: Columbia UP, 1982.

4: 1925–2000:
From Mann to the Millennium

THE LAST SEVENTY-FIVE YEARS HAVE SEEN an explosion of interest in *Die Wahlverwandtschaften*. Alongside the increased interest, however, new controversies have arisen over its interpretation. Before the Second World War, many scholars, such as Thomas Mann, still viewed the novel in highly moral terms. Goethe, too, still held his place as a nationalist icon who represented what was "best" in the German people. After the Second World War, however, many scholars challenged highly Christian and nationalistic interpretations. For them, the novel became the story of how society threatens and indeed crushes the individual spirit. Thus, whereas the majority of the commentators during the first 130 years tended to value the concerns (whether ethical, religious, or political) of society over those of the individual, those after the war emphasized the concerns of the individual over those of society. Ottilie therefore was neither a saint nor a home-wrecker but a tragic individual caught up in the daemonic forces around and within her (Hankamer, Viëtor). And although Ottilie certainly received the lion's share of critical attention, many commentators after the Second World War discussed the other characters and examined their relationships to society (Drake, Clark, Stopp, Barnes, Schelling-Schär). Several scholars from the East (Geerdts) and the West (Danckert, Helbig) also generalized the discussion of the characters to highlight the (irreconcilable) tensions between society and the individual.

Throughout this period, scholars also gradually stopped viewing Goethe as the main authority on the novel's interpretation. Although the full force of Benjamin's philosophy did not truly emerge in the scholarship until the late 1970s and 1980s, one may already note during the postwar period a move away from viewing the novel primarily in the light of Goethe's words and views. One of the major developments was Stöcklein's discussion of the narrator as an independent character. After this essay, scholars began to treat the narrator as a character who expresses his own opinions and prejudices, rather than Goethe's own.

In general, scholarship of the postwar period tended more and more toward the abstract. Instead of trying to uncover moral precepts, scholars attempted to unlock the clues of the novel's rich symbolism. These scholars were the first to broach such subjects as the intentional lack of closure, ambiguity, and multiplicity of meanings. And although many scholars throughout the twentieth century searched for the novel's pervasive idea (Schaeder; Stahl; Milfull; Nemec; Lillyman; Buschendorf; Adler, *Eine fast*), many more began to argue that the novel did not contain a single teaching at all, but contained several simultaneous, and at times contradictory, strands of argument (Hatfield, Staiger; cf. Miller, *Ariadne's*). By the 1980s, many scholars completely repudiated any search for meaning within the novel. For them, the complexity of *Die Wahlverwandtschaften* served primarily to illustrate the limitations of language itself.

It is, of course, difficult to characterize the scholarship of the last twenty years. *Die Wahlverwandtschaften* today enjoys tremendous scholarly popularity. Although general academic interest in Goethe has reached a low point, interest in *Die Wahlverwandtschaften* is probably higher than at any time since the period of its publication. In the late 1960s, several scholars lamented that the novel was not more widely known or appreciated in the English-speaking world (Barnes, *A Literary*). The last decades, however, have seen a steady growth in interest in the novel both here and abroad. Several prominent comparativists and theorists, including J. Hillis Miller and Tony Tanner, have examined it outside of a purely German context and thus expanded its scholarly audience. Today, one may also choose from several different English translations (Penguin, Princeton, and Oxford), and the noted Italian directors, the Taviani Brothers, have created a film adaptation, which is available with English subtitles. Of course, among Germanists the novel enjoys a special prominence. For example, in 1994 the British journal, *German Life and Letters,* devoted an entire volume to it. In many ways, this special volume gives an indication of how varied studies of the novel continue to be. *Die Wahlverwandtschaften* is examined there in terms of morality (Constantine), notions of identity (Stephenson, "Man nimmt"), computer-assisted analysis (Burgess), and comparative studies (Milne, Zecevic).

Because so many scholarly treatments of the novel are being published, it is difficult to judge which books and articles and which approaches will become central to future discussions. This difficulty is further compounded by the fact that recent interpretation on the novel are varied in approach: while some scholars attempt to forge new interpretive paths, others turn to more traditional ways of reading the novel, whether searching for a single, definitive interpretation or a moral teaching from the whole. Nevertheless, one might roughly divide the scholarship of the last few decades into three main groups: those that take discussions of Ottilie as their focal point; those that view the novel in light of recent literary theory; and those that view the novel in terms of its relationship to science and philosophy of science.

I: 1925–1945

Thomas Mann: Return to Tradition

Walter Benjamin's was not the only influential essay on *Die Wahlverwandtschaften* that was published in 1925. In that year, Thomas Mann published "Zu Goethe's *Wahlverwandtschaften*" ("Goethe, Novelist"). Unlike Benjamin's essay, which was in a sense rediscovered, Mann's essay has steadily influenced the reception since it was written. The main reasons behind the different early receptions of the two essays are obvious: (1) Mann's reputation as a writer brought several generation of readers to value his observations on other literary authors; (2) his essay is written for a general audience and is hence extremely accessible; and (3) he appeals to German pride and nationalism. Moreover, unlike Benjamin's essay, which was only recently translated into English (1996), Mann's essay was translated in 1933, only a few years after its original publication, and therefore could also enjoy a greater influence across the Atlantic. However, the differences in the recent valuation of the two essays are also obvious. While Mann no longer enjoys the same popularity as an author as he did even a generation ago, scholars throughout the humanities today read Benjamin's essay as an extremely important critical manifesto and precursor to postmodernism.

One of the most important differences between the two essays is that while Benjamin clearly has great respect for Goethe's artistry, he refuses to deify Goethe. Mann's essay, in contrast, fits very much into the tradition of the late nineteenth and early twentieth-century scholarship. He reads much of the novel through Goethe's own words on it, and he seeks to glorify Goethe as the patron saint of German art and virtue. Accordingly, he judges the novel to be both a great artistic achievement and highly moral. However, although much of Mann's essay is characteristic of earlier scholarship, his emphasis on polarities points to a more forward-looking trend. Beginning with Mann and continuing for several decades, many scholars turned to polarities to analyze various aspects of the novel, whether Vetter's discussion of gender, Reitz's analysis of Mittler as a symbol of polar mediation, Simon's portrayal of the dichotomy between responsibility and guilt, or Meessen's cataloguing of the polarities in the novel.

Mann's essay is openly and unabashedly a paean. He characterizes Goethe's novel as "ein Gebilde, so mondän wie deutsch, ein Wunderding an Geglücktheit und Reinheit der Komposition, an Reichtum der Beziehungen, Verknüpftheit, Geschlossenheit" [175; an achievement cosmopolitan as it is German, a marvel for its happy and chaste composition, its wealth of association and combination, its unity of effect: 100]. He further speaks of love for Goethe and of an obligation to help frame the readers' emotions after they have read *Die Wahlverwandtschaften*. After he offers panegyric praise of Goethe's writing style, he turns to discuss the specifics of the novel within a polar framework:

> Wir haben die Worte gebraucht, in denen die hohe Ausgewogenheit sich schon andeutet, die dem Werk seinen menschlichen Adel verleiht, und die wir hauptsächlich zur Sprache zu bringen wünschen: das Gleichgewicht von Sinnlichkeit und Sittlichkeit oder, künstlerisch gesprochen, von Plastik und Kritik, Unmittelbarkeit und Gedachtheit, in dem es schwebend ruht, und das auch mit jenem oft unbedacht gehandhabten Gegensatz von Dichter- und Schriftstellertum etwas zu schaffen hat, insofern dieser nur ein Name und Untername ist für den obersten, das Problem der Menschheit selbst aussprechenden Gegensatz von Natur und Freiheit. (177)

[What I have so far said is enough to indicate that quality in the novel which gives it its human nobility, and of which chiefly I speak: I refer to its exquisite balance. It seems to float poised between the senses and the moral — or, in the realm of aesthetics, between creation and critique, the spontaneous and the calculated. All this not quite without reference to that oft-cited, oft-abused antithesis between the man of letters and the creative artist, which, indeed, is but a phase of the larger antithesis between nature and freedom, commensurate with humanity itself. (102–3)]

Mann contrasts Goethe's use of nature and the intellect, the naive and the sentimental qualities within the work, the conflict between passion and morality, and the tension between Christian and pagan attributes. The latter polar grouping, however, is at the center of his essay. Like many of Goethe's earlier proponents, Mann argues that *Die Wahlverwandtschaften* is an ethical novel, but where previous scholars had maintained that the novel's ethical teaching is not at odds with a Christian society, Mann affirmatively argues that the novel represents the height of Christian theology.

Given Goethe's open and professed aversion to Christianity and the usual association of Goethe with neo-paganism, Mann has an uphill battle to make his point and does so via a circuitous route. He argues that Spinoza's teachings are essentially Christian, and since Goethe was a follower of Spinoza, Goethe's philosophy, too, must carry a Christian flavor. In particular, Mann argues that Goethe's concept of renunciation is not only Christian, but is particularly well-suited to elevate the German people. He tries to make the case that the novel is not simply a didactic work, but that Goethe wrote it with an "Instinktbefehl seiner besonderen nationalen Sendung, die eine wesentliche *sittigende* Sendung war" [181; instinctive compulsion of his special and national mission, which was essentially a civilizing one: 107–8]. Mann elaborates:

> Wir sprachen von einem Gefühl der Bundesgenossenschaft, das Goethe offenbar augenblicksweise im Angesichte des Christentums berührt habe. Worin bestand diese Bundesgenossenschaft und worauf bezog sie sich? Goethe neigt sich vor der "sittlichen Kultur" des Christentums, das heißt: vor seiner Humanität, seiner sittigend-antibarbarischen Tendenz. Es war die seine, und jene gelegentlichen Huldigungen entstammen ohne Zweifel der Einsicht in die Verwandtschaft der Sendung des Christentums innerhalb der völkisch-germanischen Welt mit seiner eigenen.

Hier, das ist: darin, daß er seine Aufgabe, seine nationale Beru-
fung als wesentlich zivilisatorisch begriff, liegt der tiefste und
deutscheste Sinn seiner "Entsagung." (181)

[I spoke of a sense of Christian fellowship which obviously at
moments came over Goethe. What was it, to what had it reference? Goethe bowed his head before the "ethical culture" of
Christianity; before its humanity, that is, its civilizing, anti-
barbaric spirit. It was his own. The homage he paid to it on occasion undoubtedly sprang from his insight into this truth; he as-
similated his own mission to that of Christianity within the
Germanic world. Here, then, in his conception of his life-task, his
national mission, as essentially a civilizing one, lies the profound-
est, the most Germanic meaning of his "renunciation." (108)]

For Mann, *Die Wahlverwandtschaften* is Goethe's most Christian work. To make his argument, he relies on the traditional
methodology of the nineteenth century. First, he turns to Goethe's
own words about the novel. In particular, he takes at face value
comments that might seem to be dripping with irony. Goethe
claims that he was not a heathen because he allowed Gretchen to
be condemned and Ottilie to starve to death: "ist denn das den
Leuten nicht christlich genug? Was wollen sie noch Christli-
cheres?" [is that then not Christian enough for the people? What
could they possibly want that is more Christian? (reported by
Varnhagen von Ense)].[1] Second, following the tradition of reading
Goethe's life into his works, Mann also turns to the love story with
Minna Herzlieb to explain the personal importance for Goethe of
renunciation in the novel. He therefore claims that Goethe was in
love with Ottilie because she stood for Herzlieb in his heart. And
just as Goethe had to renounce Herzlieb, so too was he forced to
kill Ottilie in the novel. Finally, Mann seeks to support his Christian view of the novel by arguing that Ottilie is truly a saint. While
he recognizes that many of Goethe's contemporaries were morally
offended by Ottilie's seeming saintly status, he nevertheless argues
in favor of it. He first turns to Goethe's autobiography to point to
Ottilie's connection to St. Odilie and then focuses upon Ottilie's
powers of renunciation:

Der Knabentraum des Studenten von der heiligen Odilie ver-
mischt sich mit der entsagenden Leidenschaft des Ergrauten für
ein junges Leben zum tragischen Gedicht, das beides feiert: die

Macht der Natur und die einer menschlichen Übernatur, die sich durch den Tod ihre Freiheit salviert. (185)

[The student's dream of the holy Odilie mingles with the resignation of the grey-haired lover to compose a tragic poem which celebrates alike the power of nature and of man, who is above nature and saves himself free through death. (114)]

Although Mann emphasized Christianity more than his predecessors, his ultimate interpretation of the novel was not that different from that of Goethe's earlier proponents. He still praises Ottilie's virtues as well as the morality of the whole and still views Goethe as a founding father of German civilization. Perhaps a more interesting aspect of his criticism — and certainly one that became more dominant in the following years — was his emphasis on the novel's polar aspects. However, while he turns to polarities primarily to address the novel's sense of balance, later critics would turn to polarities to highlight tensions and conflicts.

Focus on Polarities

One of the main sources for the growing interest in polarities in *Die Wahlverwandtschaften* is a work by Ewald Boucke, *Goethes Weltanschauung auf historischer Grundlage* (Goethe's Weltanschauung in Historical Context, 1907), which examines the importance of polarities in Goethe's writings generally. Several authors, including Reitz and Meessen, cite extensively from this book to set the framework for their own discussions. This new stress on dualistic and dynamic patterns signals a clear departure from reading the novel in moralistic terms and has enabled scholars to focus on more complex structures within the novel. And although the commentators of the 1930s did not go so far as to claim that the novel had no central message, their investigations nevertheless laid the groundwork for the future emphasis on the novel's ambiguity.

Of course, the ways in which scholars approached polarities in the 1930s differed from the way scholars viewed them in the 1980s. Whereas the scholars of the 1980s used polarities to argue for the self-contradictory and negating aspects of Goethe's works, the earlier scholars argued for the possibility of polar reconciliations and the role of mediators to bring these reconciliations about. Reitz is perhaps the best example for the earlier emphasis upon mediation and reconciliation. She begins her entire exposition with a quotation by Boucke that emphasizes Goethe's dynamic thought patterns — patterns that according to Boucke (413) included not only polar conflicts, but also polar synthesis and polar reconciliations. Reitz argues that Goethe embodied such syntheses in a string of characters that act as mediators throughout his fiction. Central to her discussion of all of these characters, and of Mittler in particular, is the notion of polarity. Mittler himself is thus seen as both an individual and a type (30), and where Mephistopheles desires to do evil, but does good, Mittler attempts to do good, but brings about misfortune (31).

Reitz's treatment of Mittler signals a new era of Mittler studies. Whereas the previous age more often than not took Mittler's words to represent the main teaching of the novel, Reitz's more critical approach to Mittler becomes the dominant one in the twentieth century. In particular, Reitz finds that his knowledge of human beings is limited (32), his rashness leads to disastrous results (31), his lack of tact limits his effectiveness (31), and his dogmatic views limit his ability to interact with the others (32). She does not, however, go so far as to discount Mittler's entire message. Although she emphasizes that his moral speeches are laced with irony, she nevertheless argues that Ottilie's death prevents one from completely dismissing his moral point of view (33).

Although polar dynamism is central to Reitz's view of the novel, her main focus remains limited to Mittler as a mediating figure. Other scholars of this period, however, examined the role of polarities more broadly. For example, a few years after Reitz's book, Meessen also turned to Boucke's characterization of polarities to interpret the novel. Meessen, however, uses polarities as a means of going beyond a moralistic interpretation. He sees the entire novel as a mystical game of the ever-changing polar relationships among the characters and argues that overarching this entire game is the greater polar conflict between love and marriage (1113). He quotes extensively from *Zur Farbenlehre* and strives to show that polarity is not a strict or reducible mathematical formula, but rather a fluid principle based upon the interactions of two opposing sides. Similarly, he does not divide the polar attributes of the characters into simplistic categories of good and bad, but instead concentrates on the dynamic nature of their interactions. Thus, Charlotte's calm, rational demeanor serves as a counterweight to Eduard's stormier one (1111), while the Captain's decisive, prudent, active personality serves to complete Eduard's more passionate, naive one (1111). Meessen also highlights the polar differences between the men and between the women (1113–15).

Meessen's exposition is thorough, and he does an excellent job in pointing out the numerous polar elements and in showing that the novel's very structure is based upon polarities. His article, however, remains largely a cataloguing of instances of polarity without discussing their philosophical or interpretive significance. His methodology — tracing one theme or aspect throughout the whole novel — is a growing trend of the time and one which Stopp characterizes as a "flat demonstration" ("Ein wahrer Narziss," 54).[2] As such, it marks a departure from reading the essay in biographical terms, but it still maintains a positivistic flavor. To a large extent, Meessen lists the facts without speculating as to their importance.

Although Stopp also characterizes Theodor Lockemann's essay, "Der Tod in Goethes *Wahlverwandtschaften*" (Death in Goethe's *Elective Affinities*, 1933), as a "flat demonstration," Lockemann's exposition in fact does not have the same positivistic flavor of Meessen's. Although written several years before Meessen's work, Lockemann's essay attempts to a much greater degree to interpret the significance of his findings rather than to list the various occurrences of death images.

Lockemann probes many of the individual death references of the novel, including Mittler's disclaimer against any association with the dead, the Captain's belief the baby's death is necessary for the happiness of the other characters, Eduard's departure for the wars as a means of placing his life on the line, the Architect's professed interest in graves and funeral monuments, and Charlotte's attempts to keep death at bay (163–67). In the process, he examines the central importance of polarities. At the center of his discussion is Ottilie (168). He juxtaposes her irrationality and mystical qualities against Mittler's highly rationalistic speeches, her self-sacrificing nature against Eduard's egotistical one, and her thoughtfulness against Luciane's superficiality. In particular, he argues for the significance of Ottilie's manner of death. Ottilie dies in an intensified state because she renounces the man she loves in order to support the moral order. She intentionally prepares herself to die with a higher ethical goal in mind. Eduard, in contrast, never reflects deeply upon death. Lockemann argues that Ottilie, who appears as a shadowy figure throughout much of the novel, becomes more and more "real" the closer she is to dying (168). Ottilie's death is not so much a representation of the inescapable end of life as a symbol of the possibility of striving toward the fulfillment of life (172).

Lockemann views Ottilie's renunciation as a moral act. His moral conclusions, however, rest upon the tradition of reading the novel in terms of Goethe's own relationship to renunciation than upon his discussion of the death images. His concluding remarks stress the biographical importance of renunciation in Goethe's advancing years. Although his moral reading of the essay is not that original, the essay as a whole was important to the reception history due to its emphasis on death symbols.

In a footnote, Lockemann indicates that he was unaware of Benjamin's article until after he had finished his own. He therefore notes only in passing the contrasting viewpoints and conclusions. Both Benjamin and Lockemann find numerous death images, but Benjamin focuses more on the symbolic images (such as mill, the lack of sunshine, etc.), while Lockemann provides a more extensive account of specific death references. Benjamin offers much more detailed analysis and many more theoretical insights than Lockemann. Lockemann's essay, nevertheless, initially had greater influence partly because, although Benjamin made the argument several years earlier, Lockemann made his case to a much larger audience, the readers of the *Jahrbuch der Goethegesellschaft* (Yearbook of the Goethe Society).

The Single Idea

The next important phase in the scholarly treatment of the novel was the search for the single, all-pervasive idea of which Goethe spoke to Eckermann (6 May 1827). This search marks a tendency in the scholarship to look for the philosophical, rather than the biographical or cultural influences upon the novel. In the process, the scholarship turned more and more to Goethe's other works. In other words, scholars of this period no longer attempted to situate the novel primarily in terms of Goethe's life experiences, but rather in terms of his main philosophical ideas.

Because the notion of the pervasive idea became such a prominent one in the literary discussions of the twentieth century (Hankamer, Stahl, Milfull, Nemec), it is instructive to see Goethe's remarks within their full context before discussing what commentators made of them. In his conversation with Eckermann, Goethe discourages the notion that he wrote his works of literature with a fixed philosophical concept in mind. He complains that people demand to know what the particular idea was behind certain compositions and explains:

Die Deutschen sind übrigens wunderliche Leute! — Sie machen sich durch ihre tiefen Gedanken und Ideen, die sie überall suchen und überall hineinlegen, das Leben schwerer als billig. — Ei! so habt doch endlich einmal die Courage, *Euch den Eindrücken hinzugeben,* Euch ergötzen zu lassen, Euch rühren zu lassen, Euch erheben zu lassen, ja Euch belehren und zu etwas Großem entflammen und ermutigen zu lassen; aber denkt nur nicht immer, es wäre Alles eitel, wenn es nicht irgend abstrakter Gedanke und Idee wäre!

Da kommen sie und fragen: welche Idee ich in meinem *Faust* zu verkörpern gesucht? — Als ob ich das selber wüßte und aussprechen könnte! — *Vom Himmel durch die Welt zur Hölle,* das wäre zur Not etwas; aber das ist keine Idee, sondern Gang der Handlung. Und ferner, daß der Teufel die Wette verliert, und daß ein aus schweren Verirrungen immerfort zum Besseren aufstrebender Mensch zu *erlösen* sei, das ist zwar ein wirksamer, Manches erklärender guter Gedanke, aber es ist keine *Idee,* die dem Ganzen und jeder einzelnen Szene im Besondern zu Grunde liege. Es hätte auch in der Tat ein schönes Ding werden müssen, wenn ich ein so reiches, buntes, und so höchst mannigfaltiges Leben, wie ich es im *Faust* zur Anschauung gebracht, auf die magere Schnur einer einzigen durchgehenden Idee hätte reihen wollen.

Es war im ganzen . . . nicht meine Art, als Poet nach Verkörperung von etwas *Abstraktem* zu streben. Ich empfing in meinem Innern *Eindrücke,* und zwar Eindrücke sinnlicher, lebensvoller, lieblicher, bunter, hundertfältiger Art, wie eine rege Einbildungskraft er mir darbot; und ich hatte als Poet weiter nichts zu tun, als solche Anschauungen und Eindrücke in mir künstlerisch zu runden und auszubilden und durch eine lebendige Darstellung so zum Vorschein zu bringen, daß Andere dieselbigen Eindrücke erhielten, wenn sie mein Dargestelltes hörten oder lasen.

Wollte ich jedoch einmal als Poet irgend eine Idee darstellen, so tat ich es in *kleinen* Gedichten, wo eine entschiedene Einheit herrschen konnte und welches zu übersehen war, wie zum Beispiel die Metamorphose der *Tiere,* die der *Pflanze,* das Gedicht *Vermächtnis,* und viele anderen. Das einzige Produkt von *größerem* Umfang, wo ich mir bewußt bin, nach Darstellung einer durchgreifenden Idee gearbeitet zu haben, wären etwa meine *Wahlverwandtschaften.* Der Roman ist dadurch für den Verstand faßlich geworden; aber ich will nicht sagen, daß er dadurch *besser* geworden wäre. Vielmehr bin ich der Meinung: *je inkommensurabeler und für den Verstand unfaßlicher eine poetische Produktion, desto besser.* (*FA* 2, 12:615–16; 6 May 1827)

[The Germans are, certainly, strange people. By their deep thoughts and ideas, which they seek in everything and fix upon everything, they make life much more burdensome than is necessary. Only have the courage to give yourself up to your impressions, allow yourself to be delighted, moved, elevated, nay instructed and inspired for something great; but do not imagine all is vanity, if it is not abstract thought and idea.

Then they come and ask, "What idea I meant to embody in my *Faust?*" as if I knew myself and could inform them. *From heaven, through the world, to hell* would indeed be something; but this is no idea, only a course of action. And further, that the devil loses the wager, and that a man, continually struggling from difficult errors towards something better, should be redeemed, is an effective, and to many, a good enlightening thought; but it is no idea which lies at the foundation of the whole, and of every individual scene. It would have been a fine thing, indeed, if I had strung so rich, varied, and highly diversified a life as I have brought to view in Faust upon the slender string of one pervading idea.

It was, in short . . . not in my line, as a poet, to strive to embody anything *abstract.* I received in my mind impressions, and those of a sensual, animated, charming, varied, hundredfold kind, just as a lively imagination presented them; and I had, as a poet, nothing more to do than artistically to round off and elaborate such views and impressions, and by means of a lively representation so to bring them forward that others might receive the same impression in hearing or reading my representation of them.

If I still wished, as a poet, to represent any idea, I would do
it in short poems, where a decided unity could prevail, and where
a complete survey would be easy, as, for instance in the "Metamorphosis of Animals," that of the plants, the poem "Bequest,"
and many others. The only production of greater extent, in
which I am conscious of having labored to set forth a pervading
idea, is probably my *Elective Affinities.* This novel has thus become comprehensible to the understanding; but I will not say
that it is therefore better. I am rather of the opinion that the
more incommensurable, and the more incomprehensible to the
understanding, a poetic production is, so much the better it is.
(Oxenford translation; 6 May 1827)]

It is ironic that Goethe's claim about the pervasive idea of *Die
Wahlverwandtschaften* comes within a conversation that generally
discourages searching for such ideas. His remarks signal an impa-
tience with a reading public that holds abstract ideas to be more
important than the emotional experience of reading the text itself.
Although some scholars, including Grete Schaeder ("Die Idee";
Gott und Welt), set the quotation in the context of Goethe's general disavowal of searching for such ideas, many subsequent scholars throughout the century do not. They turn to Goethe's
statement to justify reading the novel in terms of one concept or
idea. And while Goethe certainly opens the door for such exposi-
tions by claiming to have written the work according to a pervasive
idea, the context of the whole — even in the case of *Die Wahlverwandtschaften* — discourages such an exploration. One might also
take Goethean irony into account in interpreting this passage. That
he deems *Die Wahlverwandtschaften,* a work about which his readers could not even agree on its basic message and themes, as inferior because of its comprehensibility, should certainly give one
pause. In addition, one must consider the possibility of Goethean
irony in the claim that the novel was written with only one idea in
mind. Rather than seeing this novel as a simple, unified composition, most critics, even those negatively disposed towards it, have
categorized it as quite complex.

Schaeder's essay, "Die Idee der *Wahlverwandtschaften*" (The
Idea of the *Elective Affinities,* 1941) is one of the most important
early attempts to place the philosophy of the novel within the
greater context of Goethe's intellectual development. In other words,
whereas countless biographers attempted to situate the novel ac-

cording to specific events in Goethe's life, or where others, such as Walzel and François-Poncet, tried to show the possible historical and social influences upon the novel, Schaeder attempts to situate the novel within the context of Goethe's philosophical ideas. Specifically, she turns to Goethe's natural philosophy, especially in light of Spinoza's influence upon his thought, to discuss the philosophical meaning of the novel as a whole. However, Schaeder does not make a complete break from reading the novel in a moral light because she ultimately links Goethe's natural philosophy with Christian ideals.

Schaeder argues throughout her article as well as her book that Goethe had a very religious conception of the world: God and nature are one in the same in that both are the source of creation and creativity. She therefore stresses the importance of Goethe's natural studies and his concept of natural law as a key to unlock the kingdom of art (*Gott und Welt,* 130, 153–60). Thus, she grounds much of her interpretation of *Die Wahlverwandtschaften* upon principles found in Goethe's scientific works. She argues that Goethe's nature studies, as well as *Die Wahlverwandtschaften* and much of his poetry, are attempts to recognize the language of God within nature and to reconcile the two poles of God and the world (*Gott und Welt,* 7–9).

Schaeder begins her essay ("Die Idee") by quoting Goethe's statements to Eckermann (6 May 1827) and then attempts to define what Goethe meant by the term "idea." Although Goethe attributes to the general reading public the desire to find the "idea" underlying the whole of his individual works, Schaeder claims that he is not using the word in a common way. Rather, he uses it in the sense of the Platonic ideal, namely the way he and Schiller would use it to signify a kind of archetype, the coherence of the whole, or that which determined how the various parts formed a whole ("Die Idee," 182).

Schaeder's particular interpretation of the term "idea" rests largely upon her idealization of Goethe's science. Whereas Goethe turned to archetypes as consciously artificial constructs that enabled the study of natural organisms which were constantly in flux,[3] Schaeder interprets these archetypes as akin to Platonic ideas. Because she views Goethe's concept of archetypes as part of the tradition of Platonic Idealism, she tends to emphasize the static and hierarchical aspects of his science. In the process, she ignores the subversive aspects of his scientific theories, which in large part challenge the Greek views of static natural law. Thus, whereas Goethe's science was Romantic in the sense that it sought to challenge an ordered and patterned view of the world, she stresses the ordered aspects of nature in Goethe's natural philosophy. Her idealization of his scientific works, moreover, corresponds to her attempt to read the novel in moral terms. She wishes to ground a moral view of the world, as the ancient Greeks had done in their natural philosophy, on an understanding of the workings of nature. Her perspective, however, is more religious than philosophical. She argues in her book that Goethe's nature studies are not an attempt to ground a natural philosophy, but rather that they have a religious and moral purpose.

In turning to *Die Wahlverwandtschaften*, Schaeder builds up to this position by first linking the novel to the natural scientific poems that Goethe mentions alongside his novel as containing a pervasive idea, "Die Metamorphose der Tiere" (The Metamorphosis of Animals, 1806) and "Die Metamorphose der Pflanzen (The Metamorphosis of Plants, 1798). She then categorizes these works as dialogues between the scientific researcher and the poet (183). The scientist provides the archetypal phenomena from which the poet builds the context of the visible and the invisible worlds (183). In order to discover the archetypal phenomenon underlying *Die Wahlverwandtschaften*, Schaeder accordingly turns to several of Goethe's scientific works. She argues that the archetypal phenomenon is to the scientist what the symbol is to the poet: both signify the cleft between idea and experience. She places two archetypal phenomenon at the center of the discussion, polarity and intensification, and argues that just as colors arise through the interactions of light and darkness in the *Farbenlehre,* so too does the human soul form through its interactions with polar forces. She contends that for Goethe the concept of morality arises from the same principle that governs the organ of the eye: an organ that not only reacts to polar phenomena, but one that is able to create its own polar phenomena. The eye seeks to create a totality and harmony for itself by producing complementary colors. (For example, if the eye stares at a green object for a given time, it will produce an after-image of the complementary color of red). Similarly, human beings attempt to fashion a harmony for themselves by creating moral laws (195–96).

Although Schaeder grounds Goethean morality in natural principles, her conclusions echo those of Mann. She contends that no other work by Goethe comes so close to Christian doctrines ("Die Idee," 201; *Gott und Welt,* 299). She therefore also takes at face value Goethe's denial that he was a heathen because he killed off Gretchen and Ottilie (*Gott und Welt,* 299). She cites the quotation as proof of Goethe's morality and as evidence against those readers who "misinterpreted" Goethe's efforts to teach by negative example (*Gott und Welt,* 299). Therefore, despite her attempts to base a new reading of the novel on Goethe's natural philosophy, her conclusion agrees with the earlier moralistic readers. Ottilie, for Schaeder, as for many of those commentators who argue for the morality of the novel, becomes a heroic figure — a figure that symbolizes the triumph of morality over nature.

Schaeder's approach is echoed throughout much of the criticism of the time. E. L. Stahl's 1946 article "*Die Wahlverwandtschaften*" similarly looks for the pervasive idea of the whole (71) and emphasizes a moral interpretation. His approach, however, represents more of a transition to the next scholarly phase. Although he emphasizes certain traditional moral readings, he nevertheless rejects viewing the novel primarily as a didactic work. Instead, he reads it as the story of one tragic individual, Ottilie, as she faces an internal and highly personal battle between inclination and duty (80–81). In choosing to die, she "proves her resolution not to submit to the inimical power of fate" (84). This slight switch in emphasis — from reading the novel as a social commentary to reading it as the story of one individual — is characteristic of many articles written after the Second World War as commentators became increasingly uncomfortable with making pronouncements based upon societal values.

Paul Hankamer's book, *Spiel der Mächte* (1943), shows an even greater discomfort with reading the novel in terms of a moral teaching. Hankamer's work shares several common characteristics with Schaeder's. He searches for the pervasive idea and links it to Goethe's concept of the archetypal phenomena found in his scientific works (209–16, 276). Hankamer's influential book, however, takes several new interpretive turns. Most importantly, he rejects the notion that the central concept of the book addresses Christian morality. Instead, he argues that Goethe's concept of the daemonic is at its heart.[4] Ottilie therefore becomes a tragic figure not because she seeks to uphold the Christian belief in the sanctity of marriage, but because the daemonic forces in her own life, which can never be overcome, drive her to suicide. He thus disputes that the novel addresses social criticism at all. Ottilie's renunciation is not Christian, but highly personal. She acts according to an oath that she made with herself (288, 317): "Sie opfert ihr Leben, um lieben zu dürfen, ohne sich als geistpersönliches Wesen aufgeben zu müssen" (289) [She sacrifices her life, in order to be allowed to love, without having to give herself up as a spiritually personal being]. Her sacrifice, her act of renunciation, only applies to this life. She keeps her promise to herself by committing suicide. She does not, however, give up her love for Eduard (317), which the narrator implies will continue into the next life.

Hankamer's essay was also influential for several other reasons besides this emphasis on the daemonic. In particular, it laid the groundwork for the reevaluation of the role of the narrator. Although Hankamer at times still equates the narrator with Goethe and does not treat him as a separate character to the extent that Stöcklein does a few years later in 1949, he nevertheless highlights the narrator's ironic stance. In addition, Hankamer frequently asks his reader to reassesses commonly held truths about the novel. For example, he reconsiders the general tendency to condemn Eduard's character and questions the nineteenth century's unqualified praise for Charlotte and the Captain's moral uprightness (248).

II: 1945–1970

Postwar Approaches

Interest in *Die Wahlverwandtschaften* grew tremendously in both the U.S. and Europe during the postwar period. Many of the scholars that would become influential throughout the rest of the twentieth century in Germanic studies wrote on the novel, including Karl Maurer, Henry Hatfield, Paul Stöcklein, Karl Viëtor, Benno von Wiese, and Victor Lange. And while many of the topics remained the same — the issue of morality, the role of the polarity, the connection between Goethe's life and the novel — the tone of much of the postwar scholarship changed: it became much less moralistic and began to emphasize more and more the novel's ironies. Postwar scholars stressed its moral ambiguities and the difficulties that its structure and symbols posed for interpretation. They thus rejected the "one idea" approach and turned instead to the richness of Goethe's varied uses of symbolism. In their works, one begins to see the seeds of postmodern interpretations that examine the novel in terms of its contradictory symbols and lines of argument. And although many of the scholars, such as Schaeder (*Gott und Welt*), still highly revered Goethe and looked to his works for spiritual guidance, it was no longer assumed that Goethe was a German demigod. Many of the German authors show a new distance to their national poet. *Die Wahlverwandtschaften* was therefore no longer touted as a didactic or moral (or for that matter, an immoral) text, but rather as a complex aesthetic object.

One of the most influential articles of this period was Henry C. Hatfield's "Towards the Interpretation of *Die Wahlverwandtschaften*" (1948). Hatfield seems to follow a more traditional line of scholarship when he argues that moral questions are at the center of the book. However, he does not assume that we ought to embrace the morality of the novel or even conversely to condemn it. Instead, he contends that *Die Wahlverwandtschaften* contains neither an absolute defense of marriage nor a philosophical attack on it. Indeed, one of the essay's main contributions is its attempt to explain the controversial reception of the novel. He thus takes the modern step of examining the reader's role in determining a particular interpretation: "when a reader's moral and religious convictions are involved, he is not likely to be an objective judge" (104). Several generations of readers, according to Hatfield, had let their emotions get carried away. Although he tends to side more with those who see a moral teaching (largely because this kind of reading seemed to have been endorsed by Goethe), he warns that "certain friendly interpreters, in forcing Goethe's work into an over-didactic mold, are [as] guilty of . . . narrow moralizing" as those who wish to condemn the novel as immoral (105).

Although Hatfield does not completely depart from the earlier tradition in that he still supports his claims by turning to biographical facts (in particular Goethe's attraction to Herzlieb), he nonetheless paints a much more complex and rich image of the novel's morality than either those who condemned it or those who praised it.[5] Hatfield points to the very end of the novel, the promise of a reunion between Eduard and Ottilie, as evidence that the moral law of marriage does not ultimately triumph. Rather, it is the affinity that triumphs (112). Hatfield compares the novel's ending to the fate of Francesca and Paolo in Dante's *Divine Comedy*. In Dante's more Christian world, the fate of the adulterous lovers is a moving one. Nevertheless, it is still quite clear that "they are in hell, and in hell they will remain" (113). Goethe's world is quite different. As the novel draws to a close, one feels more and more sympathy for Ottilie and Eduard until one is glad that they triumph in the next world. Ottilie then acts as Gretchen does at the end of *Faust,* by drawing "Eduard upward into a realm where the bond between him and Charlotte no longer has any significance" (113). The social law of marriage is important to Goethe, but only on earth (114). It is therefore fitting that Ottilie and Eduard are punished in this life for overstepping the rules of the world. The moral rules, however, only apply to the here and now. Different laws will triumph in the next life where Eduard and Ottilie are promised a life together. Thus, love, and not morality, wins the final battle and the war. Hatfield explains:

> Goethe's position in *Die Wahlverwandtschaften* is not neutral: there are value judgments. It is not amoral: traditional norms of conduct in society are upheld, and deviation from them, even in thought, is rigorously punished. Yet, as the ending shows, it is not a glorification of marriage or of the ordinary code as such. The bond between Eduard and Charlotte dissolves into insignificance. Still less is it Christian: a passion condemned by the Church is glorified. Goethe's point of view is deeply moral, according to his own standards, but these are not the standards of many of his critics, friendly or otherwise. (114)

Finally, although Hatfield does not quote Benjamin, his essay reflects a tendency away from endorsing a single "correct" interpretation of the novel. Because interpretations will change as times change, one must constantly reevaluate works of literature. And despite Hatfield's own reliance upon biographical materials, he demands that readers not take any author's comments about his or her work at face value. Like Benjamin, Hatfield argues that the author may simply be unaware of forces in his or her own mind and therefore be unable to speak about them or even realize them (106).

Another very influential study that appeared around the same time as Hatfield's was Paul Stöcklein's "Stil und Sinn der *Wahlverwandtschaften*" (Style and Meaning of *Elective Affinities*, 1949). Stöcklein's major contribution to the history of the novel's reception is his treatment of the narrator as an independent character. Of secondary interpretative importance, but perhaps of much more historical relevance, is his subtle comparison of the characteristics of the Nazis and the German Romantics. He is one of the few scholars of this time who even broaches the topic of Germany's recent past within a commentary on *Die Wahlverwandtschaften*. (Suhrkamp is another notable exception.) Stöcklein argues, as many had previously done, that the novel was an attack on the Romantics. However, he also implicitly links the negative qualities of the Romantics with the characteristics that enabled the rise of the National Socialists in Germany.

Barnes (*A Literary*) notes that Stöcklein "was the first critic to take the function of the narrator seriously and to assess its effect on the novel" (24). Whereas earlier scholars often equated the narrator with Goethe, Stöcklein takes the narrator as a distinct character equal in importance to the four major ones. Stöcklein views the narrator with such importance because he sets the anti-Romantic tone and, most importantly, exposes and creates ironies throughout the whole story. For example, the narrator intentionally misnames both Mittler and Luciane to call attention to their true characters. Mittler is no mediator (as his attempts at mediation fail miserably), while Luciane is no illuminator, but instead brings about chaos and confusion.

Although Stöcklein sometimes takes his idea of an independent narrator to extremes (he even gives a conjectural physical sketch of the narrator and speculates that he is the Englishman's companion: 8–9, 10), his treatment of the narrator as a cool, calculating character with his own agenda did open up new directions of interpretation. First, it gave the critic a new tool with which to distance Goethe's personal voice from that of the novel. Critics began to speak of the narrator's motives and perspectives apart from Goethe's personal ones. Second, it brought a new interest in ironies in the novel, which in turn encouraged interpretations that were not centered around moral or religious issues. Third, it enabled a new appreciation for the complexity of the novel and, with it, a reassessment of the interactions among all of the characters.

Stöcklein's arguments about Goethe's anti-Romantic message, however, are more dogmatic and seem to stem from his condemnation of the National Socialists (Barnes, *A Literary*, 24; Lillyman, "Affinity," 59). He links Eduard's and Ottilie's "Romantic" flaws to characteristic traits of the followers of National Socialism. Instead of attempting to overcome their "lower," passionate natures through their "higher," rational selves, Ottilie and Eduard worship their desires and attempt to elevate them over their higher nature (31). Stöcklein also compares Eduard's and Ottilie's eroticism to the Romantic feeling for nature. He argues, for example, that Eduard's Romantic eros blinds him to the power of inner drives. Eduard, accordingly, becomes particularly enslaved by this drive because he believes himself to be free (21–22). Ottilie, too, is "sick" in her relationship to nature, and it is this relationship that ultimately leads to her death drive (30–31). Furthermore, her relationship to nature leads to a loss of individuality, which Stöcklein relates to attempts to lose oneself within a larger group, whether the army, the nation, or another community (33). Similarly, Eduard's and Ottilie's propensity toward imitation signals for Stöcklein their lack of rational, individual purpose and marks them for a path toward death (51–52). Stöcklein is particularly critical of Eduard, who often does not act on his own but according to the suggestions of others.

In contrast to his treatment of the narrator, Stöcklein's discussion of the novel's morality is traditional. He argues that the novel is a defense of the humanistic morality found within Christianity and the Platonic dialogues. He dismisses the entire chemical conversation of the novel as frivolous (27) because human beings are neither totally free creatures raised above the elements (that Charlotte holds them to be) nor completely determined beings ruled by the outside forces of nature. Instead, he argues along Platonic lines that the physical (or necessitous) and spiritual sides of human beings ideally ought to work together in harmony (28). And, like Thomas Mann, he concludes that the ultimate message is a moral one based upon Christian notions of adultery. The night of spiritual adultery, accordingly, is cited as evidence that committing adultery in one's heart is just as bad as the physical act (30).

Stöcklein's moral reading of the novel in many ways is uncharacteristic of the period. For the most part, scholars were breaking away from strict moral interpretations. Karl Viëtor's chapter on *Die Wahlverwandtschaften* in his book on Goethe (1949) is much more typical of postwar treatments. Instead of focusing upon morality, Viëtor concentrates upon the novel's tragic aspects and its dark, gloomy, mournful qualities. He argues that the novel does not expound a moral teaching, but rather displays nature's power over human beings. It illustrates the consequences of the belief that human beings are more free than they actually are, while the chemical theory displays the power of natural forces. Within this context, Viëtor stresses Ottilie's close connection to nature, as evidenced by her magnetism and her ability to divine metals underground, and argues that she feels the pull of nature more acutely than the other characters. She becomes a tragic heroine for Viëtor much in the same way as for Hankamer. Her triumph is personal and not designed to uphold a particular religious belief or societal rule.

Peter Suhrkamp's essay, "Goethes *Wahlverwandtschaften*," continues the pessimistic tone of many of the postwar writers. His disillusionment with societal forces is quite strong and is not surprising, considering that he wrote it in 1944 while a political prisoner. He tells us that his only "company" during his imprisonment was the volume of Goethe's works containing *Die Wahlverwandtschaften,* and he describes how its characters practically became the guests in his small cell (193). His opinion of his "guests" (with the exception of Ottilie) and the society that they represent is negative. He repeatedly draws parallels between the problems of his contemporary society and those in the novel. He finds the characters, as representatives of the upper classes, to be self-involved, inconstant, contradictory, and shallow. They represent for him the characteristics of his own age, of the "Zeitalter der Massen" [age of the masses], because they have lost their connection to nature, and with it, their ability to love. He points to the very first conversation between Charlotte and Eduard as indicative of how little trust there is among human beings. This conversation becomes for Suhrkamp representative of the state of society throughout the work, a society in which "Offenherzigkeit, Wohlwollen, Güte, freundschaftlicher Frohsinn, gegründetes freundliches Behagen" (196) [forthrightness, good will, goodness, friendly good humor, pleasure grounded in friendliness] are missing. He particularly criticizes the characters for their lack of productive activity.

Suhrkamp, like Stöcklein, discusses the novel's use of irony. However, Suhrkamp takes the term in its more colloquial sense to connote something humorous. He argues that Goethe uses irony to poke fun at the upper classes. For example, he views the ending of the novel as an indictment against society:

> Ist das Ende des Romans nicht doch pessimistisch? Ja — im Urteil über die Gesellschaft, die Klasse. Als hätte Goethe den heutigen Weltzustand vorausgesehen. Und diese Ironie: eine Gesellschaft, die zum Gehalt ihres Lebens die Zivilisation gemacht, sie auf ihren Hausaltar gestellt hat, betreibt den Zusammenbruch der Zivilisation! (212)

> [Is the ending of the novel thus not pessimistic? Yes, in the judgment of society, of class. It is as if Goethe had foreseen the current world condition. And this irony: a society that made civilization into the substance of its life, placed it on its private altar, pursues the collapse of civilization!]

Suhrkamp thus sees its style as highly modern and not classical. He cites the first line of the novel as evidence that one here hears the voice of a modern author, though the novel lacks the full pessimism and skepticism characteristic of truly modern works (203). What keeps it from sliding into a totally pessimistic world is the character of Ottilie. Suhrkamp individualizes the idea of morality and concentrates upon Ottilie's, rather than Goethe's own, morality. Her renunciations are not for the good of society or for the defense of any particular value. Rather, they are Ottilie's attempt, as an individual, to be true to herself, to her "path," from which she has strayed.

Symbolic Interpretations

The next major change in the scholarly approach to *Die Wahlverwandtschaften* involved an even greater departure from examining the novel either in terms of morality or a single, pervasive idea. In the 1950s and 1960s, many scholars began writing about the ambiguity and complexity of *Die Wahlverwandtschaften* (Wiese, Lange, Staiger; Barnes, *A Literary*). Although not Freudian in their methodology (and, while Wiese even overtly distanced himself from psychological approaches),[6] their emphasis upon the importance of symbols was certainly largely influenced by Freud and his followers. In addition, while postmodern interpretations are today credited with discovering the contradictory strands of structure and meaning within the text, scholars of *Die Wahlverwandtschaften* during this time also addressed such issues. Of course, many other aspects of their criticism, including their reverence for Goethe, their idealization of Ottilie, and their discussions of philosophical ideals, remained quite traditional. Nevertheless, it is striking that during this period, which is commonly assumed to be the most deeply rooted in canonical and hierarchical ideals, the predominant approach was to question, at least within the context of *Die Wahlverwandtschaften,* single, unified interpretations as well as didactic approaches that emphasized traditional, societal norms.

Benno von Wiese's essay, "Goethes *Wahlverwandtschaften*" (1951), has exerted and indeed continues to exert a great deal of influence in interpreting the novel according to its symbols. His essay was first published as a part of an appendix in what is even today one of the standard and most popular editions of Goethe's collected works, the Hamburg edition. One may still read his essay in the thirteenth edition (1993) of these works. Thus his essay is often one of the first pieces of scholarship that many readers encounter and has served as a general introduction to generations of readers.

Wiese's essay shares with other postwar critics a refusal to reduce the novel to a moral tale. In his view it defends neither adultery nor marriage. Instead, he emphasizes the complexity of its symbols and follows Benjamin in drawing attention to the numerous symbolic references to death (121). Wiese begins by arguing that *Die Wahlverwandtschaften* is a modern novel. He finds it modern, however, not because it is psychological, but because of its symbolic style. Given the frequency of symbols, however, he warns against a too simplistic or literal reading of them. For example, he rejects any interpretation of the chemical theory that reduces human actions to necessity. Unlike Freud, and perhaps in an effort to refute psychological interpretations, Wiese stresses the philosophical notion of human freedom. One cannot directly apply the chemical theory to human beings because human beings are free, and elements only appear to be so (114). He even sees Ottilie and Eduard's relationship as being outside the sphere of necessity (116) and argues that Goethe never equates love with a necessitous drive (Trieb) in his works.

Emil Staiger, too, in his influential book, *Goethe* (1956), concentrates upon the symbolic complexity of the novel. He emphasizes how the novel constantly raises questions and presents one opinion only to undermine it later. Goethe's use of numerous symbols, accordingly, serves both to draw the reader in and to keep him or her at a distance. The end effect of the novel is not to teach a particular moral message but to make the reader uncomfortable. Charlotte's rearrangement of the cemetery, the inability of the characters to avoid the very accidents against which they have tried to prepare themselves (such as drowning), and the conflicting statements about marriage (480–82) are meant to unsettle the reader. One cannot derive a moral teaching from the whole, Staiger argues, because Goethe intended to leave such issues open. However, Staiger also rejects a moral interpretation, arguing that the novel is not about marriage per se, but about a particular marriage, Charlotte and Eduard's (483). If there is a teaching, it is that each person creates his or her own fate. Eduard, for example, brings about many of the problems due to his insistence: Charlotte did not want to marry him, but his insistence made her acquiesce; his further insistence to invite the Captain, leads to Ottilie's invitation, which in turn leads to the events that follow.

Staiger often turns to polarities to demonstrate the novel's numerous ambiguities. He cites Goethe's conflicting opinions of Eduard (that he could not bear him and that he admired his capacity to love) as a prime example of the conflicting strains that are representative of the novel. Such statements, according to Staiger, do not cancel each other out or contradict each other. Rather, each reflects a different aspect of Eduard's character as seen from a different perspective (485–86). Staiger further describes how the main polar conflict of the novel, that between nature and society, reaches its climax in the birth of the baby. On the one hand, the birth should be an argument that Eduard and Charlotte should stay together. On the other hand, however, this baby's appearance makes exactly the opposite argument (496). To Staiger, this irreconcilable conflict signals Goethe's ambivalent treatment of important issues throughout the novel. Staiger's openness on such key issues as the role of marriage in society in some ways anticipates the postmodern readings at the end of the century. For Staiger, as for many of the later scholars, *Die Wahlverwandtschaften* is not a book that contains closure or straightforward teachings.

In many other ways, however, Staiger's analysis is quite traditional. Although he largely rejects the tactic of the earlier proponents who praised the novel for its moral qualities, he nevertheless returns to earlier modes of interpretation in his excessive praise of Goethe and his use of details from Goethe's life as an interpretive tool. For example, he begins the chapter on *Wahlverwandtschaften* by commenting upon Goethe's body build and cites a panegyric letter written by one of Goethe's contemporaries, who writes of Goethe's handsomeness and perfect figure, his beautiful hands, and his Jupiter-like forehead, lips, and eyes (476). This is the image, according to Staiger, that we usually have of Goethe — an image that is the object of "Verehrung" [veneration]. He further claims a connection between Goethe's appearance at this time (he had lost weight) and his literary production: it made him younger (476).

Staiger, however, most closely follows traditional scholarship in his treatment of Ottilie. Like Gundolf, he emphasizes her plant-like qualities (488–91) and like Hárnik, he also discusses the psychological significance of her locket (494). Like many of those who defended Goethe's novel against the charges of immorality, Staiger treats Ottilie as an unconscious innocent. Moreover, he believes that she contains the qualities that Goethe praised in women. She remains always the same, "wie eine Pflanze, die weiche Luft umspielt" (491) [like a plant, which plays around in the soft air].

Staiger ends his chapter by posing the question asked by many scholars of the time. What was Goethe's relationship to the Romantics? How is one to interpret Goethe's use of such Romantic elements as saints, angels, Nazarene images, and pseudo-scientific experiments (509–10)? Staiger argues that while the novel contains Romantic elements, especially its propensity to elevate everyday events and its emphasis on interiority, it is not itself a Romantic piece (512–13). He explains that the main difference is Goethe's handling of the everyday. Despite such events as the baby's appearance, Staiger argues that Goethe's novel is much more realistic than Romantic texts, "daß er bei aller Vergeistigung und Beseelung ganz realistisch bleibt und keine Unwahrscheinlichkeit zuläßt" (513–14) [that it remains realistic throughout all the spiritualization and soulfulness and never allows a single improbability]. Staiger further argues that Romantic elements are present in the novel because they were present in society during the time of its composition.

Wiese's and Staiger's emphases upon symbolic interpretations were soon challenged. Although F. J. Stopp in both of his articles from the early 1960s continues the postwar focus on the novel's complexity, he is critical of the recent studies that examine the novel's symbols. Stopp seems uncomfortable with studies that seek to distance the novel from particular messages or teachings. In particular, he is afraid that the new school of interpretation ignores the novel's message on human freedom. He especially criticizes Lockemann, Meessen, Clark, and Wiese because he believes that their emphasis on the role of symbols poses "a positive danger that such language may pre-judge the role of free will in the work" ("Ein wahrer Narziss" 55). Similarly, he also criticizes Hankamer's discussion of the daemonic as placing too little emphasis on the role rational causality plays in the novel (56). To avoid the "mistakes" of earlier critics and to add another dimension to the study of the novel, Stopp in his own works ties the novel's symbols to particular teachings. His work therefore illustrates a growing tension in *Wahlverwandtschaften* studies. On the one hand, studies of this period show a greater propensity to address the complexities and the ambiguities of the novel. On the other hand, some critics show a reluctance to abandon the search for particular morals or teachings within its pages.

The Analysis of Structure

Although most of the postwar scholarly treatments concentrate upon analyzing symbols, a different sort of scholarship was also fairly prevalent, especially in Germany. Scholars such as Hans M. Wolff, Hennig Brinkmann, and to a somewhat lesser extent Kurt May centered their analyses on the structural and linguistic aspects of the novel. In many ways, this approach was like nineteenth-century positivism in that it strove to base analysis on factual data.

These scholars differed from more straightforward positivistic approaches, however, in that they attempted to use this more "hard" evidence to support particular theoretical conjectures.

One of the more controversial attempts to examine the language and background materials was Wolff's 1952 book, *Goethe in der Periode der Wahlverwandtschaften (1802–1809)* (Goethe During the Period of the *Elective Affinities,* 1802–1809). Here Wolff argues that it is possible to reconstruct the novella upon which *Die Wahlverwandtschaften* is based (i.e., the one that Goethe initially intended to include in his *Wilhelm Meister* novel) and that this reconstruction is essential to understanding the novel. He concludes from his research that Goethe's ethical views changed drastically from the time he started working on the novella to when he turned it into a finished novel. The basic problem with Wolff's approach, of course, is that Goethe did not leave behind an actual manuscript of the earlier novella. Wolff's conjectures on the earlier novella therefore rely upon diary entries and letters as well as a careful reading of the novel. He argues that a close analysis of the text of *Die Wahlverwandtschaften* illuminates inconsistencies that point to an earlier version with a different perspective. Wolff then followed up this attempt with his 1955 book, *Goethes "Novelle" Die Wahlverwandtschaften: Ein Rekonstruktionsversuch* (Goethe's "Novella" *The Elective Affinities:* A Reconstruction Attempt). There, he publishes what he believes to be the original "condensed" version of the novel, the novella "version" that existed before Goethe lengthened it into a novel.[7]

Wolff's studies set off a lively debate. Hans Jaeger's 1959 article, "Goethe's 'Novelle' *Die Wahlverwandtschaften?*," thoroughly criticizes Wolff's conclusions.[8] What is striking about Jaeger's criticisms, however, is that he does not so much question the endeavor itself as Wolff's conclusions. Thus, Jaeger himself engages in his own reconstruction attempts. Jaeger first questions many of the "discrepancies" that lead Wolff to excise so much of the text. He then challenges some of the new interpretations that Wolff is forced to develop in the face of so much missing text. He finds Wolff's analysis of the novel's ending to be particularly problematic. Ottilie's guilt no longer derives from her part in the child's death, but rather from having slept with Eduard. Jaeger argues:

Who can conceive a night of love with Ottilie not saying a single word and, under these circumstances, continuing her silence until her death except for the writing of a letter? Wolff had to keep both her silence and her letter, of course, since Goethe mentions the letter in his diary . . . Nor does Ottilie's subsequent behavior toward Eduard indicate a feeling of guilt as we might expect it after an illicit, adulterous night of love. . . . Wolff . . . had to leave a gap where the novel describes Ottilie's death, because her death too could not be motivated in the same way as in the final version. Thus, instead of eliminating discrepancies, the large cut has created new difficulties, above all the dilemma that the concluding two and a half chapters no longer fit. (17–18)

Jaeger also disputes that the earlier novella differed greatly from the final product. He refers extensively to the outlines that Goethe used when writing the novel to demonstrate that "the first draft must have been the same as that of the second version" (27).

Although several scholars of the period (Jaeger, Geerdts, Danckert) reacted to Wolff's studies, Wolff's rather creative and far-fetched approach did not have a lasting influence. Scholars were quick to dismiss his second book, and his first book is probably best remembered and cited for his suggestion that Silvie von Ziegesar (and not Minna Herzlieb) is the novel's inspiration.

The Individual Versus Society

Following the postwar trend, several scholars of the 1960s and 1970s wrote studies on the conflict between individuals and society. While this approach may sound reminiscent of the earliest critics who juxtaposed the concerns of duty and passion, the emphasis in this later criticism was quite different. Indeed, one can judge the vast change in values by contrasting the approaches of both ages. Goethe's earliest critics and proponents judged the novel in terms of whether it supported or undermined the social institution of marriage. Commentators during the latter part of the twentieth century valued the concerns of the individual above those of society and indeed viewed society itself with greater suspicion. For example, Hans Jürgen Geerdts emphasizes the negative influences of society upon the individual. While this approach is perhaps not surprising given the author's Marxist perspective, several scholars from the West, including Danckert and Helbig also reexamine the conflicts between the individual and society.[9]

Werner Danckert's book, *Offenes und geschlossenes Leben: Zwei Daseinsaspekte in Goethes Weltschau* (Open and Closed Life: Two Aspects of Being in Goethe's Worldview, 1963), analyzes the individual's relation to society. Although he discusses numerous aspects of polarities within *Die Wahlverwandtschaften*, Danckert, as his title indicates, concentrates especially upon polarities associated with openness (of the individual) and closedness (of society). Like Staiger, he views the numerous symbols within the book as both opening and closing the possibility of meaning (54). Danckert argues that Goethe would never have spoken about hidden meanings and secrets within his novel if, in the end, it had a simple, moralistic message (72). Thus, he contends that the character Mittler clearly does not speak in Goethe's voice or bear the moral message of the whole. Instead he is so grotesque (cf. Staiger 483) that Goethe could never have intended his words to be taken seriously (98). He is similarly critical of Charlotte, who represents the negative side of "closed" society: she believes herself to act reasonably, but in reality acts without instinct (100).

For Danckert, the main conflict of the novel is between "open" nature (symbolized especially by the power of Ottilie's love) and "closed" society (symbolized by laws and conventions). The entire novel is thus characterized as the pulse between these two forces. He takes, for example, Charlotte and the School Master's discussion about opening up walled gardens as representative of the conflict between open and protected spaces (21, 75). This example becomes but one of many that symbolize the dynamic movement from one polar extreme to another (73).

Central to Danckert's discussion is the symbolic importance of Ottilie, who represents for him the tragic aspects of the individual's irreconcilable conflict with society (129). The power of her individual eros (that which he characterizes as open) remains in stark conflict with the forces of convention (or those forces that he characterizes as closed). He draws parallels between her and her saintly namesake: both are blind (Ottilie figuratively so), regain sight (Ottilie's eyes are opened after the baby's death), heal the sick, and remain virgins (39–40). In keeping with the theme of his book, Danckert emphasizes Ottilie's dual nature. She is both a natural being and a type of religious icon and as such represents the Goethean "idea" of the feminine. Danckert also offers a new interpretation of Ottilie's death. While many scholars blame Mittler's words for pushing the weakened Ottilie to her grave, Danckert notes that Nanny's words, too, precipitate Ottilie's death. He breaks Ottilie's death into two phases. She is first stricken when she hears the discussion of the commandment against adultery, but is then far more affected when she sees the materials from her box laid out throughout the room and hears them likened to bridal clothing (64–65).

Louis Ferdinand Helbig's 1972 *Der Einzelne und die Gesell-schaft in Goethes Wahlverwandtschaften* (The Individual and Society in Goethe's *Wahlverwandtschaften*) follows very much in the tradition of Danckert. In contrast to the older German scholarship, which Helbig characterizes as being concerned with the more general, impersonal principles of marriage and society, fate and accident, Helbig sets out to examine the dynamic relationship between the individual and society (10, 13–14). Further, whereas Geerdts examines how society determines the consciousness of the characters (11), Helbig, following Reiss, promises to look at their inner natures (11).[10] Helbig concentrates especially upon Ottilie, and following Schelling-Schär, he believes that she possesses the greatest degree of self-knowledge (13). In addition, he argues that Ottilie is the only character who demonstrates any character development (14). She struggles for individual development against the static forces of societal conventions, and her death is tragic not only because she has failed to resolve the conflict between the individual and society in a fruitful way, but also because society misunderstands her life and death. Whereas she strove towards individual change and growth, society objectifies her into a static icon.

Although several scholars addressed societal issues during the 1960s and 1970s, social criticism was not a prominent approach. This is especially surprising for this period given that *Die Wahlver-wandtschaften* is so often viewed as a novel of social criticism (cf. Ryan 251). Instead, a much more characteristic approach to the novel during this time favored a strict textual analysis. H. G. Barnes was one of the most influential scholars who favored this methodology.

H. G. Barnes's Textual Analysis

Barnes was one of the most cited (and most criticized) writers on *Die Wahlverwandtschaften* during the late 1950s and throughout the 1960s. Although like many of his contemporaries he stressed the novel's ambiguity, his work differed from earlier scholarship in several ways, including his interpretive methodology, his emphasis on the role of prefiguration, and his reassessment of several accepted doctrines regarding the characters. He is also harshly critical of his predecessors' search for the pervasive idea (*A Literary*, 41).

The tone of Barnes's book is aggressive. His introduction lays out his disagreements with earlier scholars on several scores and seeks to establish his own individual niche in the scholarship in several different areas. Most importantly, he breaks away from his predecessors by rejecting an approach that reads the novel in terms of Goethe's life and times or even in terms of Goethe's other works. Barnes argues that the only way to approach *Die Wahlverwandtschaften* is through close textual analysis — to treat it as an aesthetic object independent of its historical period and Goethe's life. He complains that "literary-historical" approaches have only "impeded" the treatment of *Die Wahlverwandtschaften* as a work of art (19). He proposes instead an approach that concentrates on the work in isolation from any background materials: "Any interpretation of this novel which claims to be valid should be based on the work itself, and on the whole work" (26).

In contrast to the general postwar tendency to see the novel as an anti-Romantic work (Stöcklein, Geerdts), Barnes views the story as Romantic (2, 4, 20). He further disagrees with those critics who view the novel as classical and instead writes that Schiller's death had "emancipated" Goethe from his classical phase (2). Barnes attempts to establish the correspondence between the Romantic images of the novel and Goethe's aesthetic (40). He blames the novel's "un-romantic" and "moralistic" narrator for slanting and misrepresenting the events and therefore traces earlier misinterpretations of the novel's meaning to the narrator (2, 13). He hopes that his book will set straight the "false judgements" endorsed by the narrator so that the interpretation of the novel will not be distorted (27). In his discussion of the narrator as an independent character, Barnes is clearly following in Stöcklein's footsteps. However, where Stöcklein emphasizes the narrator's role in creating levels of irony, Barnes criticizes the narrator's perspective.

One of Barnes's main innovations is his insistence that the only way to read the novel as a whole to view it through the "narrative device" of prefiguration (26). Only by examining the symbols that prefigure later events can the reader circumnavigate "the tendentious influence of the narrator" and discover new complexities of the whole. For example, Barnes links all three *tableaux vivants* to future events: the blinded Belisarius "foreshadows that Ottilie will be blinded by passion"; Esther's fainting spell "points forward" to Ottilie's trance after the baby's death; and the paternal admonition "symbolizes Ottilie's need of admonition" (45). Perhaps his most radical claim regards the chemical theory of elective affinities. The chemical theory has no philosophical function, he argues, whether to elucidate Goethe's natural philosophy or to analyze the relationship between human beings and nature. Instead, the theory becomes for Barnes a means by which "to heighten the ambiguity of the whole and to foreshadow in ironic fashion later phases of the plot" (31). In other words, the chemical theory's only function is to illustrate the personalities of the characters and to predict their interactions with one another (31–32).

Barnes attempts throughout his book to reevaluate many of the standard readings of the characters. Eduard becomes the true hero of the novel (as he also is to several later scholars, including Peacock and Atkins), while Charlotte is no longer seen in a predominantly positive light. He blames the narrator for creating false impressions of the characters by dwelling too much on Eduard's faults while indulgently overlooking Charlotte's (100, 113–20, 161, 179, 186). Most striking, however, is Barnes's interpretation of Ottilie's death. In contrast to most critics, he argues that she does not commit suicide (23). In essence, he argues that Ottilie has no need to commit suicide because her love of Eduard has transcended earthly desire. That Ottilie places her father's portrait in the trunk with mementos of her relationship with Eduard suggests that "she is no longer conscious of a dividing gulf between her love of Eduard and her love of God" (66, 154–58). Ottilie's death is not a suicide but is rather "occasioned by Mittler" (67). Mittler's words against adultery do not hasten her death because she feels guilty, but because they "merely reveal to her the false light [in which] her present relationship with Eduard must appear to the outside world" (68). He takes Mittler's words on adultery and murder to be ironic when applied to Ottilie because throughout the narrative (and here Barnes takes the narrator's words at face value) "she is presented as 'das Kind' [the child]" and therefore could not be conscious of such things (68).

Hans Reiss's 1969 English reworking of his earlier German book (1963) serves as a foil to many of Barnes's points. Although Reiss became aware of Barnes's book only shortly before his own had gone to press, Reiss was able to include extensive comments upon Barnes's approach in the endnotes. He finds Barnes's treatment of the narrator "extreme," arguing instead that the narrator is detached and not biased (212).[11] In fact, Reiss emphasizes the independent nature of the narrator's commentary (155–59). He further questions Barnes's elevation of Eduard to heroic status, and reiterates, as commentators have done for generations, Eduard's limited perspective and egotism (197, 212, 218). He also disagrees with Barnes's statement that Charlotte's true defect is "lack of true love" and calls into question Barnes's saintly characterization of Ottilie (219).

Reiss's own treatment of the novel is largely traditional and indeed shows a tendency to return to earlier, more moralistic interpretations that were characteristic before the war. Thus, he discounts the chemical theory's applicability to human beings, for "the law of nature does not rule unchallenged" in the human sphere "for there morality and free will are also important" (145, 176–77). Reiss therefore also reads the novel as a negative commentary on Romantic marriage practices (149). Ottilie is a tragic figure due to her inner conflict. She respects "the laws of religion and of society" and the "sacred quality of marriage," yet she also loves Eduard deeply (177). He sees no distinction between her rules and the rules of moral law (199). And although Reiss questions whether in the end the novel "can be called a tragedy of marriage" (184) or whether it is even a Christian novel (207), he nevertheless tends to emphasize its moral role. However, Reiss shares with Barnes, as with many of the postwar writers (Staiger, Wiese), a heightened interest in symbolic readings of the novel that stress its ambiguity (152–53, 161).

III: Recent Trends and Developments

The last twenty years have seen a tremendous interest in *Die Wahl-verwandtschaften*. As interest in the novel has grown, so have the conflicts surrounding its interpretation. The culture wars of the 1980s certainly influenced interpretive approaches. Several decon-structionists argued that *Die Wahlverwandtschaften* aptly illustrated the limitations of language and reason and that the novel was a model for the failings of the Western philosophical tradition. These scholars further continued along the path that Benjamin had laid out regarding the author's relationship to the text. They no longer centered the discussion on authorial intent, but rather argued that the novel's true significance arose from its inability to sustain a single interpretation. Such deconstructionist readings were in turn quickly attacked. Several scholars questioned the deconstruction-ists' approach to language and symbols in the novel and argued that deconstructionists were falling into the very language trap against which the novel warns. They argued that the novel's symbols were not illustrative of the shortcomings of reason, but rather a rejection of a Newtonian type of reductive symbolism — a type of symbolism which they then equated with deconstruction itself.

And while the theoretical debates that began in the late 1970s still continue today, a more predominant recent trend is to read the novel in intertextual and interdisciplinary terms. Many current scholars concentrate upon the novel's intertextual elements and address the social, cultural, or philosophical influences upon the novel. For example, Gabrielle Bersier's recent book examines the elements of parody within *Die Wahlverwandtschaften* by tracing Goethe's intertextual conversation with the Romantics. In addi-tion, many recent scholars have examined Goethe's novel against the backdrop of the science and natural philosophy of his day. While earlier scholars, such as Schaeder, had linked Goethe's sci-entific principles to his novel, they tended to equate his scientific studies with an appreciation for God. More recent scholars have looked to the specific details of Goethe's science and the influences shaping his philosophy. As a consequence, they have developed a much more complex and chaotic view of Goethe's science and its role within the novel.

Before turning to the branches of scholarship that investigate these theoretical approaches, I will begin by first turning to a more traditional subject, namely Ottilie. While scholars have shown an almost unbroken interest in her since the date of the novel's publication, recent scholarly treatments display several key changes within critical approaches of the last few decades.

Ottilie Revisited

The analysis of Ottilie's character has occupied scholars since the time of the novel's publication. Those early scholars who were favorably disposed toward the novel tended to view her as a moral being due to her ability to overcome the strongest of passions and sacrifice herself in order to save a marriage. Conversely, many who condemned the novel viewed Ottilie with suspicion. They questioned the morality of elevating such a woman to saintly status. Although much of the scholarship of the first half of the century viewed Ottilie in a positive light (with the important exception of Benjamin), by the mid-twentieth century, despite Staiger's encomiums (and those of others, including Schelling-Schär, Helbig, and to a somewhat lesser extent, Stopp), several scholars of the period began to view Ottilie more critically.[12] Rather than viewing her as an ideal character or moral icon, scholars in the mid-century began to view her as a pathological character. This tendency to demystify Ottilie continued into the last decades of the twentieth century and culminated in a complete repudiation of her idealized image. Indeed, by the end of the century, several scholars argued that Ottilie's qualities are not to be universally praised, but ought to be condemned for their close connection to oppressive patriarchal norms.

In the 1980s and 1990s, numerous articles on Ottilie appeared (Lillyman; Anton; Hörisch, "Die Himmelfahrt"; Gelley; Bersier, "Ottilies verlorenes"; Puszkar; Wels; Egger; McIsaac). For the most part these articles illustrate Benjamin's influence in questioning Ottilie's status as either a saint or an exemplary character.[13] In the early 1980s, several scholars tried to refute the earlier scholarship that canonized Ottilie. Several of the essays in Bolz's edited volume thus develop a more pathological image of Ottilie. For example, Jochen Hörisch ("Die Himmelfahrt") emphasizes the symbolic importance not of her morality or her saintly iconography, but rather the troubling aspects of the symbolism associated with her anorexia, which in his interpretation becomes a system of signs (see also Bolz, "Analysen," 69). Numerous works of this period also paint a completely new picture of Ottilie's symbolic importance. For example, neither Norbert Puszkar nor Peter M. McIsaac see Ottilie as a moral or spiritual model of human behavior. Instead they view her actions, especially her withdrawal into silence, as being representative of the imposition of crippling patriarchal standards.

While scholars generally tended to distance themselves from idealized views of Ottilie in the 1980s and 1990s, they differed in their approaches. William J. Lillyman, for example, does not turn to the developments within literary theory, but rather discovers a new Ottilie through close textual analysis. In two of his articles, he examines two root causes for Ottilie's elevated status in the eyes of many readers: the narrator's love for Ottilie slants the story in her favor ("Affinity"), and her own language about herself creates a saintly image ("Monasticism"). He contends that "an important reason" for the lack of critical consensus on the entire novel "has been the failure to obtain an adequate understanding of the central character, Ottilie" ("Monasticism," 347). Rather than treating the narrator as a father figure (Stöcklein) or as unromantic (Barnes, *A Literary*), Lillyman argues that the narrator is as much in love with Ottilie as many of the other male characters in the novel and indeed "displays the same mixture of rational and irrational attributes found in the major characters" ("Affinity," 47). In short, Lillyman discounts many of the narrator's descriptions of Ottilie as the hyperbole of a man in love.

Lillyman, however, stops short of attributing to the narrator the creation of Ottilie's saintly image ("Affinity," 58). He traces Ottilie's inclination toward the monastic life, in word and deed, to show "the problematic nature of her own — not Goethe's or his narrator's — representation of herself as a saint, her very own 'lebendes Bild'" ("Monasticism," 349). He sees the characteristics of her famous "Bahn" or path as monastic: "self-denial, abstinence, service, humility, and reticence are all clearly associated with a state of poverty and dependence, whether this state be secular or religious" (354). Her later silence, too, ought to be seen in "accordance with the monastic principle of silence" (356). Her love for

Eduard thus becomes "an implicit breaking of the central monastic vow of chastity" (355). Like Danckert, Lillyman ultimately blames Ottilie's death on two causes: Mittler's words against adultery and Nanny's identification of the clothing as bridal (358). Both incidents remind Ottilie how far she has strayed from her path.

Gabrielle Bersier, in her 1988 article, "Ottilies verlorenes Paradies" (Ottilie's lost Paradise), also questions the propensity of earlier scholarship to see Ottilie as a saint, a Madonna figure of the early Renaissance, or even a daemonic figure. Bersier questions whether Goethe could ever have intended to idealize the figure of Ottilie to the extent that she was idealized in the pre-war scholarship (151). To see Ottilie's character in a new light, Bersier draws parallels between her and two of her predecessors — Wieland's Tilia and Brentano's Otilie — and argues that Goethe's Ottilie is a transitional figure. On the one hand, her similarities to Wieland's character emphasize her function as a "pädagogisches Frauenideal der Empfindsamkeit, ideale zukünftige Mutter, Gattin und Hausfrau" (139) [pedagogical feminine ideal, ideal future mother, spouse, and housewife]. As such, Bersier finds her to be much more reminiscent of Rousseau's Sophie than a Madonna figure from the Renaissance (139). On the other hand, a comparison between Ottilie and Brentano's character points to Ottilie's Romantic, parapsychological tendencies (140). Bersier argues that Ottilie stands between these two polar sisters and thus represents the intellectual transition from the Enlightenment to Romanticism (142). In light of her comparisons, Bersier argues for a more pathological reading of Ottilie. Thus instead of seeing Ottilie's death (as many of the early scholars did) as the triumph of the spirit over the body/nature, Bersier views it more critically. She views Ottilie's attempts to overcome the physiological as an escape from the real and an attempt to create a second, imaginary world — a world, however, that remains an optical illusion (154).

Several recent scholars have turned to comparisons between Ottilie and Luciane, especially in their participation in *tableaux vivants,* as a means of both criticizing society for its treatment of women and demystifying Ottilie's character. Rather than concentrating on the differences between the two female characters (as do other scholars, such as Dunkle), Norbert Puszkar emphasizes their similarities. Both characters, as Puszkar reminds us, are viewed as attractive when silent (403–7). The narrator tells us that Luciane was at her best during the *tableaux vivants*, while Eduard first finds Ottilie entertaining even though she has scarcely opened her mouth. Puszkar notes that the very themes of the paintings emphasize patriarchal norms and aesthetics. Luciane plays female figures that are powerless, unconscious, and subject to paternal authority.[14] Puszkar argues that for Goethe, beauty, which is feminine, is seldom compatible with speech (405). More recently, Peter M. McIsaac has also written about the notion of silence and its function within a political aesthetic (1997). In his 1997 article, McIsaac generally claims "that a *museum function* describes ways in which a given culture valorizes, acquires and discards, organizes, displays, and hides the objects that relate its art and history, and that this function finds expression in narrative projects of the time as well" (347). In particular, he wishes to show "how collecting and exhibiting induce behavior in Ottilie that conforms to an aesthetic that locates beauty in feminine self-denial and paralysis" (348).

Like Puszkar, McIsaac turns to the *tableaux vivants* with a critical eye. He notes that the narrator changes his prior negative assessment of Luciane due to her "petrification" within the living pictures (350). He argues that the "aesthetic ideal in these pictures finds beauty in female silence and paralysis. . . . The tableaux succeed as entertainment precisely because Luciane emulates a 'beautiful' femininity" (351). He similarly views Ottilie's participation in the nativity scene as ultimately providing Ottilie with the lesson of keeping quiet: "Ottilie's body is forced to articulate her emotions, which she then contains by maintaining a static and predetermined position. The sign of her pain, her tears, goes unheeded by the architect, who only stops the performance once the baby moves" (352). By forcing Ottilie to participate in the nativity scene, Ottilie must directly face how unworthy she is, in light of her love for Eduard, to play the Virgin Mary. That she is able to do so implies for McIsaac how severely Ottilie must curb her emotions. He therefore sees her participation as laying the "groundwork for Ottilie's eventual refusal to speak and eat after little Otto's death" (353). McIsaac questions the claim that the "virtues" that lead to Ottilie's death arise by nature and suggests instead that "Ottilie's death occurred at least in part due to the shortcomings of her culture" (354).

Thus, reactions to Ottilie provide one of the best measures for how radically interpretations of the novel have changed since it was first published. Initially, Goethe's readers either praised Ottilie's actions as the triumph of human will over natural necessity or they condemned her for her adulterous love of Eduard. Today, scholars are critical of the societal norms that required her to deny her love and forced her into the actions that are now condemned but which were once considered heroic.

Literary Theory

The growing influence of literary theory in academe throughout the 1980s and 1990s is reflected in many of the books and articles written about *Die Wahlverwandtschaften* during this time period. In Germany, the essays in Norbert Bolz's edited volume, Waltraud Wiethölter's influential article, and numerous more recent works, including those by Klingmann, Noyes, Konrad, Hörisch ("Die Dekonstruktion") and Twardella, place literary theory at the center of their discussions. For example, Bolz writes that *"Die Wahlverwandtschaften* dienen nicht zur Illustration von Theorien, sondern Theoreme werden als Sprengsätze in den Nischen des Texts angebracht" ("Einleitung," 16) [*Elective Affinities* does not serve as an illustration of theories, but rather theorems are laid as explosive devices in the niches of the text]. Wiethölter argues that the novel does not sustain one coherent interpretation, but rather three separate and complete readings: an ancient one (the story of Narcissus and Echo); a Christian one (Ottilie as a Mother Mary figure); and an amalgam of both traditions (alchemy) (7).[15] In her 1995 book, *Goethes Wahlverwandtschaften und das Dilemma des Logozentrismus* (Goethe's *Elective Affinities* and the Dilemma of Logocentrism), rather than examining the question of which force wins in the end, the passionate or the moral, Susanne Konrad places polarities themselves at the center of her discussion. In her investigation, she follows Derrida's concept of logocentrism and argues that Goethe's novel illustrates how logocentric premises influence the course of action (3).

The most influential deconstructionist criticism in Germany to date has been Bolz's edited volume. It was a pathbreaking book in that its contributors consciously sought (much as Benjamin had done) to break with more traditional scholarly trends. In the introduction, Bolz announces a task for a new *Germanistik*. This task is to break with the tradition that still seeks to find unity, closure, and meaning within texts. Bolz's volume is in many ways a kind of manifesto for reading *Die Wahlverwandtschaften* in light of the literary and cultural theories that were popular in the 1980s, including those by Adorno, Lacan, Foucault, Derrida, and especially Benjamin. Indeed, as Ryan notes in her review of the volume, "several essays are less interpretations of the novel than commentaries on Benjamin" (253).

The essays in the volume are quite varied and include Richard Faber's discussion of the social and historical context of landscaping, Herbert Anton's analysis of the symbolic relevance of the "living pictures" (especially in respect to their ability to mediate between realms), F. Kittler's treatment of Ottilie and the Captain in light of eighteenth-century "pädagogische Produktion von Beamten und Müttern" (262) [pedagogical production of officials and mothers], and Jochen Hörisch's discussion of Ottilie's anorexia. One of the most cited essays within the volume is Heinz Schlaffer's "Namen und Buchstaben in Goethes *Wahlverwandtschaften* (Names and Letters in Goethe's *Elective Affinities*). This essay first appeared in 1972 (although Schlaffer added a section to it for this volume) and takes to task the idea of searching for a single, pervasive idea. Schlaffer turns to some of the traditional tools of interpretation (closely examining the symbolic importance of names as well as the alchemical and mythological references) to show the impossibility of uncovering a secret and unified meaning of the whole. Instead, he seeks to demonstrate throughout his essay the disjunction between the various levels of the text and the pervasive irony of the whole.

More recently in Germany, several authors view *Die Wahlverwandtschaften* as a text that demonstrates the inadequacies of language. Hörisch's article "Die Dekonstruktion der Sprache und der Advent neuer Medien in Goethes *Wahlverwandtschaften*" (The Deconstruction of Language and the Advent of New Media in Goethe's *Elective Affinities*, 1998) is one of the more innovative readings. He points to numerous instances in which speech fails in the novel. He argues that the deaths are occasioned by false speaking, writing, or reading and that the unusual number of ambiguous sentences show the lack of dependability of language.

Most importantly, he contends that the attempts to make things better through speech — as the Englishman and his Assistant try to do by telling a story — only make matters worse. He postulates, however, that Goethe sees a technical alternative to language, the *camera obscura,* which does not fail or cause pain. Thus, where the Englishman's words and his Assistant's story cause only pain, the activities surrounding the technological apparatus of the *camera obscura* lead to no catastrophes, and indeed, its images bring knowledge and pleasure.

Scholarship in the last twenty years in the English-speaking world has also concentrated upon literary theory, whether utilizing it (Tanner, Miller, Brodsky, Muenzer) or questioning some of its suppositions (Nygaard; Stephenson, "Theorizing"). What is especially significant in the reception history of *Die Wahlverwandtschaften* is that scholars such as Tanner and Miller brought new readers from the English-speaking world to the novel.

Tony Tanner's book, *Adultery in the Novel: Contract and Transgression,* treats *Die Wahlverwandtschaften* alongside such novels as Rousseau's *La Nouvelle Héloïse* and Flaubert's *Madame Bovary.* Tanner begins his discussion by noting the various levels of *Die Wahlverwandtschaften.* It could be "variously described as a study in the geometry of changing relationships, in the syntax of problematical arrangements within the grammar of middle-class society, or as the topography of shifting attractions and separations among four people" (179). What Tanner finds interesting about the novel's treatment of these issues is that they are not only presented for the reader to interpret, but are analyzed by the characters themselves within the novel. Tanner gives several examples of how this process works. He notes that the book begins with Eduard's grafting of shoots, "which in turn precipitates a conversation considering the possibility of bringing new people into the house, or, as we say, 'grafting' them onto the existing arrangement" (180). These various levels are never static, but in constant motion, leading from one topic to another and back again.

Where numerous commentators have examined the abundant use of metaphors within the novel as interpretive tools, Tanner emphasizes their function for the characters themselves. In his view, the characters' use of language creates a trap from which they cannot escape. This new way of viewing symbols is perhaps one of the most innovative aspects of the deconstructionist readings of *Die Wahlverwandtschaften* (Nygaard). The symbols thus become telling not only of Goethe's historical and literary influences (Buschendorf), but also of the propensity that the characters have to interpret their own lives. In other words, not only do we as readers have to be conscious of our own tendency to "read" into the text, but part of the experience of reading *Die Wahlverwandt-schaften* is to watch how the characters perform this very function. In examining the metaphors, Tanner stresses their relationship to the idleness of "bourgeois" characters:

> But in the bourgeois house of Goethe's novel, tableaux, pictures, discussions, and experiments are essentially used as distractions to fill up empty time. They are not functionally related to the condition of the characters' existence. . . . Bourgeois human nature, I suggest, becomes a texture for metaphor, or more generally for areas of signification that are not immediately functional within their living situation. Thus, images from chemistry, art, evolution, topography fill up the void time created by idleness; and since the characters do not set them to work, *they* set the characters to work. In this way the property owners become paradoxically owned by the metaphors they play with, or by the redundancy of signs and projections that they make use of during their leisure hours. In so doing, they effectively help to create the situations and patterns in which their unused energies will find formal expressions. (212–13)

Tanner argues that the characters have too much meaning in their lives, that what they need is "a reprieve from excessive meaning." They have become trapped by the formulas that surround their lives, and they therefore are no longer free from their "totally formulated environment" (222). The irony, of course, is that the characters themselves have created these metaphors that inhibit their freedom. That they are bored makes them fill up their time with the metaphors that in the end determine their actions.

Throughout his text, Tanner addresses the movements of the characters and their creations of new kinds of "singleness" and "apartness," whether in joining what should be separated or separating what should be united. Once again, language serves a negative function. For example, following Lacan, Tanner further argues how the process of naming enslaves the characters. Names (especially because the four main characters and the baby share the root,

"Otto") serve to circumscribe the characters and hence unite what should be kept separate. That the characters share the same name binds them more to language than is usually the case with a name. What should indicate a certain kind of uniqueness, a person's individual name, instead becomes the means of losing one's identity.

In addition to examining those instances in which the characters try to unite what is separate, Tanner also examines those instances that should bind the characters but which actually separate them. Eduard and Charlotte's love-making ought to unite them, but it instead their brings about "untogetherness." Their marriage "legalizes" their union in that they are within their legal rights to have a sexual relationship, yet when they awake, they feel as if they have committed a crime: "the legal may incomprehensibly turn into its supposed opposite and become the very thing it was formulated to prohibit and exclude" (195).

Tanner emphasizes, however, that although Ottilie and Eduard follow a different pattern in their relationship, it too is doomed to failure. They unite not to form a new entity, but to create a zero, an absence, a void. Ottilie joins with Eduard only by sacrificing her individuality. Their union, as a consequence, "is a mark, not of a relationship based on symmetrical differences and reciprocities, but rather of one based on identity, and thus no relationship at all. . . . Two want to become one and to be done with difference and separation. But two cannot become one. They can only become zero" (197). Ottilie, he explains, is drawn to "a negation of energy" and is so "lacking in substance," that it "seems to enable her to cede herself completely to another" (219).

In his exposition, Tanner concentrates on the failure of language to enable the characters to find happiness and fulfillment. He closely links their personal tragedies to their relationship with language. J. Hillis Miller's analysis of *Die Wahlverwandtschaften* bears several similarities to Tanner's. Both re-examine and ask the reader to re-examine what the entire process of reading and re-reading such a text as *Die Wahlverwandtschaften* is all about. Like Tanner, Miller focuses upon how this "novel foregrounds its own conditions of being" (184). The reader need not look beyond the pages of the novel to discover the "keys" to its modern message. Miller argues that the "story of marriage, passion, and adultery that makes up *Die Wahlverwandtschaften* is an allegory of the laws, powers, and limitations of language" (*Ariadne's*).[16] He compares reading this novel to reading the Bible. Just as the Bible allows diametrically opposed interpretations, depending upon one's perspective, so too does Goethe's novel allow for the multiplicity of perspectives. Throughout his text, Miller contrasts such related concepts as literal and spiritual, Geist and Buchstabe, written and spoken language, figurative and literal language, and "Kunstwörter" and "Buchstaben" (170) in order to argue that these terms or lines of the novel contradict each other. Every line of the novel is both "realistic" and "allegorical" and hence the "reader is without firm ground to stand on in interpreting the novel" (210).

Miller sees numerous examples of "lines" throughout the novel: the red thread of Ottilie's diaries, Ottilie's path, Charlotte's view of her son as a link to connect her to the world, and Eduard's speech to the Captain/Major on how they should "disentangle" and "untie the knots" of the various relationships. He argues that the first lines of the novel, those describing Eduard's grafting of shoots, are representative of the whole: "Grafting is a form of anastomosis. On all its levels . . . *Die Wahlverwandtschaften* is a novel about such anastomosical crossing" (166). Miller argues, however, that these various types of crossings are intertwined, never to be reconciled: "That intertwining forbids a choice between one or the other, though they cannot be reconciled, put in hierarchy, dialectically organized, or made the themes of a coherent narrative moving from one to the other" (220–21). In other words, whereas earlier scholars tried to find ways in which to reconcile or mediate between polar oppositions, Miller sees them as being forever separated and forever opposed.

In his discussions of the various lines of anastomosis, Miller spends some time in examining the chemical theory of elective affinities. This theory for him exhibits some of the tensions between literal and figurative language that he sees throughout the text. The chemical metaphors, reduced to the proportional relations of A, B, C, and D, represent the "basic paradigm" of the novel: "human relations are like the substitutions in metaphorical expressions. Or, to put it the other way, since these metaphorical analogies are reversible: the laws of language may be dramatized in human relations" (171). Miller argues that the model of chemical unions, separations, and reunions operates on three levels:

on the level of interpersonal relations, on the level of the language, and on the level of the building of roads, paths, gardens, lakes, and houses on Edward's estate. On all three levels the paradigm seems to be the same. A literal, self-related substance is related to other such substances by lines or channels of force. These make possible transformations of that substance in which it nevertheless retains its identity. It becomes truly itself in those relations to another. This, it will be remembered, is one mode of relationship expressed by the word *anastomosis*. The title of Goethe's novel might be translated as "chosen anastomoses." (172).

In analyzing these three levels in the novel, Miller rejects the possibility of mediating between literal and figurative meanings, of reading it as "an admirable demonstration of the relations between European aestheticism and Occidental metaphysics" (173). Extending this mode of interpretation, he rejects a moral view of the novel's conclusion (174). He turns to the character of Mittler to demonstrate the problematic nature of reading the novel as a defense of marriage. Whenever Mittler tries to mediate, he only causes more suffering, and on two occasions, death. Strikingly, in light of this assessment, Miller, like many of the early critics, links Goethe's opinions on marriage with Mittler's (177).

Miller also turns to the use of reading and writing within the novel as a means of showing the impossibility of reconciliations between such opposing notions as the written and spoken language. He turns to the several instances of Eduard's reading aloud. The first time, Eduard is inordinately angry when Charlotte reads over his shoulder: he so identifies with the text that he feels torn in two. However, when Ottilie does so, he does not mind, for as they "are one person, his reading aloud while she looks over his shoulder is a single act performed by a single unified consciousness" (182). Miller describes their relationship as empty:

> Edward has gone to Ottilie because of a lack in himself. He has sought in her as all true Narcissistic lovers do proof of his own existence and confirmation of his manhood. He has sought not just his own face in the mirror but an image that will tell him he exists and is a man. Instead Ottilie lifts the veil to reveal an imitation confirming his lack of substance and power. This dooms both to death. (206–7)

Like Tanner, Miller emphasizes the empty and narcissistic quality of this union. Ottilie, for both scholars, is a "zero" (Miller 217; Tanner 197). Miller even reads Ottilie's "daemon" as "Ottilie's metaphysical personification of her projection of herself into Edward, [as a] reflex of his Narcissistic love for her" (219).

For Miller, narcissism describes not only Ottilie and Eduard's relationship, but is also a central motif of the novel. Human beings act narcissistically throughout the novel: funeral monuments, portraits, chemical theories, all "are opportunities" for man to "display his propensity to see everything as figure or in figure, to see figuratively" (199). And as narcissism is at its roots not only an empty union, but also a destructive one, so the central message of the novel is about the inability of reconciliations, whether among the characters or between literal and spiritual language.

Several years after the publication of some of the most influential poststructuralist and deconstructionist texts (Bolz; Wiethölter; Tanner; and Miller, "A 'Buchstäbliches'"), certain scholars, including Loisa Nygaard and R. H. Stephenson ("Theorizing"), began to quarrel with the idea that *Die Wahlverwandtschaften* is a model deconstructionist text. Nygaard, for example, contends that "none" of the deconstructionist readings "are adequate to explain the complex and subtle ways in which the symbols actually function in a work like *Die Wahlverwandtschaften*" (58). She further argues that "there is a profound irony to the application of this particular methodology [deconstruction] to this particular work, for the novel offers a critique of the very trends in our culture of which this movement represents the culmination" (58).

Nygaard develops her point by turning to Goethe's scientific treatise, *Zur Farbenlehre,* and concludes:

> What most perturbs Goethe about Newtonian science is that again and again, it allows the *symbol* to displace what it represents, the *sign* to displace the phenomenon as the real focus of attention. The practice of science in this school increasingly becomes the manipulation of abstract signs, the plotting of points and coordinates, the juggling of formulas and equations rather than the attentive observation of the dynamics of physical processes in their natural context. (71)

She argues that both Goethe's *Farbenlehre* and his *Wahlverwandtschaften* "are concerned with the problem of signs and representations, both are critical of a penchant in our culture toward reductive symbolization, and both trace the tendency of symbol to displace reality, the signifier the signified in certain areas of human experience" (71). She further contends that Goethe's attack of Newtonian science may especially be extended to apply to structuralists and poststructuralists as they "have deep roots" in precisely this tradition (73). In addition, these "new schools of thought also reflect another pattern of behavior that Goethe criticized directly in the *Farbenlehre,* more obliquely in *Die Wahlverwandtschaften:* one can trace through both movements a shift in emphasis from the *phenomenon* to the *sign,* and from the *signified* to the *signifier*" (72). Here, Nygaard is particularly critical of Schlaffer, Schreiber, Bolz ("Ästhetisches"), and Miller. In other words, whereas deconstructionists such as Tanner and Miller view *Die Wahlverwandtschaften* as a text that supports and prefigures postmodern views of language, Nygaard argues the opposite. She argues that Goethe's text shows the shortcomings of emphasizing symbols at the expense of concrete phenomena.

R. H. Stephenson takes a different tack in his criticisms of poststructuralism in his article, "Theorizing to Some Purpose." Instead of taking on deconstruction per se, he argues against its exclusivity and contends that other modes of research must be taken into account, especially when dealing with aesthetic texts (381). While setting aside the question of the philosophical soundness of poststructuralism, Stephenson argues that such approaches "can do nothing to further scholarship as a practical enquiry" (381). He therefore wishes to separate "distinct if ultimately related areas of valid intellectual activity: philosophical speculation and practical enquiry" (387). In his mind, philosophical speculation ought not to be the only way in which we approach literature. Instead, "practical inquiry" remains for him the more fruitful means of approaching aesthetic works. In order to demonstrate his point, he contrasts Schiller's and Derrida's concept of play. He concludes that Schiller "is concerned" with the "freedom felt in aesthetic *experience,* to whose elucidation he subordinates his abstract argumentation" (384). Stephenson argues that Derrida, in contrast to Schiller, is more concerned with "abstract argumentation itself, or, more accurately, the intimate interrelationship of language and discursive *thought*" (384). Thus, when Stephenson turns to his exposition of Goethe's works, he highlights the experience of reading them. He categorizes Goethe's classical works as having "a direct sensuous and physical appeal and [being] as real, as palpable, as any other object of our senses." He further argues that aesthetic activity, as defined by Weimar Classicism, is "at the very centre of all man's creativity, every man-made form . . . is rooted in what Goethe called the individual's *Lebensform* — 'the form of life' that is an organic-aesthetic precipitate of the encounter of self and world" (386). He argues that aesthetic objects exist and thus may be approached through both theoretical and historical modes of inquiry.

The latter part of Stephenson's essay is a direct attack against Miller's 1979 article on *Die Wahlverwandtschaften*. Stephenson is harshly critical of Miller's approach, questioning his main thesis, his identification of Goethe with the characters, his deafness to the "pervasive irony of the novel," and "a curious absence of anything approaching literary *theory,* in the sense of a general account of the differential properties of a work of fiction couched in language" (389). Stephenson's main critique of deconstruction is its approach to aesthetics: "The essence of the aesthetic use of language lies, after all, in the coordination effected between giving meaning and sound and look. The play of meanings that deconstructionist criticism entertains will simply not mesh with the sound-look relations established to yield import, and we are left with a mere welter of literally meaningless configurations" (391). Thus, Stephenson argues that the reader is not left in the end with an absence or zero that signals the larger inadequacy of language, but quite the opposite. He argues that the aesthetics of the novel create a realm of meaning that is not accounted for in deconstructionist readings.

More recent studies, while taking earlier theoretical approaches into account, have forged new interpretive paths. An excellent example of this recent trend is Gabrielle Bersier's book, *Goethes Rätselparodie der Romantik.*[17] Bersier argues that the Romantic understanding of parody is at the heart of Goethe's novel. Thus, while numerous scholars have noted Goethe's use of irony, her approach is quite new in that it focuses upon parody (51). In addition, unlike most earlier scholars, who interpret the novel according to thematic issues, she reads the novel in terms of its intertextuality and self-reflexivity. In the process, she finds several new connections between *Die Wahlverwandtschaften* and Romantic literary and theoretical works.

Throughout her book, she carefully traces Goethe's knowledge and active engagement with disparate Romantic sources and demonstrates that numerous aspects of the novel are in fact parodic representations of individual Romantics and their theories. For example, she places the significance of Eduard's name within the context of a long line of Romantic heroes (59–60) as well as linking several of his characteristics to those of Friedrich Schlegel. Similarly, she traces the discussion of narcissism back to an Athenäum fragment (113), while Eduard's "alpha and omega" reference finds its source in Schlegel's review of a Stolberg text (115).

In contrast to the deconstructionists, who, as a general rule, approached *Die Wahlverwandtschaften* primarily through textual analysis, more recent scholarship, as Bersier's book illustrates, has begun again to expand its interpretive horizons and look beyond the boundaries of the text itself. Of course, the theorists of the 1980s consciously sought to limit their investigation as a means of breaking free of the more traditional Goethe scholarship. More recent scholarship, in turn, has tried to broaden its approach and show the book's engagement with and connection to its larger cultural or intellectual milieu. McIsaac's article on Ottilie, discussed above, is but one example of the recent attempt to link events in the novel to cultural propensities of the time. Indeed, one of the main recent trends in scholarship is to look at the novel within the context of eighteenth-century science and natural philosophy.

Goethe and Science

Scholarship on Goethe during the 1980s and 1990s saw an increased interest in his scientific and natural philosophical works. Scholars re-examined his arguments against Newton (Sepper, Höpfner, Ribe, Schönherr), his conception of the history of science (Fink; Stephenson, *Goethe's Conception*), his place within the history of science (Amrine, Mayr), his influence upon chaos theory (Gleick), his status as a precursor to Darwin (Wenzel, Cornell) and his philosophy of gender (Koerner; Tantillo, "Goethe's Botany"). During this same time period, many scholars also addressed the relationship between science and *Die Wahlverwandtschaften*, in terms of Goethe's relationship to the science of his day (Adler, Selbmann, Müller-Sievers, Yee), the connection between his scientific works and his understanding of signs and symbols (Brodsky, Nygaard), the influence of earlier natural philosophers upon his thought (Ehrhardt), and the relationship between his own scientific works and the novel (Tantillo, "Deficit Spending," "Polarity"). At stake in much of this scholarship is Goethe's scientific critique (especially his argument against reductive, Newtonian science), his understanding of the role of human beings within nature as a whole, and his vision of a dynamic, creative nature that breaks and creates rules as much as it follows them. In light of these issues, scholars have questioned some of the more traditional views of the novel and some of the more recent interpretive conclusions, including Goethe's endorsement of set and hierarchical laws, whether applied to chemical elements or human beings; the notion that human beings are "raised" above the rest of nature because they are "free," while elements are not; and the applicability of Goethe's polar principle to deconstructionist readings.

Not surprisingly, much of the scholarship examining scientific themes within the novel addresses the chemical theory of elective affinities. Jeremy Adler wrote some of the most important studies of this period on the topic.[18] His 1987 book and 1990 article extensively examine Goethe's relationship to the chemistry of his time. Whereas most scholars link the source of the theory to Torbern Bergman's chemical treatise, Adler argues that the novel shows the influences of numerous different scientific traditions, from pre-Socratic to Newtonian. He argues that *Die Wahlverwandtschaften* not only uses the scientific discourses of its time, but that it also critiques those discourses ("Goethe's Use," 264). He sets out to prove that the chemical theory does not simply have a symbolic or aesthetic function, but rather that the novel "powerfully combines science — that is, natural philosophy — with literature" (263). His examination of the novel illustrates that Eduard's interpretation of the chemical theory — a formulaic reduction that applies the laws of chemistry to human beings — has its source in Newtonianism. Eduard's simplistic interpretation, during the course of the novel, is discredited, because "no one formula can account for what occurs. Affinity, the novel appears to assert, proves to be a more complex phenomenon than any single theory would allow" (276).

Several years before Adler, Claudia Brodsky (1982) also examined the symbolic importance of the chemical theory. She, however, does not turn to the historical influences upon Goethe's work, but rather to Goethe's *Zur Farbenlehre*. She juxtaposes the scientific language of *Zur Farbenlehre* against that of *Die Wahlverwandtschaften:* "The question of whether 'Wahlverwandtschaften' refers to relations between people or in nature refers *Die Wahlverwandtschaften* to the major corpus of Goethe's own 'natural science' writings, *Zur Farbenlehre*. While the novel tells a story of relationships of love, the *Farbenlehre* speculates upon observations of color relations" (1149). She further argues that the comparison of these two texts yields fruitful results as both "are major prose texts written by the poet who continues to figure most actively in the unreconciled aesthetics (as well as incompatible philosophies) associated with Classicism and Romanticism" (1150). She concludes that both the scientific treatise and the chemical theory are based upon "error": "The 'natural science' of color finally defines itself as a system based on inherent, investigative error. The failure of those engaged in 'Wahlverwandtschaften' to understand or mend their ways may be seen as the consequence of original errors of passion" (1172). Like many of the other theorists of the 1980s, Brodsky writes about the impossibility of reconciliation and hence the inherent failure of the system presented within the novel.

More recently, Kevin Yee (1997) has turned to the chemical analogy in order to offer a reassessment of the Captain's character. Arguing that the Captain "generally only receives scant attention from the critics," Yee maintains that the Captain acts as a catalyst, "who propels, accelerates, and alters the reaction without being affected himself" (59). Yee gives several examples to support his thesis. Charlotte and Eduard's marriage begins to disintegrate after the Captain's arrival as Eduard even moves his room in order to be closer to the Captain; Eduard and the Captain forge a bond that excludes Charlotte; the Captain's presence precipitates Ottilie's invitation to the manor; and the Captain's bond to Charlotte helps strengthen the relationship between Eduard and Ottilie. The Captain's role as a catalyst thus demonstrates the complexity of the meaning of the chemical affinities: "The implied 'correct' outcome of the human reaction (a simple exchange of partners), which was predicted much like a chemical reaction, is avoided because the Captain is a catalyst and not a normal reactant . . . [Goethe's] presentation of the Captain, the wild card in the mix of reactants, saves for humanity the possibility of freedom" (70). For Yee, understanding the chemical theory enables the reader to unlock one of the main messages of the novel.

Examinations of the link between science and *Die Wahlverwandtschaften* are, of course, by no means limited to discussions of the chemical theory. In my own work, I attempt to re-examine *Die Wahlverwandtschaften* in light of Goethe's natural philosophy. My 1994 article, "Deficit Spending and Fiscal Restraint," examines the applicability of Goethe's little-discussed theory of compensation to the novel.[19] In my more recent article, "Polarity and Productivity in Goethe's *Wahlverwandtschaften*," I turn to Goethe's use of the polar principle throughout his scientific corpus as a means or re-evaluating the role of polarities within the novel. Thus, while numerous commentators have viewed the novel in terms of the dichotomy between duty and passion or the individual and society, I argue that "Goethe's scientific texts point to another important dichotomy in the novel — that between productive and destructive polar desire" (310). Goethe's scientific works, therefore, "provide a compelling criticism of the chemical theory as it is interpreted by the characters in the novel" (310). During the course of the article, I examine the theory in terms of his understanding of the family and argue that he proposes an open philosophy which is based upon his understanding of biological growth and which stresses individual creativity and fulfillment (310). This openness is further reflected within the interpretation of the chemical theory by the characters. The text presents the reader not with one chemical theory, but three: "each of the three characters . . . holds a different perspective on the chemical theory, and each perspective is mirrored in his or her own views of family structure: Eduard is interested in the separation or the 'divorcing' of the elements; Charlotte in their marriage; and the Captain in their freedom of movement" (317). Thus despite the fact that on the surface it appears if these theories should contradict one another, each theory is completely valid and true for the character who is expressing it.

Other scholars look more broadly at the scientific paradigms of Goethe's day in order to examine the novel. For example, Helmut Müller-Sievers examines the novel against the backdrop of the "epigenetic turn." He traces the eighteenth-century reproductive theory of epigenesis back to Aristotle, who used the principle to account for organic self-generation "under the guidance of a formative drive" (3). Müller-Sievers argues that the manner in which the various disciplines turned to epigenesis as a kind of model "provides an altogether unique means by which to understand the momentous and irrevocable changes in philosophy, language philosophy, and literature at the end of the eighteenth and the beginning of the nineteenth century" (4). The epigenetic model, according to Müller-Sievers, failed in each of these categories. His final chapter in large part examines *Die Wahlverwandtschaften* in light of the culmination of this failure. As he explains in the introduction:

> The persistence of this failure [of the epigenetic model], the broken promises of harmony between body and mind, between nature and freedom, between language and self, are thematic in what Goethe called his "best book," *Elective Affinities*. The motivation to close this study with punctual interpretations of a romantic novel, then, comes not from the conviction that literature, as the most comprehensive dimension, contains or even sublates all other discourses, but that it represents the failure of reconciliation and containment in the most comprehensive way. This is not due to any superior insight on the part of the poet . . ., but to the romantic project of literature, which is that failure. (8–9)

His examination of *Die Wahlverwandtschaften* centers on its treatment of marriage, arguing that the novel demonstrates its impossibility: "marriage fails to become explicable in the terms of the underlying discourse of generation" (122). Müller-Sievers, like most of the authors who write on the novel during the closing decades of the twentieth century, thus focuses upon the novel's negative aspects — its failure. But where the earlier deconstructionists examined that failure in light of the limitations of language, Müller-Sievers turns to a different and more scientific model to argue for the characters' inability, despite all their efforts, to succeed in their relationships.

A Last Look: Variety and Continuity

The sheer number and disparate viewpoints of recent scholarly works on *Die Wahlverwandtschaften* make generalizations quite difficult. I have attempted, however, to illustrate some of the more prevalent of the approaches, in particular those which reevaluate the character of Ottilie as a critique of eighteenth-century society, which treat the novel in light of literary theory, and which examine it within a larger cultural or intellectual framework. However, even within these approaches, as I have argued above, there remains little scholarly agreement. Critics still disagree on Ottilie's role and function, on the novel's ultimate "message," and on the relevance of its natural philosophy. And while the emphases have changed since 1809, many of the issues have not. Critics still discuss the morality of the book, but whereas Abeken or Eckermann praised Ottilie's renunciation as a moral act, McIsaac and Puszkar criticize the society that required such renunciation. For two hundred years, readers of *Die Wahlverwandtschaften* have questioned whether it contains a teaching, but while Rehberg and de Valenti condemned the novel for its failure to provide moral guidance, Miller and Tanner praise it for its open-endedness. Similarly, reviewers have always discussed the role of nature within *Die Wahlverwandtschaften*. Goethe's contemporaries, however, viewed nature in a negative light because they tended to equate nature with the passions. As a consequence, they argued that morality required human beings to struggle against natural forces. More recent scholarship, in contrast, views nature as a more abstract or culturally determined force and seeks instead to situate the novel within scientific and philosophical contexts.

This study has attempted to examine how these various reactions to *Die Wahlverwandtschaften* have reflected the changes towards Goethe, cultural, moral and aesthetic attitudes, and literary criticism generally. If anything, a review of the literature on *Die Wahlverwandtschaften* over the past two hundred years shows that this novel will undoubtedly continue to perplex and intrigue scholars from many different backgrounds and points of view in the years to come.

Notes

[1] The irony does not appear lost to Varnhagen von Ense, who cites this passage in the same context as Goethe's response to Knebel after he had complained about the morality of the book: Goethe maintained that he had not written it for Knebel, but for young girls.

[2] Stopp includes Meessen, Lockemann, Clark, and Wiese in this characterization. He describes their inquiries as "useful two-dimensional exercises" that fail to "reveal something of the *inner* dynamism of the action" (54).

[3] For example, Goethe discusses archetypal forms in his essays on comparative anatomy. He suggests creating an archetype so that scientists will be better able to compare disparate forms. They need such static points of comparison because nature is in a constant state of flux, and without such created "types," the comparisons become more difficult. Therefore, where the doctrine of Platonic forms teaches that if we study various forms and phenomena, we will be able to identify an underlying *similarity* of form, Goethe uses his type to discover and highlight the *differences* between individuals as well as species. In opposition to the mathematical formulas of Newton and the mechanistic philosophy of Descartes, Goethe reminds scientists that they must be willing to change their constructs as nature itself changes. The type is not to become permanent. Nature cannot be reduced to the simplest terms of algebra or plotted onto a graph, because it is capricious and ever-changing. In an introductory essay to his morphology journal, he instructs the scientist to be as fluid as nature itself:

> Das Gebildete wird sogleich wieder umgebildet, und wir haben uns, wenn wir einigermaßen zum lebendigen Anschaun der Natur gelangen wollen, selbst so beweglich und bildsam zu erhalten, nach dem Beispiele mit dem sie uns vorgeht. ("Die Absicht eingeleitet," *FA* 1, 24:392)
>
> [When something has acquired a form it metamorphoses immediately to a new one. If we wish to arrive at some living perception of nature we ourselves must remain as quick and flexible as nature and follow the examples she gives. (12:64)]

[4] Barnes notes that Hankamer's book departs from his earlier work which emphasized Christian ideals. He further postulates that Hankamer's turn to the daemonic "doubtless reflects Hankamer's dismay at the military triumphs of National Socialism" (22).

[5] Most importantly, Hatfield is quite critical of Mann's Christian interpretation. He agrees that Goethe uses Catholic symbols throughout the novel, but questions whether they represent a "fundamentally Christian" teaching (107).

Hatfield turns to Goethe's quote of "what could be more Christian" than letting Ottilie and Gretchen die, but argues, in opposition to Mann, that this statement contains "biting sarcasm" (107).

[6] Drake is the most notable exception.

[7] Jaeger summarizes the cuts that Wolff makes in order to arrive at his novella prototype: "His most extensive excisions are the omission of chapters I, 9–11 and the fifteen chapters from the end of I, 17 to the beginning of II, 15. . . . 'Wahlverwandtschaft' is at work only between Eduard and Ottilie. Thus we have a mere triangle and the Captain actually plays a secondary role. There is no night of love for Eduard and Charlotte, no birth and death of their child. . . . What happens at the meeting in the inn Wolff leaves open by leaving a gap. But he assumes that Ottilie has probably yielded to Eduard's desire for consummation of their love" (14).

[8] Jaeger notes that few scholars endorsed Wolff's thesis (14). Geerdts, in writing of Wolff's first book, is critical of its use of biographical as opposed to aesthetic arguments (218–19). Danckert finds Wolff's methodology highly questionable (37).

[9] See also Nemec, who examines the conflict between the smaller worlds of the individual and the household against the larger forces of society.

[10] For a contrasting view, see also Vaget.

[11] Kahn too questions some of Barnes's more extreme views of the narrator. Kahn points to several key passages and argues that they may not be the words of the narrator, but rather the thoughts of the characters presented in free indirect discourse (erlebte Rede). For example, in the case of Eduard's walk with Ottilie, when the narrator reports that Eduard nearly desired that Ottilie would trip so that he could catch her, Kahn argues that the words are not the narrator's own, but rather his report of Eduard's thoughts (271). Lillyman, however, in turn questions many of the passages which Kahn identifies as narrated monologue ("Affinity," 50, 57–58).

[12] A good example of an early revision of Ottilie's character is Patricia Drake's article, "Ottilie Revisited." Although she does not cite him, she follows in Hárnik's footsteps in trying to psychoanalyze Ottilie's character. She treats Ottilie as a mentally unstable young woman whose "uneasy sense of inferiority," "desperate desire for security," and "sick sense of inadequacy" (248–49, 251) drive her actions. In his "The Metamorphosis of Character in *Die Wahlverwandtschaften*," Clark also paints a less idealized image of Ottilie. He compares each of the named main characters to types of plants in the "Metamorphose": Charlotte is the "completely normal" progressive plant because she generally follows the prescribed rules of society (246–47); Eduard is the retrogressive plant first because, although he is an adult, he acts as if he were a child, and second because he tries to go back in time to rekindle his earlier

relationship with Charlotte (247–49); and Ottilie represents the development of "monstrous" plants in the sense that her final acts, like these plants, "excite wonder" in the observer (250). He does not view her, by any means, as a saint. Her "beatification" is ironic: "between the miraculous and the freakish there is but a short step" (250).

[13] Bersier discusses in some detail the approaches that scholars have taken over the years in interpreting Ottilie (*Goethes Rätselparodie*, 45–55). She notes that the interpretation of Ottilie has been central to the question of Goethe's relationship to the Romantics.

[14] Recent scholarship questions whether Gerard ter Borch's painting is really a family scene at all. It may instead be a bordello scene. See Maierhofer (363–82).

[15] For an attempt to recombine these three separate readings, see Seibt and Scholz.

[16] In my analysis of Miller, I will cite exclusively from his book as both articles are closely related to it: he expanded his 1979 article for his book and his 1992 article is "another version" of the "material contained" in his book ("Interlude," 121).

[17] In her recent review article on Goethe scholarship, Becker-Cantarino writes that this "unpretentious study belongs among the best of Goethe interpretations in recent years" (191).

[18] Of course, several earlier scholars also focused their discussions on the meaning of the chemical theory (see, for example, Milfull and Allemann), but Adler's is the most comprehensive study.

[19] I argue that we gain a new perspective of the characters' flaws and their relationship to each other by applying the theory of compensation to their actions.

Works Cited

Adler, Jeremy. *'Eine fast magische Anziehungskraft': Goethes Wahlver-wandtschaften und die Chemie seiner Zeit*. Munich: C. H. Beck, 1987.

———. "Goethe's Use of Chemical Theory in His *Elective Affinities*." *Romanticism and the Sciences*. Ed. Andrew Cunningham and Nicholas Jardine. Cambridge: Cambridge UP, 1990.

Allemann, Beda. "Zur Funktion der chemischen Gleichnisrede in Goethes *Wahlverwandtschaften*." *Untersuchungen zur Literatur als Geschichte: Festschrift für Benno von Wiese*. Ed. Vincent J. Günther et al. Berlin: Erich Schmidt Verlag, 1973.

Amrine, Frederick, Francis Zucker, and Harvey Wheeler, eds. *Goethe and the Sciences: A Reappraisal.* Boston Studies in the Philosophy of Science. Vol. 97. Boston: D. Reidel Publishing Co., 1987.

Anton, Herbert. "Rettende Bilder. Ottiliens Tagebuch und Goethes Dichtungsverständnis." *Goethes Wahlverwandtschaften: Kritische Modelle und Diskursanalysen zum Mythos Literatur.* Ed. Norbert W. Bolz. Hildesheim: Gerstenberg Verlag, 1981. 169–91.

Atkins, Stuart. "*Die Wahlverwandtschaften:* Novel of German Classicism." *German Quarterly* 53 (1980): 1–45.

Barnes, H. G. "Bildhafte Darstellung in den *Wahlverwandtschaften.*" *Deutsche Vierteljahrsschrift* 30 (1956): 41–70.

———. "Ambiguity in *Die Wahlverwandtschaften.*" *The Era of Goethe: Essays Presented to James Boyd.* Oxford: Blackwell, 1959. 1–16.

———. "Goethes *Wahlverwandtschaften* vor der katholischen Kritik." *Literaturwissenschaftliches Jahrbuch.* Neue Folge 1 (1960): 53–65.

———. *Goethe's Die Wahlverwandtschaften: A Literary Interpretation.* Oxford: Clarendon Press, 1967.

Becker-Cantarino, Barbara. "Review Article: Goethe — New Scholarship." *German Quarterly* 73 (2000): 185–93.

Benjamin, Walter. "Goethes *Wahlverwandtschaften.*" *Neue deutsche Beiträge* (1924/25). Quoted here from *Walter Benjamin: Gesammelte Schriften* I, i. Ed. Rolf Tiedemann and Hermann Schweppenhäuser. Frankfurt: Suhrkamp, 1974. English from *Walter Benjamin: Selected Writings (1913–1926).* Vol. 1. Ed. Marcus Bullock and Michael W. Jennings. Essay trans. Stanley Corngold. Cambridge: Belknap Press, 1996.

Bersier, Gabrielle. "Ottilies verlorenes Paradies. Zur Funktion der Allegorie in den *Wahlverwandtschaften:* Wieland — Brentano — Goethe." *Goethe Yearbook* 4 (1988): 137–60.

———. *Goethes Rätselparodie der Romantik. Eine neue Lesart der Wahlverwandtschaften.* Untersuchungen zur deutschen Literaturgeschichte. Vol. 90. Tübingen: Max Niemeyer Verlag, 1997.

Bloch, Andreas. "Goethes *Die Wahlverwandtschaften* (von 1809) — die Ehe im Werk und in der Wirklichkeit." *Zeitschrift für das gesamte Familienrecht* 40 (1993): 1409–13.

Bolz, Norbert W., ed. *Goethes Wahlverwandtschaften: Kritische Modelle und Diskursanalysen zum Mythos Literatur.* Hildesheim: Gerstenberg Verlag, 1981.

———. "Einleitung. Goethes *Wahlverwandtschaften* — Analysen zum Mythos Literatur." *Goethes Wahlverwandtschaften: Kritische Modelle und Diskursanalysen zum Mythos Literatur.* Ed. Norbert W. Bolz. Hildesheim: Gerstenberg Verlag, 1981. 7–20.

———. "Ästhetisches Opfer: Die Formen der Wünsche in Goethes *Wahlverwandtschaften.*" *Goethes Wahlverwandtschaften: Kritische Modelle und Diskursanalysen zum Mythos Literatur.* Ed. Norbert W. Bolz. Hildesheim: Gerstenberg Verlag, 1981. 64–90.

Boucke, Ewald A. *Goethes Weltanschauung auf historischer Grundlage. Ein Beitrag zur Geschichte der dynamischen Denkrichtung und Gegensatzlehre.* Stuttgart: E. Hauff, 1907.

Brinkmann, Hennig. "Zur Sprache der *Wahlverwandtschaften.*" *Festschrift für Jost Trier zum 60. Geburtstag.* Meisenheim a. G.: Anton Hain, 1954. 254–76. Also published in Brinkmann's *Studien zur Geschichte der deutschen Sprache und Literatur.* 2 vols. Düsseldorf: Pädagogischer Verlag Schwan, 1965/66. Quoted here from Rösch 1975.

Brodsky, Claudia. "The Coloring of Relations: *Die Wahlverwandtschaften* as Farbenlehre." *Modern Language Notes* 97 (1982): 1147–79.

Burgess, Gordon J. A. "The Book in the Machine: First Report on a Computer-Assisted Analysis of *Die Wahlverwandtschaften.*" *German Life and Letters* 47 (1994): 418–31.

Buschendorf, Bernhard. *Goethes mythische Denkform. Zur Ikonographie der Wahlverwandtschaften.* Frankfurt: Suhrkamp, 1986.

Clark, Robert T., Jr. "The Metamorphosis of Character in *Die Wahlverwandtschaften.*" *Germanic Review* 29 (1954): 243–53.

Constantine, David. "Rights and Wrongs in Goethe's *Die Wahlverwandtschaften.*" *German Life and Letters* 47 (1994): 387–99.

Cornell, John F. "Faustian Phenomena: Teleology in Goethe's Interpretation of Plants and Animals." *Journal of Medicine and Philosophy* 15 (1990): 481–92.

Danckert, Werner. *Offenes und geschlossenes Leben: Zwei Daseinsaspekte in Goethes Weltschau.* Bonn: H. Bouvier und Co. Verlag, 1963.

Drake, Patricia. "Ottilie Revisited." *German Quarterly* 26 (1953): 248–57.

Dunkle, Harvey. "Monkey Business in Goethe's *Faust, Die Wahlverwandtschaften,* and Science." *Goethe Yearbook* 4 (1988): 123–35.

Egger, Irmgard. "'. . . ihre große Mäßigkeit': Diätetik und Askese in Goethes Roman *Die Wahlverwandtschaften.*" *Goethe Jahrbuch* 114 (1997): 253–63.

Faber, Richard. "Parkleben. Zur sozialen Idyllik Goethes." *Goethes Wahlverwandtschaften: Kritische Modelle und Diskursanalysen zum Mythos Literatur.* Ed. Norbert W. Bolz. Hildesheim: Gerstenberg Verlag, 1981. 91–168.

Fink, Karl J. *Goethe's History of Science.* Cambridge: Cambridge UP, 1991.

François-Poncet, André. *Les Affinités Électives.* Paris: F. Alcan, 1910. Quoted here from the 1951 German translation: *Goethes Wahlverwandtschaften: Versuch eines kritischen Kommentars.* Mainz: Florian Kupferberg Verlag.

Geerdts, Hans Jürgen. *Goethes Roman "Die Wahlverwandtschaften": Eine Analyse seiner künstlerischen Struktur, seiner historischen Bezogenheiten und seines Ideengehaltes.* Weimar: Aufbau Verlag, 1958. Quoted here from the 3rd ed., 1974.

Gilli, Marita. "Das Verschweigen der Geschichte in Goethes *Wahlverwandtschaften* oder Wie man der Geschichte nicht entfliehen kann." *Sie, und nicht Wir.* Ed. Arno Herzig, Inge Stephan, and Hans G. Winter. Hamburg: Doelling und Galitz, 1989. 553–65.

Gleick, James. *Chaos: Making a New Science.* New York: Penguin Books, 1988.

Gundolf, Friedrich. *Goethe.* Berlin: Bondi, 1916. Quoted here from the 4th ed., 1918.

Hankamer, Paul. *Spiel der Mächte: Ein Kapitel aus Goethes Leben und Goethes Welt.* Tübingen: Rainer Wunderlich Verlag, 1943.

Hárnik, J. "Psychoanalytisches aus und über Goethes *Wahlverwandtschaften.*" *Imago Zeitschrift für Anwendung der Psychoanalyse auf die Geisteswissenschaften* 1 (1912): 507–518.

Harper, Anthony J. "Mysterium Conjunctionis: On the Attraction of 'Chymical Weddings.'" *German Life and Letters* 47 (1994): 449–55.

Hatfield, Henry C. "Towards the Interpretation of *Die Wahlverwandtschaften.*" *The Germanic Review* 22 (1948): 104–14.

Helbig, Louis Ferdinand. *Der Einzelne und die Gesellschaft in Goethes Wahlverwandtschaften.* Bonn: Bouvier Verlag, 1972.

Höpfner, Felix. *Wissenschaft wider die Zeit: Goethes Farbenlehre aus rezeptionsgeschichtlicher Sicht.* Heidelberg: Carl Winter Universitätsverlag, 1990.

Hörisch, Jochen. "'Die Himmelfahrt der bösen Lust' in Goethes *Wahlverwandtschaften:* Versuch über Ottliliens Anorexie." *Goethes Wahlverwandtschaften: Kritische Modelle und Diskursanalysen zum Mythos Literatur.* Ed. Norbert W. Bolz. Hildesheim: Gerstenberg Verlag, 1981. 308–22.

———. "Die Dekonstruktion der Sprache und der Advent neuer Medien in Goethes *Wahlverwandtschaften.*" *Merkur* 52 (1998): 826–39.

Jaeger, Hans. "Goethe's 'Novelle' *Die Wahlverwandtschaften?*" *The Germanic Review* 34 (1959): 14–38.

Kahn, Ludwig W. "Erlebte Rede in Goethes *Wahlverwandtschaften.*" *PMLA* 89 (1974): 268–77.

Kittler, Friedrich A. "Ottilie Hauptmann." *Goethes Wahlverwandtschaften: Kritische Modelle und Diskursanalysen zum Mythos Literatur.* Ed. Norbert W. Bolz. Hildesheim: Gerstenberg Verlag, 1981. 260–75.

Klingmann, Ulrich. "Recht der Einbildungskraft und Recht des Wirklichen: Goethes *Wahlverwandtschaften* in poststrukturalistischer Sicht." *Monatshefte* 80 (1988): 172–86.

Köhler, Astrid. *Salonkultur im klassischen Weimar: Geselligkeit als Lebensform und literarisches Konzept.* Stuttgart: M & P Verlag, 1996.

Koerner, Lisbet. "Goethe's Botany: Lessons of a Feminine Science." *Isis* 84 (1993): 470–95.

Konrad, Susanne. *Goethes Wahlverwandtschaften und das Dilemma des Logozentrismus.* Heidelberg: Universitätsverlag Carl Winter, 1995.

Lange, Victor. "Goethe's Craft of Fiction." *PEGS.* New Series, 22 (1953): 31–63.

Lillyman, William J. "Affinity, Innocence, and Tragedy: The Narrator and Ottilie in Goethe's *Die Wahlverwandtschaften.*" *German Quarterly* 53 (1980): 46–63.

———. "Monasticism, *Tableau Vivant,* and Romanticism: Ottilie in Goethe's *Die Wahlverwandtschaften.*" *JEGP* 81 (1982): 347–66.

———. "Analogies for Love: Goethe's *Die Wahlverwandtschaften* and Plato's *Symposium.*" *Goethe's Narrative Fiction: The Irvine Goethe Symposium.* Ed. William J. Lillyman. New York: Walter de Gruyter, 1982. 128–44.

Lockemann, Theodor. "Der Tod in Goethes *Wahlverwandtschaften.*" *Jahrbuch der Goethegesellschaft* 19 (1933): 48–61.

Maierhofer, Waltraud. "Vier Bilder und vielfältige Bezüge: die sogennante 'Väterliche Ermahnung' und die Figuren in den *Wahlverwandtschaften*." *Ethik und Ästhetik. Werke und Werte in der Literatur vom 18. bis zum 20. Jahrhundert.* Ed. Richard Fisher. Frankfurt: Peter Lang, 1995. 363–82.

Mann, Thomas. "Zu Goethe's 'Wahlverwandtschaften.'" *Die Neue Rundschau* 36 (1925): 391–401. Quoted here from *Gesammelte Werke in zwölf Bänden.* Vol. 9. Frankfurt: S. Fischer, 1960. 174–86. English from *Past Masters and Other Papers.* "Goethe, Novelist." Trans. H. T. Lowe-Porter. New York: Alfred A. Knopf, 1933. 99–114.

Maurer, Karl. "Goethe's 'Elective Affinities.'" *The Modern Language Review* 42 (1947): 342–52.

May, Kurt. "Goethes *Wahlverwandtschaften* als tragischer Roman." *Form und Bedeutung: Interpretationen deutscher Dichtung des 18. und 19. Jahrhunderts.* Stuttgart: Ernst Klett Verlag, 1957.

Mayr, Ernst. *The Growth of Biological Thought: Diversity, Evolution, and Inheritance.* Cambridge: Belknap Press of Harvard UP, 1982.

McIsaac, Peter M. "Exhibiting Ottilie: Collecting as a Disciplinary Regime in Goethe's *Wahlverwandtschaften*." *German Quarterly* 70 (1997): 347–57.

Meessen, Hubert J. "Goethes Polaritätsidee und *Die Wahlverwandtschaften*." *PMLA* 54 (1939): 1105–23.

Milfull, John. "The 'Idea' of Goethe's *Wahlverwandtschaften*." *Germanic Review* 47 (1972): 83–94.

Miller, J. Hillis. "A 'Buchstäbliches' Reading of *The Elective Affinities*." *Glyph* 6 (1979): 1–23.

———. *Ariadne's Thread: Story Lines.* New Haven: Yale UP, 1992.

———. "Interlude as Anastomosis in *Die Wahlverwandtschaften*." *Goethe Yearbook* 6 (1992): 115–22.

Milne, C. Audrey. "*The Elective Affinities* in Exile: *Der Ehering*." *German Life and Letters* 47 (1994): 456–68.

Muenzer, Clark. *Figures of Identity.* University Park: Pennsylvania State UP, 1984.

Müller-Sievers, Helmut. *Self-Generation: Biology, Philosophy, and Literature Around 1800.* Stanford: Stanford UP, 1997.

Nemec, Friedrich. *Die Ökonomie der Wahlverwandtschaften.* Münchner Germanistische Beiträge. Vol. 10. Munich: Fink Verlag, 1973.

Noyes, John. "Die blinde Wahl. Symbol, Wahl und Verwandtschaft in Goethes *Die Wahlverwandtschaften*." *Deutsche Vierteljahrsschrift* 45 (1991): 132–51.

Nygaard, Loisa. "'Bild' and 'Sinnbild': The Problem of the Symbol in Goethe's *Wahlverwandtschaften*." *The Germanic Review* 63 (1988): 58–76.

Osten, Manfred. "'Mit dem Gewissen verheiratet': Ein Versuch über die Gestalt der Ottilie in Goethes *Wahlverwandtschaften*." *Goethe und Forster: Studien zum gegenständlichen Dichten*. Ed. Detlef Rasmussen. Bonn: Bouvier Verlag, 1985. 150–63.

Peacock, R. "The Ethics of Goethe's *Die Wahlverwandtschaften*." *Modern Language Review* 71 (1976): 330–43.

Plenderleith, H. Jane. "Sex, Lies and *Die Wahlverwandtschaften*." *German Life and Letters* 47 (1994): 407–17.

Puszkar, Norbert. "Frauen und Bilder: Luciane und Ottilie." *Neophilologus* 73 (1989): 397–410.

Reiss, Hans. *Goethes Romane*. Bern: Francke Verlag, 1963.

———. *Goethe's Novels*. Revised translation of *Goethes Romane*. New York: St. Martin's Press, 1969.

Reitz, Gertrud. *Die Gestalt des Mittlers in Goethes Dichtung*. Frankfurter Quellen und Forschungen zur germanischen und romanischen Philologie. Ed. Erhard Lommatzsch, Hans Naumann, and Franz Schultz. Frankfurt: Mortiz Diesterweg, 1932. Quoted here from the 1973 facsimile reprint, Hildesheim: Dr. H. A. Gerstenberg.

Ribe, Neil M. "Goethe's Critique of Newton: A Reconsideration." *Studies in History and Philosophy of Science*. 16 (1985): 315–35.

Rösch, Ewald. *Goethes Roman "Die Wahlverwandtschaften."* *Wege der Forschung*. Vol. 113. Darmstadt: Wissenschaftliche Buchgesellschaft, 1975.

Ryan, Judith. Review of *Goethes Wahlverwandtschaften: Kritische Modelle und Diskursanalysen zum Mythos Literatur,* ed. Norbert W. Bolz. *Goethe Yearbook* 2 (1984): 250–53.

Schaeder, Grete. "Die Idee der *Wahlverwandtschaften*." *Goethe: Neue Folge des Jahrbuchs der Goethe-Gesellschaft* 6 (1941): 182–215.

———. *Gott und Welt: Drei Kapitel Goethescher Weltanschauung*. Hameln: Fritz Seifert, 1947.

Schelling-Schär, Esther. *Die Gestalt der Ottilie: Zu Goethes Wahlver-wandtschaften.* Zürcher Beiträge zur deutschen Literatur- und Geistes-geschichte. Vol. 36. Zurich: Atlantis Verlag, 1969.

Schlaffer, Heinz. "Namen und Buchstaben in Goethes *Wahlverwandt-schaften.*" *Goethes Wahlverwandtschaften: Kritische Modelle und Dis-kursanalysen zum Mythos Literatur.* Ed. Norbert W. Bolz. Hildesheim: Gerstenberg Verlag, 1981. 211–29. This an expanded version of the article published in 1972 in the *Jahrbuch der Jean-Paul-Gesellschaft* 7:84–102.

Schönherr, Hartmut. *Einheit und Werden: Goethes Newton-Polemik als sy-stematische Konsequenz seiner Naturkonzeption.* Würzburg: Königshau-sen & Neumann, 1993.

Schreiber, Jens. "Die Zeichen der Liebe." *Goethes Wahlverwandtschaften: Kritische Modelle und Diskursanalysen zum Mythos Literatur.* Ed. Nor-bert W. Bolz. Hildesheim: Gerstenberg Verlag, 1981. 276–307.

Schwan, Werner. *Goethes Wahlverwandtschaften: Das nicht erreichte So-ziale.* Munich: Fink Verlag, 1983.

Seibt, Gustav and Oliver R. Scholz. "Zur Funktion des Mythos in *Die Wahl-verwandtschaften.*" *Deutsche Vierteljahrsschrift* 59 (1985): 609–30.

Selbmann, Rolf. "Auf den Menschen reimt sich die ganze Natur. Über das Verhältnis von Chemie und Literatur im 19. Jahrhundert." *Eupho-rion* 90 (1996): 153–65.

Sepper, Dennis. *Goethe Contra Newton: Polemics and the Project for a New Science of Color.* Cambridge: Cambridge UP, 1988.

Simon, Lilli. *Verantwortung und Schuld in Goethes Roman.* Erlangen: Palm & Enke, 1934.

Sirc, Susan. "Monkeys, Monuments and Miracles: Aspects of Imitation of Word and Image in *Die Wahlverwandtschaften.*" *German Life and Let-ters* 47 (1994): 432–48.

Stahl, E. L. "*Die Wahlverwandtschaften.*" *PEGS* 15 (1946): 71–95.

Staiger, Emil. *Goethe.* Vol. 2: 1786–1814. Zurich: Atlantis Verlag, 1956.

Stephenson, R. H. "Theorizing to some Purpose: 'Deconstruction' in the Light of Goethe and Schiller's Aesthetics — The Case of *Die Wahlver-wandtschaften.*" *Modern Language Review* 84 (1989): 381–92.

———. "'Man nimmt in der Welt jeden, wofür er sich gibt': The Presen-tation of Self in Goethe's *Die Wahlverwandtschaften.*" *German Life and Letters* 47 (1994): 400–406.

————. *Goethe's Conception of Knowledge and Science*. Edinburgh: Edinburgh UP, 1995.

Stöcklein, Paul. *Wege zum späten Goethe: Dichtung — Gedanke — Zeichnung — Interpretationen*. Hamburg: Marion von Schröder Verlag, 1949.

Stopp, F. J. "'Ein wahrer Narziss': Reflections on the Eduard-Ottilie Relationship in Goethe's *Wahlverwandtschaften*." *PEGS* 29 (1960): 52–85.

————. "Ottilie and 'das innere Licht.'" *German Studies Presented to Walter Horace Bruford*. London: George G. Harrap & Co., 1962. 117–22.

Suhrkamp, Peter. "Goethes *Wahlverwandtschaften*." *Ausgewählte Schriften zur Zeit- und Geistesgeschichte*. Frankfurt: Suhrkamp, 1951. Quoted here from Rösch 1975.

Tanner, Tony. *Adultery in the Novel: Contract and Transgression*. Baltimore: The Johns Hopkins UP, 1979.

Tantillo, Astrida Orle. "Deficit Spending and Fiscal Restraint: Balancing the Budget in *Die Wahlverwandtschaften*." *Goethe Yearbook* 7 (1994): 40–61.

————. "Goethe's Botany and His Philosophy of Gender." *Eighteenth-Century Life* 22 (1998): 123:38.

————. "Polarity and Productivity in Goethe's *Wahlverwandtschaften*." *Seminar* 36 (2000): 310–25.

Taviani, Paolo and Vittorio. *"Elective Affinities."* Rai Radiotelevisione Italiana, 1996. English subtitled version from Fox Lorber 1998.

Twardella, Johannes. "Experimente im Treibhaus der Moderne. Versuch einer Kommunikationstheoretischen Analyse von Goethes *Wahlverwandtschaften*." *Neophilologus* 83 (1999): 445–60.

Vaget, Hans Rudolf. "Ein reicher Baron. Zum sozialgeschichtlichen Gehalt der *Wahlverwandtschaften*." *Jahrbuch der deutschen Schillergesellschaft*. 24 (1980): 123–61.

Varnhagen von Ense, Karl August. Diary Entry. 28 June 1843. Quoted here from *Karl August Varnhagen von Ense Werke*. 5 vols. Frankfurt: Deutscher Klassiker Verlag, 1994. 5:320–21. Also reprinted in *HA*, 6:641.

Vetter, August. "Wahlverwandtschaft." *Jahrbuch der Goethe-Gesellschaft* 17 (1931): 98–113.

Viëtor, Karl. *Goethe: Dichtung/Wissenschaft/Weltbild*. Bern: A. Francke Verlag, 1949. English from *Goethe the Poet*. Trans. Moses Hadas. Cambridge: Harvard UP, 1949.

Walzel, Oskar F. "Goethes 'Wahlverwandtschaften' im Rahmen ihrer Zeit." *Goethe Jahrbuch* 27 (1906): 166–206.

Wels, Volkhard. "Eine Auslegung von Goethes *Wahlverwandtschaften* nach ihrer theologischen Begrifflichkeit." *Euphorion* 88 (1994): 406–17.

Wenzel, Manfred. "Goethe und Darwin — Der Streit um Goethes Stellung zum Darwinismus in der Rezeptionsgeschichte der morphologischen Schriften." *Goethe Jahrbuch* 100 (1983): 145–58.

Wiese, Benno von. "Goethes *Wahlverwandtschaften.*" Vol. 6. Hamburg: Christian Wegner Verlag, 1951. Cited here from Wiese's *Der Mensch in der Dichtung: Studien zur deutschen und europäischen Literatur.* Düsseldorf: August Bagel Verlag, 1958.

Wiethölter, Waltraud. "Legenden: Zur Mythologie von Goethes *Wahlverwandtschaften.*" *Deutsche Vierteljahrsschrift* 56 (1982): 1–64.

Winkelman, John. *Goethe's Elective Affinities: An Interpretation.* New York: Peter Lang, 1987.

Wolff, Hans M. *Goethe in der Periode der Wahlverwandtschaften (1802–1809).* Munich: Leo Lehnen Verlag, 1952.

———. *Goethes "Novelle" Die Wahlverwandtschaften: Ein Rekonstruktionsversuch.* Bern: Francke Verlag, 1955.

Yee, Kevin F. "The Captain as Catalyst in Goethe's *Wahlverwandtschaften.*" *JEGP* 96 (1997): 58–70.

Zecevic, Patricia D. "The Beloved as Male Projection: A Comparative Study of *Die Wahlverwandtschaften* and *Dom Casmurro.*" *German Life and Letters* 47 (1994): 469–76.

Works Cited

Editions of Goethe's Works Cited

Goethe, Johann Wolfgang von. *Sämtliche Werke*. Ed. Hendrik Birus et al. 40 vols. Frankfurt: Deutscher Klassiker Verlag, 1985–. (Abbreviated in text as *"FA."*)

———. *Goethes Werke*. Hamburger Ausgabe. 14 vols. Ed. Erich Trunz. Originally published 1949–71. Christian Wegner Verlag. Cited here from the reissued 13th ed. Munich: Verlag C. H. Beck. (Abbreviated in the text as *"HA."*)

———. *Goethes Gespräche*. 5 vols. Ed. Wolfgang Herwig. Zurich: Artemis, 1965–87. (Abbreviated in text as *"GG."*)

———. *Conversations with Eckermann* (1984). Trans. John Oxenford. San Francisco: North Point Press reprint.

———. *Goethe's Collected Works* (1983–89). 12 vols. New York: Suhrkamp.

Chronological List of Works Consulted

Bergman, Torbern. 1775. *Disquisitio de attractionibus electivis*. Vol. 2. Nova acta Regiæ societatis scientarium upsaliensis.

Hirschfeld, Christian Cay Laurenz. 1779–85. *Theorie der Gartenkunst*. 5 vols. Leipzig: Weidmann.

[Goethe]. 4 September 1809. Advertisement for *Die Wahlverwandtschaften*. *Morgenblatt für gebildete Stände*. Cited here from *HA*, 6:639. Also reprinted in Härtl 1983, 50–51 and Braun 1885, 211.

Eichstädt, Heinrich Karl Abraham. 25 October 1809. Letter to Johann Friedrich Rochlitz. Jena. Quoted here from Härtl 1983, 65. Also reprinted in the *Goethe-Jahrbuch* 20 (1899): 273–74.

Schiller, Charlotte von. 27 October 1809. Letter to Johann Friedrich Cotta. Weimar. Quoted here from Härtl 1983, 66.

Zelter, Karl Friedrich. 27 October 1809. Letter to Goethe. Berlin. Quoted here from *Briefwechsel zwischen Goethe und Zelter in den Jahren 1796 bis 1832*. Ed. Friedrich Wilhelm Riemer. Berlin: Duncker and Humblot, 1833. Also reprinted in Härtl 1983, 65–66 and *HA*, 6:667.

Grimm, Wilhelm. 28 October 1809. Letter to Jacob Grimm. Berlin. Quoted here from *Briefwechsel zwischen Jacob und Wilhelm Grimm aus der Jugendzeit*. Ed. Herman Grimm and Gustav Hinrichs. Weimar: Böhlau, 1963. 170–71. Also reprinted in Härtl 1983, 66 and in *HA*, 6:659.

Arnim, Achim von. 5 November 1809. Letter to Bettina Brentano. Berlin. Quoted here from *Achim von Arnim und Bettina Brentano*. Ed. Reinhold Steig. Bern: Herbert Lang, 1970. 350. Also quoted in Härtl 1983, 70–71 and *HA*, 6:657.

Levin, Rahel. 14 November 1809. Letter to Rose Asser. Berlin. Quoted here from *Rahel. Ein Buch des Andenkens für ihre Freunde*. Berlin: Duncker and Humblot, 1834. 445–47. Also quoted in Härtl 1983, 73.

Wagner, Johann Ernst. 21 November 1809. Letter to August von Studnitz. Meiningen. Quoted here from *Hundert Briefe von Johann Ernst Wagner an Jean Paul Fr. Richter und August von Studnitz*. Ed. A. L. Corin. Liège: Faculté de Philosophie et Lettres, 1942. Also quoted in Härtl 1983, 79.

Grimm, Wilhelm. 24 [22] November 1809. Letter to Jacob Grimm. Halle. Quoted here from *Briefwechsel zwischen Jacob und Wilhelm Grimm aus der Jugendzeit*. Ed. Herman Grimm and Gustav Hinrichs. Weimar: Böhlau, 1963. 176–78. Also quoted in Härtl 1983, 80 and *HA*, 6:659.

Anonymous. 2 December 1809. Advertisement for the novel in *Intelligenzblatt zum Morgenblatt für gebildete Stände*. Tübingen.

Jacobi, Friedrich Heinrich. 18 December 1809. Letter to Johann Heinrich Voß. Munich. Quoted here from *Aus F. H. Jacobi's Nachlaß*. Vol. 2. Leipzig: Wilhelm Engelmann, 1869. 39–43. Also reprinted in Härtl 1983, 86 and *HA*, 6:662.

Huber, Therese. 20 December 1809. Letter to Karl August Böttiger. Günzburg. Quoted here from Härtl 1983, 86. Also reprinted in the *Goethe-Jahrbuch* 18 (1897): 128 and *HA*, 6:662.

Welcker, Friedrich Gottlieb. 21 December 1809. Letter to Caroline von Humboldt. Gießen. Quoted here from Härtl 1983, 87–88. Also reprinted in the *Goethe-Jahrbuch* 19 (1898): 199–201.

Humboldt, Wilhelm von. 23 December 1809. Letter to Friedrich Gottlieb Welcker. Erfurt. Quoted here in Härtl 1983, 88.

Savigny, Friedrich Karl von. 25 December 1809. Letter to Friedrich Creuzer. Landshut. Quoted here from Härtl 1983, 89.

[Conz, Karl Philipp]. 25–28 December 1809. "Briefe über den Goethe'schen Roman: *Die Wahlverwandtschaften.*" *Morgenblatt für gebildete Stände.* Tübingen. Quoted here from Härtl 1983, 90–99. Also reprinted in Braun 1885, 212–15.

Solger, Karl Wilhelm. 1809. "Über die *Wahlverwandtschaften.*" First published in *Solger's nachgelassene Schriften und Briefwechsel.* Ed. Ludwig Tieck and Friedrich von Raumer. Vol. 1. Leipzig 1826: 175–85. Also reprinted in Härtl 1983, 199–202, *HA*, 6:652–57, and Mandelkow (1975–84) 1:257–61.

Huber, Therese. ca. 1810. Undated letter to Emil von Herder. Günzburg. Quoted here from Härtl 1983, 203. Also reprinted in the *Goethe-Jahrbuch* 18 (1897): 130.

[Rehberg, August Wilhelm]. 1 January 1810. Review of *Die Wahlverwandtschaften* in *Allgemeine Literatur-Zeitung.* Nr. 1. Halle. Quoted here from Härtl 1983, 101–6. Also reprinted in Mandelkow (1975–84) 1:268–74 and in Braun 1885, 224–32.

[Böttiger, Karl August]. 2 January 1810. "Ueber Göthe's *Wahlverwandtschaften.*" *Zeitung für die elegante Welt.* Nr. 2. Leipzig. Quoted here from Härtl 1983, 107–9. Also reprinted in Braun 1885, 232–36.

Jacobi, Friedrich Heinrich. 12 January 1810. Letter to Friedrich Köppen. Munich. Quoted here from *Aus F. H. Jacobi's Nachlaß.* Vol. 2. Leipzig: Wilhelm Engelmann, 1869. 44–45. Also reprinted in Härtl 1983, 112–13 and *HA*, 6:662–63.

Schlegel, Friedrich. 16 January 1810. Letter to August Wilhelm Schlegel. Vienna. Quoted here from *Krisenjahre der Frühromantik. Briefe aus dem Schlegelkreis.* Ed. Josef Körner. Vol. 2. Vienna, 1937. 100–105. Also reprinted in Härtl 1983, 113.

[Delbrück, Johann Friedrich Ferdinand]. 18 and 19 January 1810. "*Die Wahlverwandtschaften.* Ein Roman von Goethe." *Jenaische Allgemeine Literatur-Zeitung.* No. 16 and 17. Quoted here from Härtl 1983, 114–21.

[Abeken, Bernhard Rudolf]. 22–24 January 1810. Ueber Goethes *Wahlverwandtschaften.* (Fragmente aus einem Briefe). *Morgenblatt für gebildete Stände.* No. 19–21. Tübingen. Quoted here from Härtl 1983, 121–27. Also reprinted in *HA*, 6:644–51 and Mandelkow (1975–84) 1:262–74.

Böttiger, Karl August. 28 January 1810. Letter to Johann Friedrich Rochlitz. Dresden. Quoted here from the *Goethe-Jahrbuch* 18 (1897): 152. Also reprinted in Härtl 1983, 128.

Knebel, Henriette von. 7 February 1810. Letter to Karl Ludwig von Knebel. Weimar. Quoted here from *Aus Karl Ludwig von Knebels Briefwechsel mit seiner Schwester 1774–1813.* Ed. Heinrich Düntzer. Jena: Friedrich Mauke, 1858. 411. Also reprinted in Härtl 1983, 129.

Stein, Charlotte von. 7 February 1810. Letter to Friedrich von Stein. Weimar. Quoted here from *Goethe in vertraulichen Briefen seiner Zeitgenossen: Die Zeit Napoleons 1803–1816.* Ed. Wilhelm Bode. Berlin: Mittler & Sohn, 1921. 238. Also reprinted in Härtl 1983, 129.

Wieland, Christoph Martin. 10 February 1810. Letter to Charlotte Geßner. Weimar. Quoted here from *Goethe in vertraulichen Briefen seiner Zeitgenossen: Die Zeit Napoleons 1803–1816.* Ed. Wilhelm Bode. Berlin: Mittler & Sohn, 1921. 238–39. Also reprinted in Härtl 1983, 137 and *HA,* 6:663.

Schelling, Friedrich Wilhelm Joseph. 12 February 1810. Letter to Pauline Gotter. Stuttgart. Quoted here from Härtl 1983, 137.

Savigny, Friedrich Karl von. 27 February 1810. Letter to Clemens Brentano. Landshut. Quoted here from Härtl 1983, 140.

Humboldt, Wilhelm von. 6 March 1810. Letter to Caroline von Humboldt. Berlin. Quoted here from Härtl 1983, 141. Also reprinted in *HA,* 6:664.

Anonymous. 23 March 1810. "Französisches Urtheil über Goethes *Wahlverwandtschaften.*" *Morgenblatt für gebildete Stände.* No. 71. Tübingen. Quoted here from Härtl 1983, 146–50.

[Bartholdy, Jacob Salomon]. 23 March 1810. "Göthe's *Wahlverwandtschaften.* Ein Roman in 2 Bändchen." *Oesterreichischer Beobachter.* Quoted here from Härtl 1983, 144–50.

Gries, Johann Diederich. 23 March 1810. Letter to Bernhard Rudolf Abeken. Jena. Quoted here from Härtl 1983, 150–51.

Jean Paul. 24 March 1810. Letter to Karl Ludwig von Knebel. Bayreuth. Quoted here from Härtl 1983, 151.

Abeken, Bernhard Rudolf. 26–30 March [1810]. Letter to Heinrich Voß. Jena. Quoted here from Härtl 1983, 151–52.

Schlegel, August Wilhelm. 10 May 1810. Letter to Julie Schlegel. Quoted here from Härtl 1983, 155.

[Schlegel, Friedrich]. 21 May 1810. "Über Liebe und Ehe in Beziehung auf Goethe's *Wahlverwandtschaften.*" *Oesterreichischer Beobachter.* Beylage 11 zu Nr. 35. Wien. Quoted here from the *Goethe-Jahrbuch* 27 (1906): 252–54. Also reprinted in Härtl 1983, 156–57.

Passow, Franz. 14 June 1810. Letter to Ernst Breem. Weimar. Quoted here from Passow's *Leben und Briefe.* Ed. Albrecht Wachler. Breslau: Ferdinand Hirt, 1839. Also cited in Härtl 1983, 157–58.

Wieland, Christoph Martin. 15 June 1810. Letter to the Countess Elisabeth von Solms-Laubach. Weimar. Quoted here from Härtl 1983, 158–59.

Unger, Friederike Helene. 20 June 1810. Letter to August Wilhelm Schlegel. Berlin Quoted here from *Krisenjahre der Frühromantik. Briefe aus dem Schlegelkreis.* Vol. 3. Ed. Josef Körner. Bern: Francke Verlag, 1958. 461. Also reprinted in Härtl 1983, 159.

Gerlach, Wilhelm von. 30 June 1810. Letter to Leopold von Gerlach. Berlin. Quoted here from *Aus den Jahren preussischer Not und Erneuerung: Tagebücher und Briefe der Gebrüder Gerlach und ihres Kreises 1805–1820.* Ed. Hans Joachim Schoeps. Berlin: Haude und Spenersche Verlagsbuchhandlung, 1963. 460–62. Also reprinted in Härtl 1983, 160.

Anonymous. 14 July 1810. "Ein Paar Worte über eine Recension von Goethes *Wahlverwandtschaften* und über eine andere des ersten Buchs der *Wanderjahre Wilhelm Meisters.* (Aus einem Briefe)." *Morgenblatt für gebildete Stände.* Tübingen. No. 168. Quoted here from Härtl 1983, 161–63.

Wieland, Christoph Martin. 16 July 1810. Letter to Karl August Böttiger. Weimar. Quoted here from Härtl 1983, 164–65.

Riemer, Friedrich Wilhelm. 11 August 1810. Diary Entry. Teplitz. Quoted here from Härtl 1983, 166.

Gerlach, Leopold von. 14 August 1810. Letter to Wilhelm von Gerlach. Heidelberg. Quoted here from *Aus den Jahren preussischer Not und Erneuerung: Tagebücher und Briefe der Gebrüder Gerlach und ihres Kreises 1805–1820.* Ed. Hans Joachim Schoeps. Berlin: Haude und Spenersche Verlagsbuchhandlung, 1963. 468–69. Also reprinted in Härtl 1983, 167.

[Böttiger, Karl August]. 1810. "*Die Wahlverwandtschaften;* ein Roman von Göthe." *Bibliothek der redenden und bildenden Künste.* Leipzig. Quoted here from Härtl 1983, 176–98. Also reprinted in Braun 1885, 265–69.

Werner, Zacharias. 23 April 1811. Letter to Goethe. Rome. Quoted here from Härtl 1983, 216–17. Also reprinted in *HA*, 6:664–65.

Anonymous. 1812. "*Elective Affinities;* a Novel by Goëthe." *The American Review of History and Politics and General Repository of Literature and State Papers* 3:51–69.

Horn, Franz. 1812. *Die schöne Litteratur Deutschlands, während des achtzehnten Jahrhunderts.* Berlin. Quoted here from Härtl 1983, 225.

Staël-Holstein, Anne Germaine de. 1814. *Deutschland.* Trans. into German by Friedrich Buchholz. Berlin. Quoted here from Härtl 1983, 246–47.

[Wagner, Adolph?]. 1814. "*Die Wahlverwandtschaften.*" *Heidelbergische Jahrbücher der Literatur.* No. 12–13. Quoted here from Härtl 1983, 230–45.

[Conz, Karl Philipp]. 11–13 December 1817. "Noch einige Bemerkungen über Göthe's *Wahlverwandtschaften.*" *Zeitung für die elegante Welt.* Leipzig. Quoted here from Härtl 1983, 250–56.

[Meißner, Konrad Benjamin]. 1817. "Roman." *Conversations-Lexikon oder Hand-Wörterbuch für die gebildeten Stände.* 2nd ed. Vol. 8. Leipzig-Altenburg. Quoted here from Härtl 1983, 256–57.

[Pustkuchen, Johann Friedrich Wilhelm]. 1821. *Wilhelm Meisters Wanderjahre. Erster Theil.* Quedlinburg and Leipzig. Quoted here from Härtl 1983, 270–73. Also reprinted in Mandelkow (1975–84) 1:316–29.

Varnhagen von Ense, Rahel Levin. May 1823. Diary Entry. Berlin. Quoted here from Hannah Arendt's *Rahel Varnhagen. Lebensgeschichte einer deutschen Jüdin aus der Romantik.* Munich: R. Piper & Co., 1959. 259–60. Also reprinted in Härtl 1983, 226.

Eckermann, Johann Peter. 1824. "Bemerkungen über Goethe's *Wahlverwandtschaften.*" *Beyträge zur Poesie mit besonderer Hinweisung auf Goethe.* Stuttgart: Cotta.

[Meißner, Konrad Benjamin]. 1824. "Roman." *Allgemeine deutsche Real-Encyklopädie für die gebildeten Stände. (Conversations-Lexikon).* Bd. 8. 6. Original-Auflage. Leipzig: F. A. Brockhaus. Cited here from the 7th ed., 1830. Also reprinted in Härtl 1983, 309–310.

Menzel, Wolfgang. 1824. "Göthe und Schiller." *Europäische Blätter oder das Interessanteste aus Literatur und Leben für die gebildete Lesewelt.* Ed. Wolfgang Menzel. Zürich. Quoted here from Härtl 1983, 308–9. Also reprinted in Mandelkow (1975–84) 1:363–67.

Diepenbrock-Grüter, Ludwig von. 20 November 1826. Diary Entry. Lüneburg. Quoted here from *Begegnungen mit Heine. Berichte der Zeitgenossen*. Ed. Michael Werner. Hamburg: Hoffmann und Campe, 1973. 145–46. Also reprinted in Härtl 1983, 323.

Wessenberg, Ignaz Heinrich von. 1826. *Ueber den sittlichen Einfluß der Romane. Ein Versuch*. Constanz: W. Wallis, 1826. Also reprinted in Härtl 1983, 323–25.

Menzel, Wolfgang. 1828. *Die deutsche Literatur*. 2nd ed. Vol. 3. Stuttgart: Hallberger'sche Verlagshandlung, 1836. 368–74. Also reprinted in Härtl 1983, 330–31.

Carlyle, Thomas. 3 November 1829. Letter to Goethe. Craigenputtoch, Dumfries. Quoted here from *The Collected Letters of Thomas and Jane Welsh Carlyle*. Duke-Edinburgh Edition. Ed. Charles Richard Sanders and Kenneth J. Fielding. Durham, NC: Duke UP, 1976.

Ancillon, Friedrich. 1831. *Philosophie und Poesie (=Zur Vermittlung der Extreme in den Meinungen*. Zweiter Theil). Berlin. Quoted here from Härtl 1983, 376.

Valenti, Ernst Joseph Gustav de. 16–30 July 1831. "Ueber Göthes *Wahlverwandtschaften*." *Evangelische Kirchen-Zeitung*. No. 57–61. Ed. Ernst Wilhelm Hengstenberg. Berlin. Quoted here from Härtl 1983, 341–75.

Carlyle, Thomas. 1832. "Death of Goethe" and "Goethe's Works." Cited here from Carlyle's *Critical and Miscellaneous Essays* (1872). 7 vols. London: Chapman and Hall.

Rötscher, Heinrich Theodor. 1838. "Die 'Wahlverwandtschaften' von Goethe in ihrer weltgeschichtlichen Bedeutung, ihrem sittlichen und künstlerischen Werthe nach entwickelt." *Abhandlungen zur Philosophie der Kunst* 2. Abtheilung. Berlin: Duncker und Humblot.

Grillparzer, Franz. 1841. Diary entry #3538. Cited here from *Sämtliche Werke*. Vol. 10. Vienna: Kunstverlag Anton Schroll & Co., 1909. 319–20.

Weiße, Christian Hermann. 1841. "Ueber Göthe's *Wahlverwandtschaften* und ihre neuesten Beurtheilungen." *Blätter für literarische Unterhaltung*. Quoted here from Weiße's *Kleine Schriften zur Aesthetik und ästhetischen Kritik* (1867). Ed. Rudolf Seydel. Leipzig: Breitkopf und Härtel.

Gervinus, G[eorg] G[ottfried]. 1842. *Geschichte der deutschen Dichtung V: Neuere Geschichte der poetischen National-Literatur der Deutschen. Zweiter Theil: Von Göthes Jugend bis zur Zeit der Befreiungskriege*. Leipzig: Engelmann.

Varnhagen von Ense, Karl August. 1843. Diary Entry. Quoted here from *Karl August Varnhagen von Ense Werke*. 5 vols. Frankfurt: Deutscher Klassiker Verlag, 1994. 5:320–21. Also reprinted in *HA*, 6:641.

Hebbel, Friedrich. 1844. "Vorwort" zur *Maria Magdalene*. Hamburg. Quoted here from *Friedrich Hebbel: Werke*. Vol. 1. Munich: Carl Hanser Verlag, 1963. 307–38. Also partially reprinted in Mandelkow (1975–84) 2:270–72. Translation by T. M. Campbell in *Hebbel-Ibsen and the Analytic Exposition*. Heidelberg: Winter, 1922.

Vilmar, A[ugust] F[riedrich] C[hristian]. 1845. *Vorlesungen über die Geschichte der deutschen National-Literatur*. Marburg: Elwert'schen Universitäts-Buchhandlung.

Rosenkranz, Karl. 1847. *Göthe und seine Werke*. Königsberg: Bornträger.

Hettner, Hermann. 1850. *Die romantische Schule in ihrem inneren Zusammenhange mit Goethe und Schiller*. Braunschweig: Bieweg. Quoted here from *Schriften zur Literatur*. Berlin: Aufbau Verlag, 1959.

Eichendorff, Joseph von. 1851. *Der deutsche Roman des 18. Jahrhunderts in seinem Verhältnis zum Christentum*. Leipzig: Brockhaus. Quoted from *Werke*. Vol. 6:468–71. Frankfurt: Deutscher Klassiker Verlag, 1993.

Lösch. 1852. "Ueber Göthe's Ottilie." *Album des literarischen Vereins in Nürnberg für 1852*. 168–84.

Schmidt, Julian. 1853. *Geschichte der Deutschen Literatur seit Lessing's Tod*. Vol. 2. Quoted here from the 4th, expanded ed., 1858. Leipzig: Friedrich Ludwig Herbig.

Lewes, George Henry. 1855. *The Life of Goethe*. Quoted from the 2nd ed., 1864. London: Smith, Elder and Co.

Haeckel, Ernst. 1868. *Natürliche Schöpfungsgeschichte*. Berlin: Georg Reimer.

M., F. K. [Friedrich Karl Meyer]. 1869. "Göthe, die *Wahlverwandtschaften* und Wilhelmine Herzlieb." *Preußische Jahrbücher*. 25:623–36.

Stahr, Adolf. March 1870. "Minna Herzlieb. Goethe's 'Ottilie' in den 'Wahlverwandtschaften.'" *Westermann's Monatshefte. Ein Familienbuch für das gesammte geistige Leben der Gegenwart* 27:664–76.

Grimm, Herman. 1877. *Goethe Vorlesungen*. Berlin: Hertz. Translation from the 1971 reprint of the 1880 English translation: *The Life and Times of Goethe*. Trans. Sarah Holland Adams. Freeport, NY: Books for Libraries Press.

Baumgartner, Alexander. 1882. *Göthe: Sein Leben und seine Werke*. 3 vols. Freiburg: Herder'sche Verlagshandlung. Quoted here from the 2nd, expanded ed., 1885–86.

Brahm, Otto. 1882. "Eine Episode in Goethes *Wahlverwandtschaften*." *Zeitschrift für deutsches Altertum und deutsche Literatur* 26: 194–97.

Scherer, Wilhelm. 1883. *Geschichte der deutschen Litteratur*. Berlin: Weidmann. Translation from the 1890 *A History of German Literature*. Trans. F. C. Conybeare. Ed. F. Max Müller. Vol. 2. New York: Charles Scribner's Sons.

Braun, Julius W. 1885. *Goethe im Urtheile seiner Zeitgenossen: Zeitungskritiken, Berichte, Notizen, Goethe und seine Werke betreffend, aus den Jahren 1772–1812*. 3 vols. Berlin: Friedrich Luckhardt.

Scherer, Wilhelm. 1885. "Goethe und Frau Rehberg, geb. Höpfner." *Goethe-Jahrbuch* 6:345–53.

Schmidt, Erich. 1885. "*Die Wahlverwandtschaften* in Frankreich." *Goethe-Jahrbuch* 6:343–44.

Calvert, George H. 1886. *Goethe: His Life and Works*. Boston: Lee and Shepard.

Nietzsche, Friedrich. 1887. *Zur Genealogie der Moral. Eine Streitschrift*. Cited here from Studienausgabe. 4 vols. Frankfurt: Fischer, 1968. English translation by Francis Golffing, New York: Doubleday, 1956.

Semler, Christian. 1887. "Goethe's *Wahlverwandtschaften* und die sittliche Weltanschauung des Dichters." *Sammlung gemeinverständlicher wissenschaftlicher Vorträge*. 18:1–48.

Bölsche, Wilhelm. 1889. "Goethes *Wahlverwandtschaften* im Lichte moderner Naturwissenschaft." *Die Gesellschaft* 5:1330–40. Quoted here from Mandelkow (1975–84) 3:170–78.

Schmidt, Julian. 1890. *Geschichte der Deutschen Litteratur von Leibniz bis auf unsere Zeit*. Vol. 4: 1797–1814. Berlin: Wilhelm Herz.

Bielschowsky, Albert. 1895. *Goethe: Sein Leben und seine Werke*. 2 vols. Quoted here from the 23rd, 1911 edition. Munich: C. H. Beck. English from the 1911 translation *The Life of Goethe*. Trans. William Cooper. New York: G. P. Putnam's Sons.

Heinemann, Karl. 1895. *Goethe*. Vol. 2. Leipzig: Seemann.

Meyer, Richard M. 1895. *Goethe*. Vol. 2. Berlin: Hofmann & Co.

Wolff, Eugen. 1895. *Goethes Leben und Werke mit besonderer Rücksicht auf Goethes Bedeutung für die Gegenwart*. Kiel and Leipzig: Lipsius & Tischer.

Witkowski, Georg. 1899. *Goethe.* Leipzig: Seemann und Gesellschaft für graphische Industrie. Quoted here from the 1923 third, expanded edition. Leipzig: Alfred Kröner.

Abeken, Bernhard Rudolf. 1904. *Goethe in meinem Leben.* Ed. Adolf Heuermann. Weimar: Böhlau. 107–115; 128–35; 228–31. Also reprinted in Härtl 1983, 204–210.

Luther, Arthur. 1905. *"Die Wahlverwandtschaften." Sechs Vorträge.* Leipzig: Oskar Hellmann.

Walzel, Oskar F. 1906. "Goethes 'Wahlverwandtschaften' im Rahmen ihrer Zeit." *Goethe-Jahrbuch* 27:166–206.

Boucke, Ewald A. 1907. *Goethes Weltanschauung auf historischer Grundlage. Ein Beitrag zur Geschichte der dynamischen Denkrichtung und Gegensatzlehre.* Stuttgart: E. Hauff.

Engel, Eduard. 1909. *Goethe: Der Mann und das Werk.* 2 Vol. Berlin: Concordia Deutsche Verlagsanstalt. Quoted here from the 11th ed., 1921. Hamburg: Westermann.

François-Poncet, André. 1910. *Les Affinités Électives.* Paris: F. Alcan. Quoted here from the 1951 German translation: *Goethes Wahlverwandtschaften: Versuch eines kritischen Kommentars.* Mainz: Florian Kupferberg Verlag.

Hárnik, J. 1912. "Psychoanalytisches aus und über Goethes *Wahlverwandtschaften.*" *Imago Zeitschrift für Anwendung der Psychoanalyse auf die Geisteswissenschaften* 1:507–18.

Grimm, Ludwig Emil. 1913. *Erinnerungen aus meinem Leben (1794–1823).* Ed. Adolf Stoll. Leipzig. Quoted here from the 1950 edition. Kassel: Bärenreiter Verlag. Also reprinted in Härtl 1983, 213.

Brandes, Georg. 1915. *Wolfgang Goethe.* 2 vols. Copenhagen: Gyldental. Quoted here from the 1925 English edition. Trans. Allen W. Porterfield. New York: Frank-Maurice.

Snider, Denton J. 1915. *Goethe's Life-Poem: As Set Forth in His Life and Works.* St. Louis: Sigma Publishing Co.

Gundolf, Friedrich. 1916. *Goethe.* Berlin: Bondi. Quoted here from the 4th ed., 1918.

Benjamin, Walter. ca. 1917. "Bemerkung über Gundolf: Goethe." Unpublished during Benjamin's lifetime. Quoted here from *Walter Benjamin: Gesammelte Schriften* I, 3. Ed. Rolf Tiedemann and Hermann Schweppenhäuser. Frankfurt: Suhrkamp. 1974. English from *Walter Benjamin: Selected Writings (1913–1926).* Vol. 1. Ed. Marcus Bullock and Michael W. Jennings. Essay trans. Stanley Corngold. Cambridge: Belknap Press, 1996.

Thomas, Calvin. 1917. *Goethe.* New York: Holt and Company.

Hofmannsthal, Hugo von. 11 November 1923. Letter to Florens Christian Rang. Cited in *Die neue Rundschau* 70 (1959): 439–40.

Benjamin, Walter. 1924/25. "Goethes *Wahlverwandtschaften.*" *Neue deutsche Beiträge.* Quoted here from *Walter Benjamin: Gesammelte Schriften* I, i. Ed. Rolf Tiedemann and Hermann Schweppenhäuser. Frankfurt: Suhrkamp, 1974. English from *Walter Benjamin: Selected Writings (1913–1926).* Vol. 1. Ed. Marcus Bullock and Michael w. Jennings. Essay trans. Stanley Corngold. Cambridge: Belknap Press, 1996.

Mann, Thomas. 1925. "Zu Goethe's '*Wahlverwandtschaften.*'" *Die neue Rundschau* 36:391–401. Quoted here from *Gesammelte Werke in zwölf Bänden.* Vol. 9. Frankfurt: S. Fischer, 1960. 174–86. Also reprinted in Rösch 1975. English from *Past Masters and Other Papers.* "Goethe, Novelist." Trans. H. T. Lowe-Porter. New York: Alfred A. Knopf, 1933. 99–114.

Sommerfeld, Martin. 1926. "Goethes *Wahlverwandtschaften* im 19. Jahrhundert." Jahrbuch d. fr. dt. Hochstifts. 203–50.

Vetter, August. 1931. "Wahlverwandtschaft." *Jahrbuch der Goethe-Gesellschaft* 17:98–113.

Reitz, Gertrud. 1932. *Die Gestalt des Mittlers in Goethes Dichtung.* Frankfurter Quellen und Forschungen zur germanischen und romanischen Philologie. Ed. Erhard Lommatzsch, Hans Naumann, and Franz Schultz. Frankfurt: Mortiz Diesterweg. Quoted here from the 1973 facsimile reprint, Hildesheim: Dr. H. A. Gerstenberg.

Lockemann, Theodor. 1933. "Der Tod in Goethes *Wahlverwandtschaften.*" *Jahrbuch der Goethegesellschaft.* 19:48–61. Also reprinted in Rösch 1975.

Mann, Thomas. 1933. "Goethe, Novelist." [Translation of "Zu Goethe's *Wahlverwandtschaften*" (1925)] *Past Masters and Other Papers.* Trans. H. T. Lowe-Porter. New York: Alfred A. Knopf, 1933. 99–114.

Simon, Lilli. 1934. *Verantwortung und Schuld in Goethes Roman.* Erlangen: Palm & Enke.

Blankenagel, John C. 1936. "An Early American Review of *Die Wahlverwandtschaften.*" *JEGP* 35:383–89.

Meessen, Hubert J. 1939. "Goethes Polaritätsidee und *Die Wahlverwandtschaften.*" *PMLA* 54:1105–23.

Schaeder, Grete. 1941. "Die Idee der *Wahlverwandtschaften*." *Goethe: Neue Folge des Jahrbuchs der Goethe-Gesellschaft* 6:182–215.

Hankamer, Paul. 1943. *Spiel der Mächte: Ein Kapitel aus Goethes Leben und Goethes Welt.* Tübingen: Rainer Wunderlich Verlag.

Stahl, E. L. 1946. "*Die Wahlverwandtschaften.*" *PEGS* 15:71–95.

Maurer, Karl. 1947. "Goethe's 'Elective Affinities.'" *The Modern Language Review* 42:342–52.

Schaeder, Grete. 1947. *Gott und Welt: Drei Kapitel Goethescher Weltanschauung.* Hameln: Fritz Seifert.

Hatfield, Henry C. 1948. "Towards the Interpretation of *Die Wahlverwandtschaften.*" *The Germanic Review* 22:104–14. Also reprinted (in German translation) in Rösch 1975.

Stöcklein, Paul. 1949. *Wege zum späten Goethe: Dichtung — Gedanke — Zeichnung — Interpretationen.* Hamburg: Marion von Schröder Verlag. Also reprinted in 1984, Darmstadt: Wissenschaftliche Buchgesellschaft.

Viëtor, Karl. 1949. *Goethe: Dichtung/Wissenschaft/Weltbild.* Bern: A. Francke Verlag. English from the 1949 *Goethe the Poet.* Trans. Moses Hadas. Cambridge: Harvard UP.

Suhrkamp, Peter. 1951. "Goethes *Wahlverwandtschaften.*" *Ausgewählte Schriften zur Zeit- und Geistesgeschichte.* Frankfurt: Suhrkamp. Quoted here from Rösch 1975.

Wiese, Benno von. 1951. "Goethes *Wahlverwandtschaften.*" Vol. 6. Hamburg: Christian Wegner Verlag. Cited here from Wiese's *Der Mensch in der Dichtung: Studien zur deutschen und europäischen Literatur.* Düsseldorf: August Bagel Verlag, 1958.

Wolff, Hans M. 1952. *Goethe in der Periode der Wahlverwandtschaften (1802–1809).* Munich: Leo Lehnen Verlag.

Drake, Patricia. 1953. "Ottilie Revisited." *German Quarterly* 26:248–57.

Lange, Victor. 1953. "Goethe's Craft of Fiction." *PEGS,* New Series, 22:31–63.

Brinkmann, Hennig. 1954. "Zur Sprache der *Wahlverwandtschaften.*" *Festschrift für Jost Trier zum 60. Geburtstag.* Meisenheim a. G.: Anton Hain. 254–76. Also published in Brinkmann's *Studien zur Geschichte der deutschen Sprache und Literatur.* 2 vols. Düsseldorf: Pädagogischer Verlag Schwan, 1965/66. Quoted here from Rösch 1975.

Clark, Robert T., Jr. 1954. "The Metamorphosis of Character in *Die Wahlverwandtschaften.*" *Germanic Review* 29:243–53.

Wolff, Hans M. 1955. *Goethes 'Novelle' Die Wahlverwandtschaften: Ein Rekonstruktionsversuch*. Bern: Francke Verlag.

Barnes, H. G. 1956. "Bildhafte Darstellung in den *Wahlverwandtschaften*." *Deutsche Vierteljahrsschrift* 30:41–70.

Staiger, Emil. 1956. *Goethe*. Vol. 2: 1786–1814. Zurich: Atlantis Verlag.

May, Kurt. 1957. "Goethes *Wahlverwandtschaften* als tragischer Roman." *Form und Bedeutung: Interpretationen deutscher Dichtung des 18. und 19. Jahrhunderts*. Stuttgart: Ernst Klett Verlag.

Geerdts, Hans Jürgen. 1958. *Goethes Roman "Die Wahlverwandtschaften": Eine Analyse seiner künstlerischen Struktur, seiner historischen Bezogenheiten und seines Ideengehaltes*. Weimar: Aufbau Verlag. Quoted here from the 3rd ed., 1974.

Barnes, H. G. 1959. "Ambiguity in *Die Wahlverwandtschaften*." *The Era of Goethe: Essays presented to James Boyd*. Oxford: Blackwell. 1–16. Also reprinted (in German translation) in Rösch 1975.

Jaeger, Hans. 1959. "Goethe's 'Novelle' *Die Wahlverwandtschaften?*" *The Germanic Review* 34:14–38.

Barnes, H. G. 1960. "Goethes *Wahlverwandtschaften* vor der katholischen Kritik." *Literaturwissenschaftliches Jahrbuch*. Neue Folge 1:53–65.

Stopp, F. J. 1960. "'Ein wahrer Narziss': Reflections on the Eduard-Ottilie Relationship in Goethe's *Wahlverwandtschaften*." *PEGS* 29:52–85.

Leppmann, Wolfgang. 1961. *The German Image of Goethe*. Oxford: Clarendon Press.

Stopp, F. J. 1962. "Ottilie and 'das innere Licht.'" *German Studies Presented to Walter Horace Bruford*. London: George G. Harrap & Co. 117–22.

Danckert, Werner. 1963. *Offenes und geschlossenes Leben: Zwei Daseinsaspekte in Goethes Weltschau*. Bonn: H. Bouvier und Co. Verlag.

Reiss, Hans. 1963. *Goethes Romane*. Bern: Francke Verlag.

Barnes, H. G. 1967. *Goethe's Die Wahlverwandtschaften: A Literary Interpretation*. Oxford: Clarendon Press.

Gray, Ronald D. 1967. *Goethe: A Critical Introduction*. Cambridge: Cambridge UP.

Reiss, Hans. 1969. *Goethe's Novels*. Revised translation of Reiss (1963). New York: St. Martin's Press.

Schelling-Schär, Esther. 1969. *Die Gestalt der Ottilie: Zu Goethes Wahl-verwandtschaften.* Zürcher Beiträge zur deutschen Literatur- und Geistesgeschichte. Vol. 36. Zurich: Atlantis Verlag.

Milfull, John. 1971–72. "The Function of the Novelle 'Die wunderlichen Nachbarskinder' in Goethe's *Die Wahlverwandtschaften.*" *German Life and Letters* 25:1–5.

Helbig, Louis Ferdinand. 1972. *Der Einzelne und die Gesellschaft in Goethes Wahlverwandtschaften.* Bonn: Bouvier Verlag.

Milfull, John. 1972. "The 'Idea' of Goethe's *Wahlverwandtschaften.*" *Germanic Review* 47:83–94.

Allemann, Beda. 1973. "Zur Funktion der chemischen Gleichnisrede in Goethes *Wahlverwandtschaften.*" *Untersuchungen zur Literatur als Geschichte: Festschrift für Benno von Wiese.* Ed. Vincent J. Günther et al. Berlin: Erich Schmidt Verlag.

Nemec, Friedrich. 1973. *Die Ökonomie der Wahlverwandtschaften.* Münchner Germanistische Beiträge. Vol. 10. Munich: Fink Verlag.

Kahn, Ludwig W. 1974. "Erlebte Rede in Goethes *Wahlverwandtschaften.*" *PMLA* 89:268–77.

Mandelkow, Karl Robert. 1975–1984. *Goethe im Urteil seiner Kritiker: Dokumente zur Wirkungsgeschichte Goethes in Deutschland.* 4 vols. Munich: C. H. Beck.

Rösch, Ewald. 1975. *Goethes Roman 'Die Wahlverwandtschaften.'* Wege der Forschung. Vol. 113. Darmstadt: Wissenschaftliche Buchgesellschaft.

Brown, Jane K. 1976. "*Die Wahlverwandtschaften* and the English Novel of Manners." *Comparative Literature* 28:97–108.

Peacock, R. 1976. "The Ethics of Goethe's *Die Wahlverwandtschaften.*" *Modern Language Review* 71:330–43.

Blessin, Stefan. 1979. *Die Romane Goethes.* Königstein: Athenäum Verlag.

Miller, J. Hillis. 1979. "A 'Buchstäbliches' Reading of *The Elective Affinities.*" *Glyph* 6:1–23.

Tanner, Tony. 1979. *Adultery in the Novel: Contract and Transgression.* Baltimore: The Johns Hopkins UP.

Atkins, Stuart. 1980. "*Die Wahlverwandtschaften:* Novel of German Classicism." *German Quarterly* 53:1–45.

Lillyman, W. J. 1980. "Affinity, Innocence, and Tragedy: The Narrator and Ottilie in Goethe's *Die Wahlverwandtschaften.*" *German Quarterly* 53:46–63.

Mandelkow, Karl Robert. 1980. *Goethe in Deutschland I: Rezeptionsgeschichte eines Klassikers (1733–1918)*. Munich: C. H. Beck.

Vaget, Hans Rudolf. 1980. "Ein reicher Baron. Zum sozialgeschichtlichen Gehalt der *Wahlverwandtschaften*." *Jahrbuch der deutschen Schillergesellschaft* 24:123–61.

Anton, Herbert. 1981. "Rettende Bilder. Ottiliens Tagebuch und Goethes Dichtungsverständnis." *Goethes Wahlverwandtschaften: Kritische Modelle und Diskursanalysen zum Mythos Literatur*. Ed. Norbert W. Bolz. Hildesheim: Gerstenberg Verlag. 169–91.

Bolz, Norbert W. 1981. "Ästhetisches Opfer: Die Formen der Wünsche in Goethes *Wahlverwandtschaften*." *Goethes Wahlverwandtschaften: Kritische Modelle und Diskursanalysen zum Mythos Literatur*. Ed. Norbert W. Bolz. Hildesheim: Gerstenberg Verlag. 64–90.

———. 1981. "Einleitung. Goethes *Wahlverwandtschaften* — Analysen zum Mythos Literatur." *Goethes Wahlverwandtschaften: Kritische Modelle und Diskursanalysen zum Mythos Literatur*. Ed. Norbert W. Bolz. Hildesheim: Gerstenberg Verlag. 7–20.

———, ed. 1981. *Goethes Wahlverwandtschaften: Kritische Modelle und Diskursanalysen zum Mythos Literatur*. Hildesheim: Gerstenberg Verlag.

Faber, Richard. 1981. "Parkleben. Zur sozialen Idyllik Goethes." *Goethes Wahlverwandtschaften: Kritische Modelle und Diskursanalysen zum Mythos Literatur*. Ed. Norbert W. Bolz. Hildesheim: Gerstenberg Verlag. 91–168.

Hörisch, Jochen. 1981. "'Die Himmelfahrt der bösen Lust' in Goethes *Wahlverwandtschaften*: Versuch über Ottiliens Anorexie." *Goethes Wahlverwandtschaften: Kritische Modelle und Diskursanalysen zum Mythos Literatur*. Ed. Norbert W. Bolz. Hildesheim: Gerstenberg Verlag. 308–22.

Kittler, Friedrich A. 1981. "Ottilie Hauptmann." *Goethes Wahlverwandtschaften: Kritische Modelle und Diskursanalysen zum Mythos Literatur*. Ed. Norbert W. Bolz. Hildesheim: Gerstenberg Verlag. 260–75.

Mehra, Marlis. 1981. "The Art of Landscape Gardening in Goethe's Novel *Die Wahlverwandtschaften*." *Eighteenth-Century Studies* 10:239–59.

Schlaffer, Heinz. 1981. "Namen und Buchstaben in Goethes *Wahlverwandtschaften*." *Goethes Wahlverwandtschaften: Kritische Modelle und Diskursanalysen zum Mythos Literatur*. Ed. Norbert W. Bolz. Hildesheim: Gerstenberg Verlag. 211–29. Expanded version of the article published in the *Jahrbuch der Jean-Paul-Gesellschaft* 7 (1972): 84–102.

Schreiber, Jens. 1981. "Die Zeichen der Liebe." *Goethes Wahlverwandt-schaften: Kritische Modelle und Diskursanalysen zum Mythos Literatur.* Ed. Norbert W. Bolz. Hildesheim: Gerstenberg Verlag. 276–307.

Brodsky, Claudia. 1982. "The Coloring of Relations: *Die Wahlverwandt-schaften* as *Farbenlehre.*" *Modern Language Notes* 97:1147–79.

Graham, Ilse. 1982. "Wintermärchen: Goethes Roman *Die Wahlver-wandtschaften.*" *Goethe-Jahrbuch* 99:41–75.

Lillyman, William J. 1982. "Analogies for Love: Goethe's *Die Wahlver-wandtschaften* and Plato's *Symposium. Goethe's Narrative Fiction: The Irvine Goethe Symposium.* Ed. William J. Lillyman. New York: Walter de Gruyter. 128–44.

———. 1982. "Monasticism, *Tableau Vivant,* and Romanticism: Ottilie in Goethe's *Die Wahlverwandtschaften.*" *JEPG* 81:347–66.

Mayr, Ernst. 1982. *The Growth of Biological Thought: Diversity, Evolution, and Inheritance.* Cambridge: Belknap Press of Harvard UP.

Ryan, Judith. 1982. "Views from the Summerhouse: Goethe's *Wahlver-wandtschaften* and its Literary Successors." *Goethe's Narrative Fiction: The Irvine Goethe Symposium.* Ed. William J. Lillyman. New York: Wal-ter de Gruyter. 145–60.

Wiethölter, Waltraud. 1982. "Legenden: Zur Mythologie von Goethes *Wahlverwandtschaften.*" *Deutsche Vierteljahrsschrift* 56:1–64.

Wolin, Richard. 1982. *Walter Benjamin: An Aesthetics of Redemption.* New York: Columbia UP.

Härtl, Heinz. 1983. *Die Wahlverwandtschaften: Eine Dokumentation der Wirkung von Goethes Roman 1808–1832.* Weinheim: Acta humaniora.

Schwan, Werner. 1983. *Goethes Wahlverwandtschaften: Das nicht erreichte Soziale.* Munich: Fink Verlag.

Weinhold, Ulrike. 1983. "Ebenbild und Einbildung. Zur Problematik des Garten-Motivs in Goethes *Wahlverwandtschaften.*" *Neophilolgus* 67:419–31.

Wenzel, Manfred. 1983. "Goethe und Darwin — Der Streit um Goethes Stellung zum Darwinismus in der Rezeptionsgeschichte der morpholo-gischen Schriften." *Goethe-Jahrbuch* 100:145–58.

Muenzer, Clark. 1984. *Figures of Identity.* University Park: Pennsylvania State UP.

Ryan, Judith. 1984. Review of *Goethes Wahlverwandtschaften: Kritische Modelle und Diskursanalysen zum Mythos Literatur,* ed. Norbert W. Bolz. *Goethe Yearbook* 2:250–51.

Osten, Manfred. 1985. "'Mit dem Gewissen verheiratet': Ein Versuch über die Gestalt der Ottilie in Goethes *Wahlverwandtschaften.*" *Goethe und Forster: Studien zum gegenständlichen Dichten.* Ed. Detlef Rasmussen. Bonn: Bouvier Verlag. 150–63.

Ribe, Neil M. 1985. "Goethe's Critique of Newton: A Reconsideration." *Studies in History and Philosophy of Science.* 16:315–35.

Seibt, Gustav and Oliver R. Scholz. 1985. "Zur Funktion des Mythos in *Die Wahlverwandtschaften.*" *Deutsche Vierteljahrsschrift* 59:609–30.

Witte, Bernd. 1985. *Walter Benjamin.* Reinbek bei Hamburg: Rowohlt Taschenbuch Verlag.

Buschendorf, Bernhard. 1986. *Goethes mythische Denkform. Zur Ikonographie der Wahlverwandtschaften.* Frankfurt: Suhrkamp.

Gelley, Alexander. 1986. "Ottilie and Symbolic Representation in *Die Wahlverwandtschaften.*" *Orbis Litterarum* 42:248–61.

Ryan, Judith. 1986. "Kunst und Ehebruch: Zum Nachleben von Goethes *Wahlverwandtschaften.*" *Goethe Yearbook* 3:179–96.

Adler, Jeremy. 1987. *'Eine fast magische Anziehungskraft': Goethes Wahlverwandtschaften und die Chemie seiner Zeit.* Munich: C. H. Beck.

Amrine, Frederick, Francis Zucker, and Harvey Wheeler, eds. 1987. *Goethe and the Sciences: A Reappraisal.* Boston Studies in the Philosophy of Science. Vol. 97. Boston: D. Reidel Publishing Co.

Jennings, Michael W. 1987. *Dialectical Images: Walter Benjamin's Theory of Literary Criticism.* Ithaca: Cornell UP.

Winkelman, John. 1987. *Goethe's Elective Affinities: An Interpretation.* New York: Peter Lang.

Bersier, Gabrielle. 1988. "Ottilies verlorenes Paradies. Zur Funktion der Allegorie in den *Wahlverwandtschaften:* Wieland—Brentano—Goethe." *Goethe Yearbook* 4:137–60.

Dunkle, Harvey. 1988. "Monkey Business in Goethe's *Faust, Die Wahlverwandtschaften,* and Science." *Goethe Yearbook* 4:123–35.

Gleick, James. 1988. *Chaos: Making a New Science.* New York: Penguin Books.

Hohendahl, Peter Uwe. 1988. "Literary Criticism in the Epoch of Liberalism, 1820–1870." *A History of German Literary Criticism, 1730–1980.* Ed. Peter Uwe Hohendahl. Lincoln: U of Nebraska P.

Klingmann, Ulrich. 1988. "Recht der Einbildungskraft und Recht des Wirklichen: Goethes *Wahlverwandtschaften* in poststrukturalistischer Sicht." *Monatshefte* 80:172–86.

Niedermeier, Michael. 1988. "Goethes Roman *Die Wahlverwandtschaf-ten*." *Weimarer Beiträge* 34:723–45.

Nygaard, Loisa. 1988. "'Bild' and 'Sinnbild': The Problem of the Symbol in Goethe's *Wahlverwandtschaften*." *The Germanic Review* 63:58–76.

Puszkar, Norbert. 1988. "Verwandtschaft und Wahlverwandtschaft." *Goethe Yearbook* 4:161–207.

Rosen, Charles. 1988. "The Ruins of Walter Benjamin." *On Walter Benjamin: Critical Essays and Recollections.* Ed. Gary Smith. Cambridge: MIT Press. 129–75.

Sepper, Dennis. 1988. *Goethe Contra Newton: Polemics and the Project for a New Science of Color.* Cambridge: Cambridge UP.

Gilli, Marita. 1989. "Das Verschweigen der Geschichte in Goethes *Wahlverwandtschaften* oder Wie man der Geschichte nicht entfliehen kann." *Sie, und nicht Wir.* Ed. Arno Herzig, Inge Stephan, and Hans G. Winter. Hamburg: Doelling und Galitz. 553–65.

Puszkar, Norbert. 1989. "Frauen und Bilder: Luciane und Ottilie." *Neophilologus* 73:397–410.

Stephenson, R. H. 1989. "Theorizing to some Purpose: 'Deconstruction' in the Light of Goethe and Schiller's Aesthetics — The Case of *Die Wahlverwandtschaften*." *Modern Language Review* 84:381–92.

Adler, Jeremy. 1990. "Goethe's Use of Chemical Theory in His *Elective Affinities*." *Romanticism and the Sciences.* Ed. Andrew Cunningham and Nicholas Jardine. Cambridge: Cambridge UP.

Cornell, John F. 1990. "Faustian Phenomena: Teleology in Goethe's Interpretation of Plants and Animals." *Journal of Medicine and Philosophy* 15:481–92.

Höpfner, Felix. 1990. *Wissenschaft wider die Zeit: Goethes Farbenlehre aus rezeptionsgeschichtlicher Sicht.* Heidelberg: Carl Winter Universitätsverlag.

Metzger, Lore. 1990. "Spatial Relations and Subject Formation in *Wahlverwandtschaften* and *Mansfield Park. Proceedings of the XII Congress of the International Comparative Literature Association.* Munich: Iudicium Verlag. 474–79.

Steer, A. G., Jr. 1990. *Goethe's Elective Affinities: The Robe of Nessus.* Heidelberg: Carl Winter Universitätsverlag.

Fink, Karl J. 1991. *Goethe's History of Science.* Cambridge: Cambridge UP.

Noyes, John. 1991. "Die blinde Wahl. Symbol, Wahl und Verwandtschaft in Goethes *Die Wahlverwandtschaften*." *Deutsche Vierteljahrsschrift* 45:132–51.

Witte, Bernd. 1991. *Walter Benjamin: An Intellectual Biography.* Revised and enlarged English translation of Witte 1985. Trans. James Rolleston. Detroit: Wayne State UP.

Holub, Robert C. 1992. "Young Germany." *A Concise History of German Literature to 1900.* Ed. Kim Vivian. Columbia, SC: Camden House. 224–39.

Miller, J. Hillis. 1992. *Ariadne's Thread: Story Lines.* New Haven: Yale UP.

———. 1992. "Interlude as Anastomosis in *Die Wahlverwandtschaften.*" *Goethe Yearbook* 6:115–22.

Batts, Michael S. 1993. *A History of Histories of German Literature, 1835–1914.* Montreal: McGill-Queen's UP.

Beutin, Wolfgang et al. 1993. *A History of German Literature: From the Beginnings to the Present Day.* Trans. Clare Krojzl. New York: Routledge.

Bloch, Andreas. 1993. "Goethes *Die Wahlverwandtschaften* (von 1809)— die Ehe im Werk und in der Wirklichkeit." *Zeitschrift für das gesamte Familienrecht* 40:1409–13.

Koerner, Lisbet. 1993. "Goethe's Botany: Lessons of a Feminine Science." *Isis* 84:470–95.

McCole, John. 1993. *Walter Benjamin and the Antinomies of Tradition.* Ithaca: Cornell UP.

Schönherr, Hartmut. 1993. *Einheit und Werden: Goethes Newton-Polemik als systematische Konsequenz seiner Naturkonzeption.* Würzburg: Königshausen & Neumann.

Burgess, Gordon J. A. 1994. "The Book in the Machine: First Report on a Computer-Assisted Analysis of *Die Wahlverwandtschaften.*" *German Life and Letters* 47:418–31.

Constantine, David. 1994. "Rights and Wrongs in Goethe's *Die Wahlverwandtschaften.*" *German Life and Letters* 47:387–99.

Harper, Anthony J. 1994. "Mysterium Conjunctionis: On the Attraction of 'Chymical Weddings.'" *German Life and Letters* 47:449–55.

Milne, C. Audrey. 1994. "*The Elective Affinities* in Exile: *Der Ehering.*" *German Life and Letters* 47:456–68.

Plenderleith, H. Jane. 1994. "Sex, Lies and *Die Wahlverwandtschaften.*" *German Life and Letters* 47:407–17.

Sirc, Susan. 1994. "Monkeys, Monuments and Miracles: Aspects of Imitation of Word and Image in *Die Wahlverwandtschaften*." *German Life and Letters* 47:432–48.

Smith, Gary. 1994. "A Genealogy of 'Aura': Walter Benjamin's Idea of Beauty." *Artifacts, Representations and Social Practice.* Ed. C. C. Gould and R. S. Cohen. Netherlands: Kluwer Academic Publishers. 105–19.

Stephenson, Roger H. 1994. "'Man nimmt in der Welt jeden, wofür er sich gibt': The Presentation of Self in Goethe's *Die Wahlverwandtschaften*." *German Life and Letters* 47:400–406.

Tantillo, Astrida Orle. 1994. "Deficit Spending and Fiscal Restraint: Balancing the Budget in *Die Wahlverwandtschaften*." *Goethe Yearbook* 7:40–61.

Wels, Volkhard. 1994. "Eine Auslegung von Goethes *Wahlverwandtschaften* nach ihrer theologischen Begrifflichkeit." *Euphorion* 88: 406–17.

Zecevic, Patricia D. 1994. "The Beloved as Male Projection: A Comparative Study of *Die Wahlverwandtschaften* and *Dom Casmurro*." *German Life and Letters* 47:469–76.

Konrad, Susanne. 1995. *Goethes Wahlverwandtschaften und das Dilemma des Logozentrismus.* Heidelberg: Universitätsverlag Carl Winter.

Maierhofer, Waltraud. 1995. "Vier Bilder und vielfältige Bezüge: die sogennante 'Väterliche Ermahnung' und die Figuren in den *Wahlverwandtschaften*." *Ethik und Ästhetik. Werke und Werte in der Literatur vom 18. bis zum 20. Jahrhundert.* Ed. Richard Fisher. Frankfurt: Peter Lang. 363–82.

Stephenson, R. H. 1995. *Goethe's Conception of Knowledge and Science.* Edinburgh: Edinburgh UP.

Benjamin, Walter. 1996. "Goethe's *Elective Affinities*" [Translation of "Goethes *Wahlverwandtschaften*" (1924/25)]. Trans. Stanley Corngold in *Walter Benjamin: Selected Writings (1913–1926).* Vol. 1. Ed. Marcus Bullock and Michael W. Jennings. Cambridge: Belknap Press, 1996.

Blessin, Stefan. 1996. *Goethes Romane: Aufbruch in die Moderne.* Paderborn: Ferdinand Schöningh.

Brodersen, Momme. 1996. *Walter Benjamin: A Biography.* Trans. Malcolm R. Green and Ingrida Ligers. Ed. Martina Derviş. London: Verso.

Dye, Ellis. 1996. "Goethe's *Die Wahlverwandtschaften*: Romantic Metafiction." *Goethe Yearbook* 8:66–92.

Köhler, Astrid. 1996. *Salonkultur im klassischen Weimar: Geselligkeit als Lebensform und literarisches Konzept.* Stuttgart: M & P Verlag.

Selbmann, Rolf. 1996. "Auf den Menschen reimt sich die ganze Natur. Über das Verhältnis von Chemie und Literatur im 19. Jahrhundert." *Euphorion* 90:153–65.

Taviani, Paolo and Vittorio. 1996. *"Elective Affinities."* Rai Radiotelevisione Italiana. English subtitled version from Fox Lorber 1998.

Unseld, Siegfried. 1996. *Goethe and His Publishers.* Trans. Kenneth J. Northcott. Chicago: U of Chicago P.

Bersier, Gabrielle. 1997. *Goethes Rätselparodie der Romantik. Eine neue Lesart der Wahlverwandtschaften.* Untersuchungen zur deutschen Literaturgeschichte. Vol. 90. Tübingen: Max Niemeyer Verlag.

Blondeau, Denise. 1997. "Goethes Naturbegriff in den *Wahlverwandtschaften.*" *Goethe-Jahrbuch* 114:35–48.

Egger, Irmgard. 1997. "'. . . ihre große Mäßigkeit': Diätetik und Askese in Goethes Roman *Die Wahlverwandtschaften.*" *Goethe-Jahrbuch* 114:253–63.

Lippert-Adelberger, Eberhard. 1997. "Die Platanen in Goethes *Wahlverwandtschaften.* Versuch einer mariologischen Deutung." *Goethe-Jahrbuch* 114:265–75.

McIsaac, Peter M. 1997. "Exhibiting Ottilie: Collecting as a Disciplinary Regime in Goethe's *Wahlverwandtschaften. German Quarterly* 70:347–57.

Müller-Sievers, Helmut. 1997. *Self-Generation: Biology, Philosophy, and Literature Around 1800.* Stanford: Stanford UP.

Yee, Kevin F. 1997. "The Captain as Catalyst in Goethe's *Wahlverwandtschaften.*" *JEPG* 96:58–70.

Ehrhardt, Gundula. 1998. "'Wahl-Anziehung' — Herders Spinoza-Schrift und Goethes *Wahlverwandtschaften.*" *Goethe-Jahrbuch* 115:77–95.

Hörisch, Jochen. 1998. "Die Dekonstruktion der Sprache und der Advent neuer Medien in Goethes *Wahlverwandtschaften.*" *Merkur* 52:826–39.

Tantillo, Astrida Orle. 1998. "Goethe's Botany and His Philosophy of Gender." *Eighteenth-Century Life* 22:123:38.

Puecker, Brigitte. 1999. "The Material Image in Goethe's *Wahlverwandtschaften.*" *The Germanic Review* 74:195–213.

Twardella, Johannes. 1999. "Experimente im Treibhaus der Moderne. Versuch einer Kommunikationstheoretischen Analyse von Goethes *Wahlverwandtschaften.*" *Neophilologus* 83:445–60.

Becker-Cantarino, Barbara. 2000. "Review Article: Goethe — New Scholarship." *German Quarterly* 73:185–93.

Schlick, Werner. 2000. *Goethe's Die Wahlverwandtschaften: A Middle-Class Critique of Aesthetic Aristocratism.* Heidelberg: Universitätsverlag Carl Winter.

Tantillo, Astrida Orle. 2000. "Polarity and Productivity in Goethe's *Wahlverwandtschaften.*" *Seminar* 36:310–25.

Index